The Rational Peasant

We cannot help being astonished by the subtlety, the intrigue, of which a simple peasant is capable, when his wretched appearance might make one believe that he doesn't see beyond the muzzle of his buffalo.

Pierre Gourou,
Les Paysans du delta tonkinois

The
Rational
Peasant

The Political Economy
of Rural Society
in Vietnam

SAMUEL L. POPKIN

University of California Press

Berkeley • Los Angeles • London

University of California Press
Berkeley and Los Angeles, California
University of California Press, Ltd.
London, England
Copyright © 1979 by
The Regents of the University of California
ISBN 0-520-03561-5 (cloth)
ISBN 0-520-03954-8 (paper)
Library of Congress Catalog Card Number: 77-83105
Printed in the United States of America

2 3 4 5 6 7 8 9

FOR MY PARENTS

Contents

Preface

SOME REPRESENTATIONS of preindustrial society idealize life in peasant villages. These romantic portraits of peasant life are greatly overdrawn and mislead us into thinking that the transformation of these societies is forced on the peasants and is always detrimental to their collective welfare. Exaggerating the virtues of the precapitalist village also results in erroneous diagnoses of the ailments of contemporary peasant society; these diagnoses lead in turn to misguided programs to remedy the ills. To understand the historical transformations of rural society and to develop effective programs for improving peasant welfare, we need to begin with a more accurate view of peasants and their institutions.

I propose a view of the peasant as a rational problem-solver, with a sense both of his own interests and of the need to bargain with others to achieve mutually acceptable outcomes. I hope to leave the reader not with pity for peasants or with a longing to recapture their presumed innocence and simplicity, but with a respect for the intelligence with which they develop practical solutions to the complex problems of resource allocation, authority, and dispute settlement that every society faces.

It is a grave mistake to attempt to address either the moral or the practical problems of modern industrial societies by trying to reverse the process by which these societies grew out of agrarian villages. To make the peasant village an ideal for emulation is, in a sense, to impose a heavier burden on peasants than they can bear. It is vain to hope that by studying their approach to life we will somehow recapture deeper truths obscured by the veneer of civilization. On the contrary, only by abandoning any lingering illusion that village society can be a model for emulation will we gain a realistic perception of the ways our own society can be improved.

This book has its origins in field research that I conducted in Vietnam between 1966 and 1970. I first went there to study pacification programs as an employee of the Simulmatics Corporation under contract to the Department of Defense. The moral and intellectual shocks of that experience left me with a compelling desire to comprehend all that I had observed and to assess the implications of it for my personal and professional beliefs. I based my dissertation on the experience, but it forms no part of this work. Later I was able to make two more extended field trips to Vietnam, thanks to grants from the Southeast Asian Development Advisory Group of the Asia Society; the Ford Foundation, via their grant to Harvard University for faculty research; and Harvard's Center for International Affairs. In Vietnam my experiences and reactions were similar to those of Tadashi Fukutake when he did field work in China during World War II:

Although it was wartime the farmers . . . treated us with a friendliness which it is even now pleasant to recall. It was not a happy situation, however. Being in my early twenties and no lover of the army and its wars, I could not help but be conscious of the sufferings which . . . aggression was bringing to the people. . . . To plunge into village life and concentrate single-mindedly on the collection of facts was perhaps something of an escape [Tadashi Fukutake, *Asian Rural Society,* p. *vii*].

I had no intention of writing a book like this about the period prior to American intrusion in Vietnam. Indeed, I accepted the popular explanation for the decline and decay of organic, harmonious precolonial villages as an adequate basis upon which to build an understanding of the present. I spent a great deal of time, however, learning about local political history in all the villages in which I conducted research, because it was clear to me that one who did not understand the origins of the current political alignments could not explain the present revolution.

As I was beginning to write about contemporary Vietnam and to assemble the masses of interviews I had collected from past and present political activists, the Pentagon Papers were released. Today, during the bloodless seventies, it is almost impossible to recall the ensuing feeling of paranoia. Under the pretext of investigating the release of the Pentagon Papers, a federal grand jury attempted to obtain answers from me to many questions that appeared to have nothing to do with investigating the Pentagon Papers and everything to do with finding out to whom I had talked in Washington and Vietnam. Concern for respondents, and the stress of dealing with a situation not easy to distinguish from a 1950s HUAC investigation, meant that for two years my research on contemporary Vietnam was interrupted.

Still driven by a desire to understand Vietnam, I turned to a reexamination of earlier epochs. Accustomed to the meager citations on which the standard books about Vietnam were based, I was staggered to find that the libraries of Harvard contained a treasure-trove of material: the Human Relations Area File contained numerous ethnographies of value, and Widener Library contained entire sets of journals, such as the *Revue Indochinois Juridique et Economique,* which had been scarcely noticed in published works. Indeed, I note with amazement that most of the data for this book have been available in American university libraries.

With time to read and ponder, certain of the images that had burned so heavily into my mind during my field work impelled me to reexamine the standard accounts of the development of the Vietnamese revolution. I remembered days of interviews with some of

the great colonial landlords, and especially the bitterness with
which they regarded the programs to provide rural education for
"their" "childlike" peasants, now being encouraged to think for
themselves; almost confessional discussions with landlords' sons
from northern Vietnam about their exploitation of *droit du seigneur*
with tenant's daughters; talks with peasants who had participated in
the uprisings of 1930 and with persons who had been among the
founders of the Hoa Hao; visits to villages with third-generation
members of the Communist Party; long conversations with peasants
about how liberation had changed their lives. All these prompted
me to systematically reexamine Vietnam before the period of American involvement in order to establish the basis from which I can
now write about the last twenty years of the Vietnamese revolution.
Whereas I once thought that if I wrote these books I would forget
Vietnam, I now write these books so that I can live with Vietnam.

ACKNOWLEDGMENTS

First and foremost among those who made this work possible is
Susan Shirk. Through trials and tribulations she gave me the support required to persevere. It is appropriate that I write these words
on her birthday.

Norman Frohlich and Joe Oppenheimer were friends, colleagues,
and teachers. Terry Sullivan helped me to focus the assumptions
of political economy on peasant society. Brian Barry and Kristin
Luker contributed immensely to the accessibility of my theoretical
arguments, as did Ithiel Pool, who has always provided encouragement. Hue-Tam Ho Tai supplied the maps and chronology and
helped with translations, but her major contribution has been to
give me an appreciation for the history of Vietnam. Terry Rambo,
Guy Gran, and Jayne Werner provided valuable manuscripts.
William Duiker, Alexander Woodside, Nguyen Khac Vien, and
David Marr informed my understanding of Vietnamese institutions
and elites. The incisive comments of Robert Bates and Donald
McCloskey were invaluable. F. G. Bailey, Ed Friedman, Frances
Hill, Howard Rosenthal, and Michael Weisser helped improve the

argument and tone. The entire political science department at the University of California, San Diego, helped polish my final draft, as did Tom Ferguson, Robert Jervis, James Kurth, T. W. Schulz and John Gorman. Barry Popkin provided guidance on health and nutrition. Aaron Wildavsky prompted the title and format. Betsy Faught and Michele Wenzel helped keep me on schedule. Rebecca Evans kept me in tune.

At many low points in this long process, the work of other scholars presented ideas that revived my interest. The stimulus provided me by Hamza Alavi, Jerome Blum, Elizabeth Colson, Rodney Hilton, Michael Lipton, Jeffrey Paige, and Mancur Olson goes beyond any particular footnotes. And of course a study such as this is forever struggling with the agenda set by the work of Barrington Moore, Charles Tilly, Samuel Huntington, and Edward Banfield; to Ed Banfield, I offer the example of the bell tower.

A fundamental influence on my work has come from the group of scholars that are here called moral economists, particularly Eric Wolf and James C. Scott. Eric Wolf's work on corporate villages and his subsequent writings on revolution provided my starting point. If I now offer alternate concepts and conclusions, it is only because I was able to begin my work with the knowledge base he provided. James C. Scott provided unpublished manuscripts and searching criticisms. If my work ever provokes the reexamination I gave his work, I hope to be as good-natured and helpful as he has been.

In writing a book, as in making a revolution, organization is essential to communication, and I am grateful to Audrey Spiro for help in ordering this manuscript and overcoming the most egregious deficiencies in my writing style. Roy Multer typed the entire manuscript twice and kept track of revisions and corrections.

Finally, I am indebted to Samuel P. Huntington and the Harvard University Center for International Affairs for invaluable support during the early stages of this project.

La Jolla
April 30, 1978

Chronology

Tenth century Independence recovered after 1,000 years of Chinese rule. At first, Buddhist monks act as court advisors, but gradually Confucian scholars gain in importance.

Thirteenth century Three Mongol invasions repelled but leave the country weakened.

1407 Chinese invade country during dynastic dispute. There follow twenty years of Chinese rule during which documents are systematically destroyed.

1428 Independence is recovered. Le Loi, hero of struggle, establishes Le dynasty. The Vietnamese are more than ever influenced by the Chinese model. The Confucian exam system is used systematically as ladder of success.

1615 First Catholic mission in Vietnam founded by Jesuits.

1627 Le dynasty still reigns in name, but the country is split in two at Dong Hoi, with Trinh in the north and Nguyen in the south.

1679 3,000 Chinese refugees arrive in Cochinchina and begin work of colonizing the delta area.

1774 Tay Son brothers (Nguyen Nhac, Nguyen Hue, and Nguyen Lu) revolt in Binh Dinh over issue of high taxes and government corruption. Revolt spreads throughout northern Annam.

1789 Nguyen Hue expels invading Chinese armies. In 1786, Nguyen Hue entered Hanoi and deposed the Le dynasty. Attempts by Tay Son brothers to reform taxes and the land tenure system are abandoned after death of Nguyen Hue in 1792.

1802 Founding of Nguyen dynasty by Gia Long, scion of Nguyen family. Reunification of the country after 200 years of partition.

1817–1822 Vinh Te canal built along present Cambodian border: an important step in colonization of western Cochinchina. Military plantations established in 1840s and 1850s.

1847 French frigate bombards Da Nang (Tourane).

1849 Cholera epidemic kills 600,000 throughout country and destroys crops. New military plantations established to resettle population. Founding of Buu Son Ky Huong sect in western Cochinchina.

1860–1867 Creation of Cochinchina out of six southern provinces. Eastern provinces annexed in 1862, western provinces in 1867. Abolition of military colonies; confiscation and auctioning off of public lands and lands belonging to "rebels" or fleeing peasants.

1863 *Cochinchina:* Regulations governing property rights promulgated. Extended to Tonkin in 1888 and to Annam in 1897 when emperor renounces ultimate property rights of the crown.

1867 Cochinchina ceded to the French.

1879 First civilian government replaces government by admirals.

1881 *Cochinchina:* Official abolition of corvée, to be replaced by increased tax. Value of corvée increased in 1897 and again the following year when corvée and personal tax are amalgamated. But de facto corvée continues well into 1930s as public projects create demand for manpower. Corvée amalgamated with tax in 1908 in Annam, in 1920 in Tonkin.

1884 *Cochinchina:* Tax receipt used as ID card. This measure is extended to Tonkin in 1897 and to Annam in 1913.

1884–1885 French protectorate established over Tonkin and Annam.

1885 *Tonkin and Annam:* Can Vuong movement of monarchic restoration led by young emperor Ham Nghi. He is captured and deported in 1888, but independent movements of opposition to French continue well into twentieth century.

1904 *Cochinchina:* Reform of village government. Notables must have prior experience in administration. Their role is expanded, and greater supervision is attempted by administration.
Annam: Founding of Duy Tan Hoi (Reform Society) by Phan Chu Trinh. Replaced in 1911 by Phan Boi Chau's Quang Phuc Hoi. Strongest in Annam and Tonkin, but its advocacy of educational reform very popular in Cochinchina.

1908 *Annam:* Scholar-led peasant revolt against taxes and corvée (works in connection with Nong Son coal mine then under way) and imposition of iron currency. Revolt spreads from Hoi An in Quang Nam to Quang Ngai, Binh Dinh, Phu Yen, Thua Thien, and Ha Tinh. Thanh Hoa and Nghe An slightly affected. Several death sentences, many deportations including Phan Chu Trinh (in exile until 1920s). *Tonkin:* Plot to poison French officers of Hanoi garrison fails; 18 death sentences. Hanoi University, founded in 1902, is closed down until 1918.

1913 *Cochinchina:* Plot to bomb public places in Saigon-Cholon area is discovered. Heaven and Earth Society leader Phan Xich Long is arrested, but 600 of his followers march to Saigon armed with sticks and amulets. Among their grievances are taxes, corvée (in connection with widening of highways), landgrabbing, and petty administrative vexations. *Tonkin:* De Tham, one of Can Vuong leaders, is captured and beheaded. Severe reprisals follow killing of two French officers in Hanoi.

1916 *Cochinchina:* 300 followers of Phan Xich Long attack Saigon prison to free him. Simultaneous risings in 13 out of 20 Cochinchinese provinces (especially in Gia Dinh, Cho Lon, My Tho, Ben Tre, Rach Gia, Tra Vinh, Long Xuyen, and Chau Doc). Main source of grievance is forcible recruitment for European front (100,000 men from Indochina). Risings are the work of sects and secret societies organized since 1911 and infiltrated by Phan Boi Chau's supporters. Thousands arrested, 38 death sentences; repression cripples sects and secret societies and allows for emergence of first modern political parties. *Annam:* Veteran of 1908 tax demonstrations Tran Cao Van persuades young emperor Duy Tan to head plot to unseat French in Annam. Duy Tan is deported and replaced by Khai Dinh. Khai Dinh dies in 1925 and is succeeded by twelve-year-old Bao Dai, who takes up his functions in 1932.

1917 *Tonkin:* Luong Ngoc Quyen uprisings in Thai Nguyen by followers of Phan Boi Chau. *Cochinchina:* Founding of Constitutionalist Party by bourgeois lawyer Bui Quang Chieu. Constitutionalists follow a moderate reformist line. High point is presentation of first *Cahier des Voeux Annamites* in 1925, advocating educational, social, and political reforms. Afterward, they are overtaken by more radical parties and become associated with bourgeois landowning and professional interests.

1918 *Tonkin:* Hanoi University reopens.
     Annam: Last Confucian exams held. (Last exams held in Tonkin in
     1915, none held in Cochinchina.)
1919 Educational reform throughout country. Single pattern of education
     imposed in three regions. From then on, French education key to
     success. However, no secondary schools are built in Annam until
     1930s. More schools to be built and staffed at villages' expense,
     leading to considerable tax increase. But in 1934–1935, estimated
     number of children in school is 400,000 out of school-age population
     of 3 million. In 1939, total number of doctors is 951 for a population
     of 18 million, though Faculty of Medicine of Hanoi University estab-
     lished in 1902. Ho Chi Minh (then known as Nguyen Ai Quoc) at
     Versailles Conference.
1920 *Tonkin:* Single tax rate for registered and nonregistered (in effect in
     Hanoi since 1919). Single tax rate extended to Annam in 1928.
1921 *Tonkin:* Village reform: creation of Council of Clan representatives.
     Council of Notables restored in 1927, Council of Clan representatives
     abolished in 1941.
1923 *Cochinchina:* French-trained Nguyen An Ninh publishes *La Cloche
     felée* advocating reforms.
1925 *Annam:* Founding of Tan Viet Cach Mang Dang (New Vietnam
     Revolutionary Party) among Confucian scholars and French-educated
     civil servants of northern Annam. Lacks a solid program and mass
     appeal, and is later absorbed into Communist Party.
1926 Death of Phan Chu Trinh, newly returned from exile, occasions huge
     demonstrations throughout the country.
     Cochinchina: Nguyen An Ninh is arrested; released in 1927, he goes
     to France until early 1928. Founding of Cao Dai sect in September
     1926. Membership stands at 200,000 by end of the year, 1 million by
     1930. Adepts are mostly peasants, but many leaders are bourgeois
     landowners or civil servants, many with French education. Early suc-
     cesses in Tonkin, Annam, Cambodia, and Laos halted by prohibi-
     tions.
1927 New Labor Code to replace obsolete code of 1913, but remains inef-
     fective until advent of Popular Front in 1936. Forcible recruitment of
     Tonkinese labor for southern rubber plantations extremely unpopular.
1927–1928 *Tonkin:* Founding of Viet Nam Quoc Dan Dang (VNQDD, or
     Vietnamese Nationalist Party) among petty civil servants and
     teachers in Hanoi. Modeled after Chinese Kuomintang.
1928 *Cochinchina:* Nguyen An Ninh Society created on foundations of
     Heaven and Earth Society and mutual-help associations in Bien Hoa,
     Cho Lon, Gia Dinh, Thu Dau Mot, and Tan An. Nguyen An Ninh

arrested in late 1928. Nguyen An Ninh Society becomes prominent in Cochinchinese mass movements of 1930–1931.

Annam: Abolition of tax exemptions.

1929 Founding of Indochinese Communist Party in Hong Kong. Split occurs in the ranks of Thanh Nien, founded in 1925 in Canton by Ho Chi Minh: one Tonkinese and one Annamese faction, both competing for support in Cochinchina. Split is healed next year.

1929–1930 *Tonkin:* Reprisals against VNQDD after assassination of coolie recruiter Bazin forces VNQDD into premature uprisings in February 1930. Yen Bay garrison kills its French officers; 535 soldiers are later "disciplined." Village of Co Am, suspected of harboring VNQDD fugitives, is bombed. Most VNQDD leaders are captured, 13 are executed.

1930–1931 *Annam:* After crop failures of 1929, peasants demand tax reductions. First demonstrations on May 1, 1930 in Nghe An escalate to demands concerning corvée and land tenure. Riots spread to Ha Tinh in August; Quang Ngai, where little damage to crops has occurred, is also affected. Biggest demonstration on September 12 with 6,000 peasants. Bomb kills 107, and another 15 later at night. Tax collectors are chased and beaten, tax rolls are burnt, rich houses and public buildings (including alcohol depot) and railway stations are destroyed, mandarins and notables are harassed. Riots subside by end of the year, but pick up again toward May 1, 1931. At height of Nghe-Tinh soviets, Communist Party membership estimated at 1,806 in Nghe An-Ha Tinh, affiliated population is 45,000 in various kinds of associations.

Cochinchina: Troubles start in May in Cao Lanh-Choi Moi area, also over issue of tax reductions. Spread to Ben Tre, Can Tho, Cho Lon, Saigon, Gia Dinh, as demands escalate to include issue of land tenure and corvée. Soviets established in Cao Lanh area in October, but movements are on the wane in November.

Tonkin: Less affected by mass movements, but workers' strikes in Hon Gay mines, Thai Binh, Hai Phong, and Nam Dinh.

1931 "White Terror." Savage repression of mass movements, including tens of thousands of arrests. Most Communist Party leaders either behind bars or in hiding. But by 1932 some returned prisoners organize action committees at village level.

1930–1933 Depression hits Indochina. Rice prices fall from high of $1.20 in 1928 to $0.20 in 1933. Child-selling to pay taxes not uncommon. Through lack of capital, 400,000 hectares of land in Cochinchina and 160,000 in Tonkin are abandoned.

1933 Abolition of corvée.

Cochinchina: Sects and Catholic church enjoy new popularity. But Cao Dai sect is affected by economic crisis and internal schisms. In 1934, Pham Cong Tac becomes leader of Tay Ninh-based branch, but in My Tho, Nguyen Ngoc Tuong forms his own branch. By 1934, there are 11 Cao Dai sects.

Creation of Single Front in Cochinchina between Paris-trained Trotskyites under leadership of Ta Thu Thau and Communists under leadership of Moscow-trained Tran van Giau. The Front publishes *La Lutte,* single most influential paper advocating sweeping reforms, trade unionism, and peasant movements.

1935 Ho Chi Minh and Le Hong Phong attend Macao Congress of the International, which calls for revolution. Le Hong Phong later arrested and dies in prison.

     Cochinchina: strikes by up to 2,000 bus drivers in Saigon, Cho Lon, Gia Dinh, and Bien Hoa to demand higher wages and right to form union.

1936–1938 *Cochinchina:* New wave of mass movements under liberal policies of Popular Front. Affected areas sensibly the same as in 1930–1931. Estimated number of action committees is 600, most common form is youth, peasants, women's associations. Demand for reform of land tenure, reduction in taxes, right to unionize.

1937 *Cochinchina:* Split between Trotskyists and Communists over how to combat mounting threat of fascism. Trotskyists remain in control of *La Lutte* and retain popularity in the South. But Communists control network of cells. Cao Dai sect openly sides with Japanese and creates its own administrative apparatus on French model.

1939 Demonstrations throughout the country, especially on July 14. Trotskyists win all three seats on Cochinchinese Council. But they and the Communists are outlawed after outbreak of World War II.

     Cochinchina: Founding of Hoa Hao sect in July. By end of the year, it numbers tens of thousands of adepts. Founder Huynh Phu So interned in a psychiatric hospital in mid 1940, then under house-arrest in Bac Lieu until he is rescued by Japanese in October 1942.

1940 *Tonkin:* Uprisings in northern Tonkin by pro-Japanese Phuc Quoc and Dai Viet parties in anticipation of Japanese entry into Indochina.

     Cochinchina: Communist southern general uprisings suppressed by French. With 6,000 arrests, dozens of executions, the party network is almost entirely wiped out. Cao Dai oratories closed down. In 1941, French troops occupy Tay Ninh, and Pham Cong Tac is deported to Madagascar.

1941 *Tonkin:* Viet Minh founded in Pac Bo. Military bases established in northern highlands, among ethnic minorities. For the first time, Vietnamese are in the majority on the Colonial Council.

1942 *Annam:* Village reforms bring Annam in line with Tonkin and Cochinchina. More schools created throughout the country. Creation of Dong Minh Hoi, government in exile, in Chungking. Dong Minh Hoi is a coalition government, with Communists in an insignificant position as Ho Chi Minh is in a Chinese prison.

1943 *Cochinchina:* Japanese woo sects. Tran Quang Vinh, head of Phnom Penh Cao Dai mission, brought back to Saigon to head Cao Dai sect. Huynh Phu So installed in Saigon under Japanese protection. Toward end of 1943, sects begin to acquire arms and to organize own self-defense forces. Communist cadres begin to trickle back to old areas, but are hampered by need for clandestine work.

1944 *Tonkin:* Widespread famine, exacerbated by export of Cochinchinese rice to Japan. Communist cadres at the forefront of relief work.

1945 March 9: Japanese depose French in Indochina. During ensuing power vacuum, Communists, other political parties, and religious sects all vie for supremacy.

Tonkin, August 18: Viet Minh enter Hanoi and depose Japanese.

Annam, August 25: Bao Dai abdicates in favor of Viet Minh.

Cochinchina, August 25: Viet Minh seize power.

September 2: Declaration of Independence and formation of Provisional Government.

1946 March 6: Creation of Democratic Republic of Vietnam. Cochinchina retains status of colony.

1

The Rational Peasant

THIS BOOK is about the impact
of colonialism, the expansion of markets, and the formation of cen
tral states on peasant society. In it I shall discuss a widely accepted
interpretation of these phenomena known as the moral economy
approach and, from different assumptions, an alternative that I shall
call the political economy approach. Applying this new viewpoint,
I shall analyze the peasant society of Vietnam in its precolonial,
colonial, and (early) revolutionary periods.

Historically, whether in colonial or noncolonial settings, the development of strong central states and the expansion of national and
international markets have been accompanied by major changes in
the forms of peasant villages and in the nature of peasant relations
with agrarian elites. Most (but not all) of the world's peasantry
today live in open villages, that is, in villages with individual responsibility for the payment of taxes, indistinct boundaries between

1

the village and the outside world, few or no restrictions on land-ownership, imprecise notions of village citizenship, and privately owned land. In contrast to the few restrictions on landownership or exchanges with persons outside the (open) village, most of the world's peasantry once lived in corporate villages—that is, in closed villages with some form of collective responsibility for the payment of taxes, clear boundaries between the village and the outside world, restrictions on landownership, a well-defined concept of village citizenship, and frequently with land that was owned or managed by the village. In the past, moreover, a peasant was likely to have multistranded relations with the landlord (or patron) from whom he rented land. In other words, the person from whom the peasant obtained land was also the person who controlled and dispensed many of the key components for farming such as credit, draft animals, housing, seeds. Often he was also the person who marketed surplus production (when there was any) for the peasant. In contrast to these multistranded ties of past landlord-peasant relations, today's peasantry is far more likely to have precise and well-defined contractual relations for obtaining these same goods and services from several different persons.

The students of rural society whom I call moral economists see the shift from corporate villages of the precapitalist era to open villages and the change from feudal, diffuse, multistranded ties between agrarian elites and peasants to single stranded, precise, and contractual ties as changes which, by exposing peasants directly to market forces, harm peasant welfare. The moral economy approach focuses on the relations between economic and social institutions. It is an economic approach not because it uses the methods of modern economists, but because it addresses important issues about markets and other economic institutions. It is moral not because it assumes peasants and elites were more moral and less calculating in pre-capitalist settings, but because it assumes that, under earlier institutions, the calculus governing behavior leads to more moral outcomes with respect to peasant welfare than under the social arrangements and institutions of modern capitalism.

When I turn to my case study of Vietnam in Chapter 3, (a case which can be read without reference to the first two chapters), I shall deal not only with the general moral economy approach to peasant societies, but also with a more romanticized local variant. To scholars of the countries with this local variant (Spain and Russia, for example), the precapitalist village is seen as a unique form attributable to special virtues of the race or culture. In the Vietnamese variant, the village is perceived as a unique local form generated by a combination of Confucian and Vietnamese virtues; the revolution occurred because colonial decrees stripped the village of the qualities and virtues it once possessed. This is romanticism; this is the "myth of the village." A way of life that may have existed only for lack of alternatives is extolled as a virtue. Peasants who had little or nothing to eat are assumed to have had a rich spiritual life. Sons who may have stayed with their fathers only in order to survive are credited with filial piety. What may have been the absence of incentives to change becomes a resistance to innovation and a defense of traditional ways. The rich who hid their wealth are perceived as having shown great modesty, and hostility among villages is converted to village solidarity. Somehow what might only have been the necessities or oppressions of one era come to be interpreted as traditional values during the next.

The general moral economy theorists with whom I deal in the next two chapters are far more sophisticated. They base their analyses of peasant institutions and their attacks on market economies not on the features of any particular race or culture, but on common challenges and crises which peasants face throughout the world. Nevertheless, these moral economists share views with the more romantic local scholars about the ways in which peasant institutions relate to or develop from the interests and concerns of individual peasants. Further, they all argue that social relations in precapitalist or noncapitalist settings are more moral than are relations in capitalist settings, and that the externally induced "breakdown" of precapitalist institutions hurts peasant welfare. I argue that moral economists base many of their claims on unsupported or unexamined premises and that crucial parts of their view of peasant institutions are without foundation.

I present a political economy alternative to moral economy not merely to clarify the historical record. The debate between moral

and political economy approaches is not simply a matter of historical revisionism, but has contemporary relevance both for the study
of revolution and for rural development. I argue that peasants are
continuously striving not merely to protect but to raise their subsistence level through long- and short-term investments, both public
and private. Their investment logic applies not only to market
exchanges but to nonmarket exchanges as well. Arguing that the
exchanges between peasants are shaped and limited by conflicts between individual and group benefits, I shall demonstrate that villages are best viewed as corporations, not communes, and that
patrons with multistranded ties to peasants are best seen as mo-
nopolists, not paternalists.

This chapter will detail the core assumptions of the moral
economy and political economy approaches to peasant society. In
the next chapter I shall compare and contrast the claims that follow
from such assumptions with material from various peasant societies. Later chapters will present the analysis of Vietnam which follows from my assumptions. The concluding chapter will summar-
ize the arguments of the book and discuss the unifying logic that,
as I shall demonstrate, underlies peasant approaches to markets,
to villages, and to revolutionary involvement.

Here I begin by developing the core assumptions of the moral
economy approach to peasant society. The moral economy approach is a set of assertions about villages, patron-client relations,
and market activity based on assumptions about peasant goals and
behavior. My account is drawn chiefly from the works of contemporary social scientists Eric Wolf, James Scott, and Joel Migdal.
There are differences among these authors in some areas, and not
all their work can be categorized as moral economy, but much of it
shares a common focus and methodological emphasis. The moral
economy perspective is found also in the work of numerous other
contemporary scholars; I cite these three as illustrative of moral
economy because they provide such insightful and systematic elaboration of its assumptions and assertions. The approach often re-
calls well-known writers of antimarket sentiment such as continen-
tal (anti-Marxist) economists like Karl Polanyi and some (*but not
all*) scholars of a Marxist persuasion such as Eric Hobsbawm.

(They are among the many scholars who incorporate portions of the moral economy perspective in their work and accordingly are cited where their views are representative of the general approach. My concern at all times is not with criticizing or labeling specific scholars but with identifying what I believe to be the core of the moral economy approach.)

But one important caveat must be noted: In order to compare the two approaches, I have recast the historical and inductive richness of moral economy thought into a deductive framework of my own construction. I cannot be sure, therefore, that any of the moral economists whose work I discuss would either recognize or agree with my statement of their assumptions or see them as the "right" set of core assumptions. Moreover, while I disagree with many of the conclusions of moral economists, it is their work that has provided the grist for this study and that has provoked many of the questions to be answered in this work. Although many of my findings cannot be incorporated into moral economy, not all of them conflict with this approach. In some areas I have serious disagreements, while in others I merely attempt to expand and clarify observations made by moral economists.

MORAL ECONOMY

An Overview

Peasant protests frequently accompany state making, commercialization of agriculture, and colonialism. Moral economists link the protest movements to a (presumed) loss of subsistence, security, and welfare by the peasantry during these changes. They interpret violence as a defensive reaction against capitalism and as an attempt to restore the precapitalist structures that provided peasant welfare. They argue that the change in welfare is due to changes in the key suprafamily institutions—the village and the patron-client relationship. They assume that peasants are antimarket, prefer common property to private, and dislike buying and selling. They also assume that peasant welfare depends on the closed corporate villages so common in precapitalist society and/or on multistranded feudal ties to those who control the land. The transition to open villages with private property and open land sales, and the transition to contractual, single-stranded ties with landlords, they argue, force peasants into the market where their welfare invariably suffers. For example, Eric Hobsbawm discusses rural protest in nineteenth-century Spain:

> The best explanation is, that the rise of social revolutionism was the consequence of the introduction of capitalist legal and social relationships. . . . It is hardly necessary to analyze the inevitably cataclysmic consequences of so unprecedented an economic revolution on the peasantry. *The rise of social revolutionism followed naturally.* [1]

Although there are variations on common themes in the works of each of its exponents, the preceding summary presents the fundamental and easily recognized characteristics of the moral economy approach. Chief among these is the view that social relations in precapitalist settings are invariably "moral" and that, whenever capitalist institutions are introduced, the fabric of the moral community is rent—in extreme cases destroyed—by the intrusion of the "cash nexus." When villages are "closed" or "corporate"—that is, with limits on the ability of nonvillagers to own land or involve themselves in the internal affairs of the village—and particularly when there is property held in common by the village (communal land), it is assumed that such communities are more humane and protective than are open villages with private property and fewer restrictions on the ability of nonvillagers to involve themselves in the local economy. Where landlord-tenant relations encompass a variety of exchanges, they are assumed to be less harsh than those confined to limited, contractual, rental arrangements. Nonmarket systems, based on a paternalistic ethos, are assumed to be more benevolent, humane, and reliable than market systems. Such common features of precapitalist society as communal property, labor exchange, burial associations, the gifts given by a patron at the birth of a child, the rent reduction after a bad harvest, make survival possible for peasants. These relationships and organizations work well enough, moral economists assume, so that before

1. Eric Hobsbawm, *Primitive Rebels*, p. 80. Emphasis added.

capitalism (or colonialism) individuals starved *if and only if* the entire community was endangered.

Within the institutions of capitalist society, in contrast, people are able to enrich themselves at the expense of the survival of others—they can avoid giving the aid and support they would have given in an earlier time. State formation, capitalism, and colonialism, the moral economists hold, harm peasant welfare, for they increase inequality and stratification and force more and more peasants into isolated and atomized positions without the insurance and protection of their traditional institutions. Capitalism turns land, labor, and wealth into commodities, and this is (for Eric Wolf) "only a short-hand formula for the liquidation of encumbering social and cultural institutions."[2] As for the peasant's "little tradition" of subsistence rights so crucial to his survival, James Scott states that "the process of commercialization and the creation of the nation state have been the assailants of the little tradition everywhere."[3] Peasant welfare is most precarious in precisely those areas where commercial progress is most impressive, Scott assumes,[4] because capitalism, commercialization of agrarian relations, and the centralizing state cut through "the integument of subsistence customs and traditional social rights to replace them with contracts, the market, and uniform laws."[5]

It is the destruction of the peasant's accustomed institutional context for reducing risks, therefore, that creates the tensions that mount toward peasant involvement in rebellion and revolution.[6] The ensuing violence reflects "defensive reactions"[7] or "desperate efforts to maintain subsistence arrangements that are under assault"[8] or to restore them once they have been lost. Peasants have a "traditional distaste of buying and selling" and a millenial dream

2. Eric Wolf, *Peasant Wars of the Twentieth Century,* p. 280.
3. James C. Scott, "Protest and Profanation—Part II," p. 217.
4. James C. Scott, *The Moral Economy of the Peasant,* p. 189.
5. Ibid., p. 2.
6. Wolf, *Peasant Wars,* p. *xv.*
7. Ibid., p. 282.
8. Scott, *Moral Economy,* p. 187. Note also Scott, "Peasant Revolution: A Dismal Science," p. 237, and "Protest and Profanation—Part I," p. 21.

of community property; peasants are opposed to capitalism and the "pre-capitalist closed economy is their utopian goal."[9]

To analyze this interpretation I shall look closely at the assumptions the moral economists make about individual peasant households, villages, and patron-client relations. And a caveat is again in order. All the authors cited present strong central claims, but they also offer numerous qualifications and hedges. Here, as I distill from their works the major arguments, the qualifications cannot receive as much attention as in the original works. However, the strong central claims—and not the qualifications—when linked together support the moral economy interpretation of peasant protest movements.

Safety First

Moral economists see security as quintessentially important because the peasant is poor and always close to the danger line, and a small drop in production can have disastrous effects on the survival of the household. This concern with subsistence and security is called the "safety-first" principle: peasants are averse to risk and focus on avoiding drops, not on maximizing expected profits. Such practices as scattered fields and the use of more than one variety of seed, for example, reflect efforts to avoid drops in income. Opportunities for gain will be eschewed if such opportunities even slightly increase the chance of falling below the subsistence line.[10]

The importance of secure floors, moral economists argue, is reflected in the systems of taxation and rent that peasants will prefer. Whereas to a secure, comfortable farmer, fixed rents and taxes provide maximum incentive to innovate and maximize production—by giving him all of the extra return from increased inputs—peasants with a concern for survival will prefer variable taxes and rents, which might over a period of years take more returns than fixed claims, but which are less onerous in bad years.[11] (As Nguyen van Vinh noted, when Vietnamese peasants demanded

---

9. Scott, "Protest and Profanation—Part II," pp. 231, 229, 245, fn. 214.
10. Scott, *Moral Economy,* pp. 5, 13–55.
11. Ibid., see in particular pp. 35–55.

agrarian reform, they were protesting not so much inequality itself, but the enslavement and dispossession brought about by fixed rents.)[12]

Market crops may offer a larger expected income than subsistence crops, but market and cash crops are assumed to increase the probability of a drop below the danger line. Since such a drop threatens long-run survival, the peasant "keeps the market at arm's length" and produces for sale "only within the context of an assured production for subsistence."[13] James Scott argues that a peasant will be seen as "demented" by his neighbors if he puts all his land into market production, not holding back a part for subsistence production for his family.[14] Rich peasants with savings and the ability to hire labor regularly can afford to engage in market production and to innovate, but poor and middle peasants (laborers, tenants, and smallholders) generally will innovate or enter into market production only when to not do so is to go under: "Peasants whose subsistence formulas are disintegrating due to climate, land shortage, or rising rents do what they can to stay afloat—this may mean switching to cash crops, taking on new debts and planting risky, miracle rice, or it may mean banditry. Much of peasant innovation has this last-gasp quality to it."[15]

The market is a last resort for the peasant, for it is assumed to be a much less certain way of meeting subsistence needs than are other local institutions. Eric Wolf argues that market production occurs only when a peasant is unable to meet his cultural needs within local institutions. If the peasant, who is oriented to local norms and roles, sells a cash crop, the money is only "to buy goods and services which he requires to subsist and to maintain his social status rather than to enlarge his scale of operations."[16] Indeed, James Scott argues that among peasants "the ethos that promoted mutual assistance was partly inspired by a rejection of the market economy. Considering the circumstances and the rigors of commercial

12. Nguyen van Vinh, *Les Reformes agraires au Vietnam*, p. 27.
13. Wolf, *Peasant Wars*, p. xiv.
14. Scott, *Moral Economy*, p. 23.
15. Ibid., p. 26. See also pp. 23–25, 205.
16. Eric Wolf, "Types of Latin American Peasantry: A Preliminary Discussion," p. 454.

agriculture, it is little wonder that many peasants, if given the option, move substantially away from production for the market."[17]

Karl Polanyi, whose ideas prompted and shaped so many of the works discussed here, makes the case against markets even stronger. As George Dalton has summarized Polanyi's thrust, subsistence livelihood "was guaranteed as a right of membership in a human community."[18] Peasants do not need markets, in Polanyi's words, because their needs are satisfied within their institutions: "the alleged propensity of man to barter, truck and exchange is almost entirely apocryphal."[19] If there is to be a labor market, "traditional institutions must be destroyed, and prevented from reforming."[20] Thus, "to include [labor and land] in the market mechanism means to subordinate the substance of society itself to the laws of the market."[21]

Although Polanyi's formulation is the most extreme, all the moral economists cited stress that individuals will go under if, and only if, their communities go under; that is, community mechanisms successfully alleviate pain and safeguard against individual crop failures through the redistribution of resources.

Villages

The village is the key institution that provides peasants with security in precapitalist society. It is a collectivity, which typically operates to assure a *"minimum income"*[22] to its inhabitants, as well as a functional unit whose internal function, in Wolf's conception, is to "equalize the life chances and life risks of its members."[23] For Joel Migdal, because peasants are so close to the line, "there developed community mechanisms to maximize security for the household."[24] Finally, in Scott's words, "the pre-capitalist com-

17. Scott and Kerkvliet, "The Politics of Survival," p. 254.

18. George Dalton, *Economic Anthropology and Development*, p. 14.

19. Karl Polanyi, *The Great Transformation*, p. 44. Note Polanyi's influence on Wolf, *Peasant Wars*, pp. 277, 282, and Scott, *Moral Economy*, p. 5, fn. 8.

20. Polanyi, *The Great Transformation*, p. 163.

21. Ibid., p. 71.

22. Scott, *Moral Economy*, p. 5. Emphasis added.

23. Eric Wolf, "Closed Corporate Communities in Meso-America and Java," p. 12.

24. Migdal, *Peasants, Politics and Revolution*, p. 72.

munity . . . was organized to minimize the risk to which its members were exposed."[25]

Village procedures reflect this overriding concern of peasants with survival, and the subsistence ethic finds social expression in the "patterns of social control and reciprocity that structure daily conduct."[26] The "right to subsistence" is the primary normative concern; the institutions peasants control are organized to insure "the weakest against ruin by making certain demands on better-off villagers."[27] Within the precapitalist village, in particular, generosity and assistance were *imposed* by peasants on their better-off neighbors, and procedures within the village guaranteed "all village families . . . a minimal subsistence niche insofar as the resources controlled by the village make this possible."[28]

Thus, in his relations with fellow villagers, the focus of the peasant is on adherence to norms and roles. In corporate villages, there is a "need to keep social relationships in equilibrium in order to maintain the steady state," and this need is "internalized in the individual as strong conscious efforts to adhere to the traditional roles, roles which were successful in maintaining the steady state in the past."[29] In this view, a peasant's starting point is "needs which are defined by his culture,"[30] and the economic goal of a household is a sufficient "level of resources to discharge its necessary ceremonial and social obligations."[31]

A common feature of many precapitalist villages is the communal management or even ownership of land, as is corporate villages. Internal allocation of collective charges imposed on the village by the state or lord is another characteristic. This local distribution of land and taxes implies "systematic participation in communal political and religious affairs."[32] This systematic participation promotes a shared collectivity and a strong village identity. This identity in turn promotes consensual decision making, controls internal conflict, and prevents the individualistic focus on gain that so dominates atomized capitalist society. Community identity limits

25. Scott, *Moral Economy,* p. 9.
27. Ibid., pp. 33, 41.
29. Wolf, "Types," p. 460.
31. Scott, *Moral Economy,* p. 9.

26. Ibid., p. 40.
28. Ibid., pp. 184, 40, 43.
30. Ibid., p. 454.
32. Wolf, "Types," p. 457.

and controls differences in wealth among peasants by pressuring the wealthy to put any surplus into feasts or other village benefits—a redistributive mechanism that "levels differences of wealth,"[33] works "against the development of large differences in wealth,"[34] or "redistribute(s) or consume(s) the surplus wealth of the richest."[35] In other words, social pressures and the desire for prestige within the village lead to an expenditure of surplus income within the village that levels income differences. Thus, if there is a short-run accumulation of resources, it will be spent on fellow villagers.

Similarly, resistance to innovation reflects a concern for the poor—an adherence to the subsistence ethic (as well as a distrust of markets): "a shared risk insurance policy . . . demanded that the village deny certain members the right to import 'progressive methods' because of the detrimental effect they could have on the poorest."[36]

Particularly important in making the case for the value of villages vis-à-vis individualist market strategies for peasant survival are the moral economists' assumptions about the response of villages, *as villages,* to increased demands on village resources, particularly from population growth. As population density increases, there is an intensification of agricultural methods including more weeding, hoeing, ploughing; more labor-intensive methods of harvesting and planting; and more sophisticated irrigation. This intensification of agricultural technique increases the role of the village in the production process, for intensification involves villagewide developments such as irrigation and drainage systems. The term that symbolizes this intensification is *agricultural involution.* But the involution process also has come to mean the *sharing and spreading of work* to make room for otherwise superfluous persons, so that the village is able to achieve "the minimization of socioeconomic contrasts . . . through that more ancient weapon of the poor: work spreading."[37]

33. Ibid., p. 458.
34. James C. Scott, "The Erosion of Patron-Client Bonds and Social Change in Rural Southeast Asia," p. 27.
35. Joel Migdal, *Peasants, Politics and Revolution,* p. 69.
36. Ibid., p. 73.
37. Clifford Geertz, *Agricultural Involution,* p. 100.

Thus, when demands on village resources increase, as long as the village is intact there is an "internal capacity to share resources" by village redistributive mechanisms through such techniques as "labor exchange which spreads the available work as far as possible."[38] A village thus strives "to guarantee its members some basic livelihood within the confines of the community."[39] In addition to the sharing or spreading of work, such village efforts also involve limits on standards of living for members of the community. Wolf argues that increased pressure on resources "leads to the establishment of a culturally recognized standard of consumption which consciously excludes cultural alternatives. By reducing alternative items of consumption, the community reduced the threat to its integrity."[40] In the same vein, Scott says that "social pressures such as jealousy and envy—or accusations of witchcraft—operated informally to discourage any desire to outdistance fellow villagers while those who did, in fact, fare somewhat better than average were pressed to redistribute their wealth."[41]

Patron-Client Relations

The other main institution in peasant society is the relation of the client or peasant (or tenant) to his lord or patron (or landlord).[42] Patron-client relations refer to dyadic relations which encompass a "broad but imprecise spectrum of mutual obligations consistent with the belief that the patron should display an almost parental concern for and responsiveness to the needs of his client and that the latter should display almost filial loyalty to the patron."[43] The continued existence of patron-client relations rests on the legitimacy of the tie for the peasant. This legitimacy, in turn, rests on the provision by the lord of fundamental subsistence rights for the

38. Scott, *Moral Economy,* p. 61; Scott and Kerkvliet, "Politics of Survival," pp. 242, 253.
39. Wolf, "Types," p. 458.
40. Ibid., pp. 458–459.
41. Scott and Kerkvliet, "Politics of Survival," p. 243.
42. Like the moral economists, I deal mainly with suprafamily institutions. However, the rapid growth of research on inheritance laws, extended and nuclear families, and demography in general will soon make possible far more attention to issues of family and population.
43. Carl Lande, "Networks and Groups in Southeast Asia," p. 105.

peasant. The terms of exchange in such relationships depend on the relative bargaining power of the two parties.

According to the moral economy perspective, the existence of patrons is linked to social norms and considerations of prestige:

> A wealthy man is pressed by villagers to assume expensive ceremonial offices, to make large religious contributions, to give personal loans and donations, and so forth. He trades some of his wealth for prestige and, by so providing for at least the minimum well being of others, he becomes a legitimate patron . . .[44]

> . . . minimum terms traditionally demanded by the peasant/client are physical security and a subsistence livelihood. This expectation is at the root of the peasantry's "paternalist moral economy", the basis of its conception of justice and equity. A breach of these minimum requirements . . . serves to undermine the legitimacy of the patron class and to provide the peasantry with a moral basis for action against agrarian elites.[45]

Although the goals or motives of the patron are never fully articulated, the emphasis of this branch of patron-client analysis (as opposed to Marxist critiques, for example) is clearly on the concepts of subsistence and legitimacy. Implicit in moral economy analyses is the proposition that the longevity and success of a lord in his role rests on the quality of the subsistence guarantee he provides his clients. The patron's route to fame or riches rests on maintaining legitimacy among his clients, and that is achieved by maintaining their subsistence guarantee. Social norms of fairness and justice must be upheld, or "subordinates will feel exploited and seize any opportunity to escape the ruling group's power or oppose it."[46] Social norms impose standards; when standards are not upheld, moral outrage and rebellion ensue. For elites, the peasantry's subsistence ethic means that they must not invade the subsistence reserves of the poor and that, furthermore, they have a positive moral obligation to provide maintenance needs in time of dearth.[47] Thus, subsistence claims apply to both villages and patrons. For the moral economists, it is the subsistence ethic that provides the

44. Scott, "The Erosion of Patron-Client Bonds and Social Change in Rural Southeast Asia," pp. 16–17.
45. Ibid., p. 7.
46. Peter Blau, *Exchange and Power in Social Life*, p. 229.
47. Scott, *Moral Economy*, p. 33.

perspective from which peasants view claims on their resources: "The peasant's criterion will be what is left after outside claims have been met—whether it is enough to maintain his basic requirements—rather than the level of the claims per se."[48] With respect to taxes or rents, what moves peasants to rebel is "the smallness of what was left rather than the amount taken."[49]

The growth of the central state, the commercialization of agriculture, and the growth of population all serve, they argue, to shift the terms of exchange against clients. In times of subsistence agriculture, weak states, and low population, such alternative sources of support as the village, along with unclaimed land on the frontier and the absence of outside backing for local powerholders, prevented the balance from moving radically in favor of the patron.[50] When the multistranded ties to patrons who provided all the essential services, insurance, and credits necessary for agriculture erode and the bonds dissolve, peasants will attempt to form new patron-client relationships with moneylenders, shopkeepers, and so forth. But whether there are multistranded ties to one patron or single-stranded ties to numerous patrons, a peasantry that can meet short-run subsistence requirements through such ties will be "effectively demobilized by virtue of its dependence links."[51] Without a short-run subsistence crisis, then, peasants will not engage in protest activities.

Conclusion

The widespread impact of moral economists on peasant studies cannot be overstated. Their analyses of danger lines, subsistence threats, and risk demonstrate that economic change or development is not merely a problem of changing "traditional" attitudes. They show that many of the norms and procedures of peasant society are embedded in considerations of subsistence and survival; they see the village as a ritual and cultural unit and also an important part of peasant economic life as a source of rights and re-

48. Ibid., p. 29.
49. Ibid., p. 11.
50. Scott, "Erosion," p. 7.
51. Scott and Kerkvliet, "Politics of Survival," p. 256.

sources. Their investigation of the services and economic goods exchanged between patrons and clients, furthermore, has focused research on the relationship between forms of patron-client exchange and peasant security.

The spate of ideas that has resulted from the moral economy approach to peasant studies, however, leaves some important questions unanswered and provides incomplete answers to still others which are central to political economy. How, to name but a few, are norms derived? What determines the "subsistence level"? How are village resources allocated? How are competing claims of need assessed and resources distributed? How is it determined whether a man who had a bad crop this year and an excellent crop last year is better or worse off than a man with an average crop for both years? (Should "income averaging" be allowed?) How is work shared? When there is pressure on resources and "work-sharing" occurs, how (and by whom) is it decided who will give up work for others? Are "need" and "inability to pay" synonymous? Who is more "needy": a young couple who cannot yet afford children, a large family with a sick child, a poor person who cannot afford a wife, an old person with irresponsible children, or an inefficient farmer whose crop failure may be due to negligence? In the case of crop failures that strike but a few peasants, how is "sloth" distinguished from an act of fate? In other words, how are needs ranked? Further, when is it the responsibility of the village, as opposed to the responsibility of family, friends, children, or patrons, to help a needy peasant? Why should a peasant, worried about the security of his family, subsidize others instead of preparing for his future by saving money or buying an animal or having another child? What assurance is there, if he does contribute to village programs to aid others, that the village will not default when he himself needs aid?

If peasants scatter their fields to reduce chances of a total crop failure, why not scatter their ties among many different patrons? Why should multistranded ties be preferable? What if a peasant depends on one person for all his needs and that person dies? What if the lord leaves everything to a profligate heir? If there is a communal ethic and effective village-leveling mechanisms, how do lords get the bargaining power over peasants necessary to raise rents? Since a landlord's bargaining power with any individual ten-

ant rests on the former's ability to redistribute the tenant's parcels
ar.ong other tenants, why don't peasants establish a norm of equal
shares and agree never to assume the parcels of a fellow tenant?
Indeed, how do landlords (and laborers without land) emerge?

If peasants are close to the line, and village office-holding requires a sacrifice of income due to the feasts involved in the leveling mechanisms, why do peasants aspire to village office? What
guarantees the village leadership in a crisis? If all surpluses are
redistributed, what incentives are there to work harder and have a
better year?

To answer these questions a new approach is required, for they
cannot be considered within models derived from the premises of
moral economists. (Moral economists are fully aware of the dis-
trusts, jealousies, frictions, rivalries, and conflicts within villages,
but argue that villages function to overcome these conflicts and to
provide the minimal guarantees and welfare on which they focus.) I
shall argue that village institutions work less well than they maintain, in large part because of conflicts between individual and group
interests, and that far more attention must be paid to motivations for
personal gain among the peasantry. I shall argue that village procedures reinforce, not level, differences and that both village procedures and the relations between peasants and lords are sources of
stratification within the peasantry.

In order to focus on the dynamics of village society and address
these issues directly, I shall begin with alternate assumptions—
assumptions that raise new questions about villages, patrons, and
markets. These questions will draw attention to data that challenge
or modify some of the conclusions of moral economists about market and nonmarket institutions, about the quality of subsistence
guarantees in precapitalist villages, and about the relationship between individual and group interests.

POLITICAL ECONOMY

Basic Assumptions

My analysis of peasant society begins with a focus on individual
decision making and an expanded conception of the role of the village in peasant economic life. Modifying the (implicit) assumptions

of moral economists, I shall consider gambles as well as risks, apply investment logic to villages and patron-client relations as well as to markets, and look at the conflicts and tradeoffs between private and collective benefits involved in both village management and the life of the peasant.

By applying theories of individual decision making to villages, we can begin to develop a deductive understanding of peasant institutions and move the analysis back one step to the level of the individual. By using the concepts of individual choice and decision making, we can discuss how and why groups of individuals decide to adopt some sets of norms while rejecting others. From this perspective, norms become problematic, and questions arise which may be otherwise overlooked. What is an enforceable norm? Under what conditions will individuals consider bending or breaking norms? By trying to analyze norms, allocation procedures, and rules deductively, we can ask, "Where do these particular norms, procedures, and rules come from?" When we theorize about how particular procedures are developed and bargains are struck, the implications for peasants of specific rules and procedures (from the universe of all possible norms and procedures) are made clear. We can ask why some procedures and norms arise in some contexts, but not in others, and this question leads to a heightened appreciation of the problems involved in developing and maintaining villagewide insurance and welfare schemes.

Investments and Gambles

Moral economists have posited that peasants have an aversion to risk when evaluating economic strategies—they prefer strategies with low but certain returns to strategies that may produce higher returns but also may have a higher risk of a disastrous drop in output. Certainly, political economists would agree that whenever a small loss would be disastrous, peasants will be extremely risk averse. Although poor and close to the margin, however, there are still many occasions when peasants do have some surplus and do make risky investments: the fact that they are poor and risk averse does not imply, either logically or factually, that they do not make investments. Peasants make long-term as well as short-term investments, and therefore have long-term and short-term investment crises, and they make risky as well as secure investments. Peasants plan and invest throughout both the crop cycle and the life cycle, and they place a high priority on investment for old age. Furthermore, besides deciding between long-term and short-term investments, peasants must choose between public and private investments, both long and short run. Peasants do decide whether to invest in children, animals, land, and other individual or family goods, on the one hand, or on the other, whether to spend their surplus through the village, on insurance or welfare programs or village improvements.

That children (in addition to everything else) are an investment is clear. In Java, for example, people feel secure only when they have their own children—whether natural or adopted—to rely on in their old age.[52] In Zambia, the family is a mutual support system within which those who possess resources can reasonably be expected to distribute them to those who do not, and children are viewed as a source of future income. It is even reasonable to rural Zambians that "a man would murder . . . were he denied access to the earnings of a youth he had supported."[53] Moreover, the value of children as old-age insurance is intimately linked to property. In Thailand, "parents hope children will repay their kindness and the trouble they took to raise them by caring for them in their old age, but they cannot rely on their children and thus the parents retain title to their property as long as they can to protect themselves."[54] Long-run security via children is intimately connected with short-run accumulation of property, including land, tools, and cattle. For any tenancy system—no matter how well off the tenants are—in the short run may threaten long-term security because of the problems of maintaining a family without property.[55] As a family firm, then, peasant couples will make tradeoffs between children and property

52. Ben White, "Production and Reproduction in a Javanese Village," chap. 9.
53. Robert Bates, *Rural Responses to Industrialization: A Study of Village Zambia*, pp. 197, 193–202, is a general elaboration of a family investment model. Bates's analysis of rural families and urban opportunities stands as a landmark.
54. Jack Potter, *Thai Peasant Social Structure*, p. 191.
55. Gerald C. Hickey, *Village in Vietnam*, p. 96, notes that patrilineages with property are more likely to have the corporate group characteristics so highly prized by villagers.

which have a long-run focus. Today, a peasant couple may refuse to incorporate labor-saving, profitable machinery if it puts their children out of work and thus deprives their "firm" of continuity and old-age security.[56] In an earlier age, European peasant couples not infrequently practiced infanticide rather than sell property, because children were easier to replace than oxen, tools, or land. Indeed, there often has been a preference for infanticide over contraception or abortion because infanticide makes possible a conscious control of the sex ratio.[57]

Given the need for investments, then, we can distinguish at least two kinds of subsistence crises. Besides the short-run subsistence crises where there is imminent starvation for the peasant couple (or a child), there is also a long-run subsistence crisis where a couple may be secure and comfortable for the short run but be without resources to build and maintain a family for either long-run security or to live a long life ("A larger daily ration is needed to keep a person alive until fifty than until forty or twenty. Staying alive is one thing, working hard is another"[58]). Moral economists have shown that during protests and rebellions peasants invariably use a language of claims focused on demands for, or the right to, a subsistence.[59] But, as I shall show, there are some groups or classes that do not revolt even when faced with a severe short-run subsistence crisis, whereas others may rebel over a much smaller short-run crisis or even revolt when there is no short-run crisis to secure a better long-run subsistence. To treat all subsistence crises as the same form of short-run crisis is to brush over the differences in demand-making ability and the ways in which subsistence levels change.

Just as peasants, despite their concern with subsistence, make

56. S. H. Franklin, *The European Peasantry: The Final Phase,* passim.

57. Norman Himes, *Medical History of Contraception,* p. 52. White, "Production and Reproduction," p. 10, notes a sex ratio of three women to every four men before and after (but not during) the Black Death, which means that at least 25 percent of all female infants were eliminated through some form of active or benign infanticide. Himes (pp. 51–52) also notes that where infanticide is practiced children may not be considered members of society, hence human, until they are past the age where parents might be forced into abandoning (or benignly neglecting) them.

58. William Letwin, "The Contradictions of Serfdom," p. 373.

59. See, as an excellent example, Scott, *Moral Economy,* chap. 5, "The Depression Rebellions."

long- and short-run investments, so there are occasions when they will make risky investments or gambles. There will be times when a person on one step of the economic ladder will have a small surplus with which to gamble in the hope of reaching the next higher step. Whenever a small amount can be lost without threatening his position, a peasant may gamble that amount for a chance at advancement. Peasant families often sent one or more children to the frontier in colonial Southeast Asia in the hope that they would strike it rich for the family. In other words, collaboration among family members may mean that many actions that would be very risky for a couple to undertake on their own can be undertaken by the larger family unit with moderate risk. As moral economists note, there are many peasant proverbs counseling caution, but there are also those that encourage the pioneer spirit, such as the Burmese proverb; "Without transfer to another village, a person cannot become great."[60] Peasants often are willing to gamble on innovations when their position is secure against the loss and when a success could measurably improve their position. There are times when a small loss would mean a big fall, but there are also times when a small loss would mean little and a win would move the peasant up one level. This is precisely the logic that William Foot Whyte found toward lotteries (during the Depression) in *Street Corner Society:* "Saving, therefore, is not a real alternative to gambling on the numbers. The small change would be dissipated in one way or another, whereas the large amounts occasionally won have real meaning for the corner boy . . . to pay off debts, to buy an outfit of clothes, to treat his friends, to give some money to his parents."[61] Thus, the pure safety-first assumption about floors must be amended to include the many long-term as well as short-term investments and gambles or risky investments as well as cautious risk-averse investments. This is the classic formulation of insurance and gambling developed in 1948 by Savage and Friedman.[62] As long as there are multiple economic levels, an interest in advancing

60. Michael Adas, *The Burma Delta: Economic Development and Social Change on an Asian Rice Frontier 1852–1941*, p. 50.
61. William Foote Whyte, *Street Corner Society*, p. 141.
62. Milton Friedman and L. J. Savage, "The Utility Analysis of Choices Involving Risk," pp. 279–304.

from one level to the next, and an interest in avoiding falls, peasants will be concerned with both *insurance* and *gambling*, that is, secure and risky investments.

Villages

Moral economy analyses of the village, as I have noted, emphasize the importance of norms and assume that the norms and procedures of villages and of patron-client exchanges are fixed and culturally determined. I expect to find, on the contrary, that norms are malleable, renegotiated, and shifting in accord with considerations of power and strategic interaction among individuals. There are always tradeoffs between conflicting and inconsistent norms.

Moral economy analyses of the village say little about how "need" is assessed. If "needy" villagers are to be helped by the village, or if influential persons are supposed to aid those in need, then it is necessary to rank-order needs in order to allocate insurance or aid. The inconsistencies and conflicts among norms suggest that norms cannot directly and simply determine actions, that decision making is involved in assessing need, and that the principles for making such comparative decisions are not easily arrived at or maintained. It is extremely difficult to rank-order norms—that is, to develop a single, stable, universally accepted social welfare function. These problems of applying norms lead to the uncertainty inherent in relying on village institutions for future welfare (and insurance). Consequently, peasants will favor personal investment in future welfare—through children and savings—rather than automatically investing in, and relying on, future reciprocity and insurance from the village.

These two dimensions of subsistence crisis—short-term subsistence and long-term investment—complicate the problem of intravillage transfers and aid. It is far easier for a scholar to hypothesize short-term transfers for people suffering short-term crises if *long-term* crises are ignored. Given long- and short-term crises, however, the peasant who has avoided the short-term crisis through skill or luck is not necessarily being asked merely to forego a modicum of luxury to ease the pain of his suffering co-villager; by giving short-term relief to a fellow villager, he is sometimes being asked to risk an insecure old age. (Or if the suffering co-villager is given short-term aid and dies anyway, there may be less cushion for the giver when his own crop fails the next year.)

The same investment logic is applied to villages as to markets. That is, contributions to the village, participation in insurance and welfare schemes, and exchanges between patron and client are all guided by investment logic, and the closer persons come to the danger point, the more cautious they will be in their investments. Villagers, after all, can default or go bankrupt. As we shall see, in a declining situation with everyone close to the danger point, villages will function *less well* as individuals become more cautious about contributing to insurance and welfare schemes with (increasingly uncertain) future payoffs and use the money for themselves and for the short run—avoiding the dangers of risky long-run village investments. In other words, the demand for insurance will rise as life becomes more risky, but supply will fall as the probability that premiums will be paid declines. This contrasts with the hypothesis of moral economists, who, emphasizing needs, would predict that the poorer the peasants and the closer to danger they come, the greater the need; hence, the more inclusive and pervasive would be the insurance and welfare schemes within the village.

Given these uncertainties, I predict that peasants will rely on private, family investments for their long-run security and that they will be interested in short-term gain vis-à-vis the village. They will attempt to improve their long-run security by moving to a position with higher income and less variance (which usually means trying to go from laborer to tenant to smallholder to landlord).[63] Economic conflict over advancement to more secure positions is therefore inevitable within the village.[64]

63. Scott, *Moral Economy,* chap. 2, emphasizes decreasing variance more and increasing income less than I do here, but the difference is one of degree. The major difference is in the implications of the long-run versus short-run and public versus private investment choices involved for the way that villages and patron-client relations operate.

64. Of course, if there were a truly efficient prestige economy in which all surplus were converted into village resources, there would be less selfish concern with advancement—and possibly also less incentive to work. But if there is truly a moral economy, it is not clear how classes and strata emerge at all.

Free Riders

Because moral economists focus on land and labor as the two factors in peasant production, they view the village primarily as a source of insurance or welfare. An enlarged view of the agricultural production process, however, leads to vastly different predictions about the economic role of the village. In addition to insurance or welfare, many other types of local collective action are characteristic of peasant society, particularly when the central state is weak. Law and order, adjudication, property rights, religious rites, irrigation and flood control, as well as taxes and labor services to state and lord are all essential to local economic life. Coordinated action is required for the provision of these goods and the distribution of the collective and divisible benefits. Political economy focuses on factors which make it difficult to achieve even mutually beneficial coordinated action. Unless the expected benefits outweigh the costs, the villager can be presumed not to contribute to collective action.

Many collective projects—such as law and order, fire-fighting, slaying marauding tigers—benefit an individual whether he contributes or not. I assume that the individual weighs his decision about participation in the supply of these public goods. When weighing his contribution, a peasant can be expected to take account of several factors relating to costs and benefits: (1) Expenditure of resources—if a peasant contributes to a collective action, he must expend valuable resources. Additionally, he may be punished for participating if the action (such as rebellion) fails. (2) Positive rewards—the value of the direct and indirect benefits. (3) Probability of his action leading to reward (efficacy)—the effectiveness of a contribution depends on its marginal contribution to the success of the endeavor. This in turn depends on how other actions aggregate, whether they bring the effort sufficiently close to success to make a contribution worthwhile. (4) Leadership viability and trust—the ultimate success of an endeavor often depends not only on the volume of resources mobilized but on the leadership skill with which they are mobilized.

Given these considerations, whenever there is coordinated action to produce collective goods, individuals may calculate they are better off not contributing. As long as they cannot be excluded from the good, there is the potential for free riders, individuals who do not contribute to the provision of goods because they believe they will receive the gain or security even if they do not participate. This divergence between the interest of the group to complete a project and the interest of an individual to benefit without contributing suggests that an individual who attaches no special personal (psychic) benefits to the act of participation and who does not view his contribution as necessary will not contribute without an incentive to do so.[65]

Collective action and the free-rider problem are crucial to comparisons between moral and political economy approaches to peasant institutions. If the moral economy views are correct, there is a community orientation whereby the free-rider and leadership problems are easily overcome by proper socialization to norms placing a high value on voluntarism. If, on the other hand, there are substantial problems of organization, individuals may withhold contributions and projects may not be undertaken or may be carried out in ways that are less than optimal. Under these conditions the political economy approach can be of value in explicating the dynamics of collective action. In fact, as we shall see, the problems of collective action are crucial to the analysis of villages and patron-client relations; it is difficult under the best of circumstances to organize peasants to provide collective goods, and the coalitions formed may be precarious.

If free-rider problems exist, as I predict, then the structure of peasant society will reflect the problems of coordinating mechanisms for the provision of collective goods. In many situations there will be arrangements for providing goods that could, if enacted, leave all better off, but that will not be successful because of the problem of free riders. There are times when many collective goods (including insurance or welfare schemes) will be provided by small groups, although large groups could do better—because neither the necessary skills nor incentive systems exist to maintain larger groups (or because cautious peasants, seeking to avert the risk posed by concentrating resources in the hands of another peasant, are unwilling to invest their resources in large-scale projects).

65. Amplification of the collective action paradigm appears in Chapter 6.

Similar issues are raised by the distribution of charges assessed by lords or states on the village and by the distribution of resources to the needy. Unless there is widespread consensus on exactly how to assess and distribute, favoritism and personal profit may influence leadership decisions. Peasant institutions, therefore, have a built-in tension: the benefits of valuable villagewide services and leadership versus the chance of personal loss from power concentrated in the hands of another peasant. In the political economy approach, there is no determinate answer to how this dilemma will be resolved. Hobbes versus Rousseau, Banfield versus Redfield, are not debates between self-interest and moral community: whether the outcome will be stability or power struggles and optimal or suboptimal provision of collective goods and services depends on leadership, shared moral codes, past performance, and numerous other variables to be discussed in this book. Both conflict and cooperation, both power struggles and widespread benefits, are inherent in village patterns of distribution and collective action.

In a world of local institutions, uncertain leadership, cautious investors, and a weak central state, village citizenship can have great motive force because membership in a village is a benefit—a license to participate in the economy of the village—in and of itself. The village need not provide welfare or insurance to be important to peasant survival; citizenship alone can bind a peasant to a village.

Further, if there is distrust and suspicion among peasants, if expanding the land under cultivation requires additional collective projects, or if it is difficult to learn the rules of collective action and cooperation within a village, there may emerge a large group of peasants who are considered ''outsiders'' and who are never granted full rights within the village. The presence of outsiders who lead lives as second-class citizens reminds us that there can be stratification even with a frontier of available land. Land may even be worthless if there is no village to provide such collective goods as self-defense, irrigation, or religious rites.

Finally, the possibility that mutual suspicion and mistrust, or the absence of skilled leadership, can impede or prevent collective action helps us to understand why there were political and religious movements that reorganized villages even in precapitalist society. These movements could improve peasant life and bring profit to the leaders by offering better local leadership and therefore less risky and more profitable collective goods. The success of both the Jesuits in precapitalist Vietnam and the Communist cadres in the twentieth century in the same country are testimony to the opportunities for leadership that can overcome free-rider problems and provide collective goods in peasant villages.

Patron-Client Relations

In addition to an expanded view of the village, I take a broader view of patron-client relations than those who assume that they are self-reinforcing, dyadic relations beneficial to both parties and that the exchanges, while governed by norms and constrained by the subsistence needs of the weaker party, are based on the relative bargaining power of the parties. I assume that the very concept of a subsistence minimum, or of the level of resources necessary to discharge obligations, is variable and endogenous to the economic system, that it is not culturally determined and fixed, and that peasants strive to improve traditional standards of living. Further, the dyadic nature of the relationship is not inherent, but is a matter of the ability of the lord or patron to individualize relations and prevent collective bargaining. This, in turn, means that resources of the patron will be invested, not only to improve the security and subsistence of the client, but to keep relations dyadic and prevent the client's acquisition of any skills that might lead to different balances of power.

Changing the terms of exchange or overthrowing lords require collective action among tenants or clients. There can be consensus among tenants as to the desirability of collective bargaining or of standards to which landed elites should be held, but the ability of tenants to hold a lord to a particular standard will depend on the ability of the group to act in concert and thus to overcome free riders.

CONCLUSION

Having detailed the core assumptions of the two approaches, I shall next compare and contrast analyses of peasant society based on the two sets of assumptions. I emphasize again that the debate over assumptions is not only a matter of historical interest, but also a matter of import for the study both of revolution and of rural development, and that the set of assumptions with which I am working here leads to precisely those data often overlooked by moral economists.

The emphasis of moral economists on stable systems upset by the penetration of markets and national governments leads to the assumption that decline, decay, erosion of bonds, or loss of legitimacy are necessary before new forms of organization will take root among peasants. I argue, however, that there is no need for dramatic subsistence crises before peasants in "feudal" or subsistence areas will support revolutionaries. Peasants in subsistence areas may be less likely to generate new organizations themselves, but when outside allies are available to provide the initial impetus they can be as revolutionary, indeed more so, than peasants in commercial centers. Further, moral economists emphasize the restorative nature of peasant protest, the fight to reclaim lost rights or privileges. This overlooks demands for the extension of rights held only by some peasants within the village, as well as the support peasants will give to movements that are able to make old practices intolerable.

The emphasis that moral economists place on floors and the assumption that only rich peasants will pursue innovation and gain generally lead to the expectation that private ownership of new technologies and innovations will be of no benefit to smallholders and tenants and that only bureaucratic approaches to development can protect peasants from the hazards of markets. But my case study of Vietnam suggests that more stratification may result from differential access to and control of the bureaucracy and other ancillary institutions of the market than from the markets themselves. Further, revolutionaries who expect peasants to have no interest in market production as long as their subsistence floor is secure are likely, as we shall see, to have problems maintaining control when peasants in liberated areas seek to enter the markets with their newly recovered surplus.

If it is accepted that peasants will innovate only as a last-gasp attempt to keep from going under, then it is easy to overlook the many occasions when peasants will innovate, in the absence of crises, in order to raise their production floors. In the same vein, if it is assumed that peasants have a fixed view of a proper income, that they will not strive to raise their income beyond that level, and that they are not interested in new forms of consumption, then it is easy to justify forcible, coercive development policies as the only means to extract a surplus from the peasantry for industrialization.

Similarly, an overly sanguine view of the ability of villages to cooperate leads to false hopes for community development schemes requiring voluntarism or a broad concern with welfare. Communal land systems are historically unstable because improved agricultural techniques require more coordination of investment than is generally possible. And peasants often will forego community welfare programs in order to avoid the conflicts that arise when they try to reach consensus on how to distribute aid: flexible systems require giving leeway to leaders and are thus systems with potential for abuse. Assuming that peasants are self-interested, I will analyze cooperation in peasant society based on task-specific incentives and calculations. In the final chapter, I will show how enlargements of Mancur Olson's approach to free riders and collective goods help to explain the considerations whereby peasants will be able to organize successfully.

Moral economists have argued that, from the perspective of peasant welfare, peasant society is moral, economically efficient, and stable. I, in contrast, will argue that none of these can be assumed. Moral economists take too benign a view of villages and patron-client ties and too harsh a view of market potential. They do not always look closely enough at the ways in which markets can benefit peasants nor at the structural factors that determine the impact a market (or a technology) will have on peasants. It is harder than they sometimes assume for peasants averse to risk (as moral economists recognize peasants to be) to make villages work well.

Fuller attention must be paid to the ways in which aversion to risk affects intravillage (as well as market) relations, and more consideration must be given to conflicts between group and individual interests; it is also necessary to differentiate among the different types of crises that threaten peasants. In the sense that peasants make moral judgments about one another, the village is indeed a moral community. I argue that peasants see in one another sufficient uncertainty or threat to make social interactions difficult.[66] Moreover, the range of persons for whom peasants make sacrifices (or for whom they do not keep strict accounts) is narrow and generally limited to family units that cook and eat together and that pool many of their day-to-day resources. Indeed, the problems of leadership and organization within peasant communities severely limit the quality of insurance and seriously restrict production. The development of new and better forms of community organization is therefore part of the appeal of new religious and political movements before, as well as during, colonialism.

Moral economists have aptly noted the ways whereby technological and market developments may be of no value to many peasants or may even decrease their welfare. They tend to ignore, however, the links between the impact of markets, on the one hand, and precapitalist village structures and patron-client relations, on the other. It is also important to look at the positive benefits of markets, especially when they are properly tamed by political and religious movements and when the auxiliary institutions of the market are reorganized.

In this political economy, as opposed to moral economy, approach, I am above all seeking a different strategy of inquiry, one which emphasizes individual decision making and strategic interaction. As Brian Barry has stated, economic theory (roughly equivalent to the political economy approach) is a method of analysis: the postulation of a number of actors with certain ends and a deductive attempt to work out how persons will act in situations which present certain alternatives, "on the assumption that they pursue their goals

66. F. G. Bailey, *Gifts and Poison*, p. 295.

rationally.''[67] In adopting an economic approach I am adopting a method. It should be clear that I am *not* committing myself to the view that individuals are solely concerned with material commodities or money incomes. By rationality I mean that individuals evaluate the possible outcomes associated with their choices in accordance with their preferences and values. In doing this, they discount the evaluation of each outcome in accordance with their subjective estimate of the likelihood of the outcome. Finally, they make the choice which they believe will maximize their expected utility.[68] Many persons equate rationality and self-interest—with self-interest defined as "interest only in one's own welfare." I most emphatically deny that persons are self-interested in this narrow sense. It is clearly the case that, at different times, peasants care about themselves, their families, their friends, and their villages. However, I do assume that a peasant is primarily concerned with the welfare and security of self and family. Whatever his broad values and objectives, when the peasant takes into account the likelihood of receiving the preferred outcomes *on the basis of individual actions,* he usually will act in a self-interested manner.

Further, I specifically focus on rationality from the point of view of the individual, for what is rational for an individual may be very different from what is rational for an entire village or collective. I shall point out the difference between the two views of rationality and show the conflicts between them. Indeed, it is frequently the case that the actions of individually rational peasants in both market and nonmarket situations do not aggregate to a "rational" village.

67. Brian Barry, *Sociologists, Economists and Democracy,* p. 5. Barry's book has greatly influenced the style and methodology of this volume. His introduction, pp. 1–12, is a superb and important discussion of the difference between sociological and economic approaches to theory. Ronald Rogowski's "Rationalist Theories of Politics" is a lucid analysis of other ventures in this approach.

68. The standard way in which discounting is assumed to take place is expected value. However, many alternatives are being developed, and no single narrow assumption is needed for the purposes of this study.

2

The Political Economy of

Peasant Society

THE CORE assumptions of both
the moral economy and political economy approaches to peasant
society have been identified in Chapter 1. Building on the political
economy assumptions, in this chapter hypotheses will be developed
about villages and patron-client relationships that will be applied in
succeeding chapters to the case of Vietnam. Contrasting political
economy predictions with those of the moral economists, and drawing on suggestive evidence from various peasant societies, this
examination of the inner workings of village and patron-client relationships will demonstrate the need for important revisions in previous interpretations of the effects on peasant society of commercial
agriculture, the growth of central states, and colonialism. In particular, precisely because insurance, welfare, and subsistence
guarantees within precapitalist villages are *limited,* a change in village structures—from closed to open villages—does not necessarily, as moral economists have asserted, result in a loss of these

32

supports, although it may change their nature. Nor is the development of linkages between the village and the wider system always—and only—initiated from outside the village, as they have further assumed.

Because villages do not provide extensive insurance or welfare, there does not have to be a crisis before peasants will involve themselves in commercial agriculture; their involvement is generally not a last-gasp response to declining situations, *but a response to new opportunities.* Indeed, the expansion of markets is frequently of particular benefit to poorer peasants, while it is large lords and patrons who prevent market involvement by peasants in order to protect their own control of the economy. These alternate views of the village and of patron-client relations generate a different analysis of peasant protests and rebellions—one that emphasizes the benefits, as well as the hazards, of markets and national development; one that stresses individual, instead of group, benefits and losses.

Moral economists have argued that the procedures within pre-capitalist, closed (or corporate) villages, where land is held in common and taxes are paid by the village, led to internal leveling and redistribution, and to villagewide insurance and welfare systems that provided subsistence guarantees for poorer villagers. In contrast, I show that the calculations of peasants driven by motives of survival in a risky environment led not to subsistence floors and extensive villagewide insurance schemes, but to procedures that generated and enforced inequality within the village. Procedures for distributing both land and tax assessments within the villages favored the wealthier peasants, and both insurance and welfare at the village level were limited. In part because of village procedures, these villages contained large numbers of persons with minimal rights and with standards of living far below what the more substantial villagers would tolerate for themselves. Because of the limited extent of insurance and this large underclass with few political or economic rights, the transition from closed to open villages did not invariably lower the levels of peasant welfare or insurance. Further, the limited abilities of peasants to generate villagewide insurance and welfare and the large underclass within the villages help explain the attractiveness to peasants of those religious and political movements that could provide the leadership necessary for increased production and for insurance and welfare.

Because moral economists have viewed closed villages as stable and autonomous, the process by which linkages develop between village and supravillage authorities has been described as "penetration." The metaphor of penetration has emphasized outside initiation and the need for force to overcome collective resistance by the village to new linkages. This reflects a misunderstanding of the internal dynamics of villages and the role which external authorities played in regulating village life and protecting the poor within villages. It also neglects the divergence between collective and individual interests and the fact that the initiators were frequently villagers seeking outside allies in local power struggles.

When problems of organization within villages are carefully examined, it becomes clear that many innovations fail (or are not adopted) not because of a positive regard for tradition or aversion to risk, but because low-quality leadership and mutual distrust preclude the requisite cost-sharing or coordination among peasants. As agricultural techniques improve, problems of coordination limit investment in, and productivity of, communal land and help explain the transfer of communal lands to private ownership.

Moral economists have interpreted the stability of patron-client ties in terms of the patron's guarantee of short-term subsistence floors for clients. In the political economy view, not only the stability of the ties but the level of the floor itself is a function of the patron's ability to keep relations dyadic, that is, to prevent collective bargaining by a united clientele or to foreclose alternate options which increase the bargaining power of peasants. In order to maintain dyadic ties and foreclose other options, the patron is often the one who prevents the spread of literacy, forcibly keeps peasants from direct involvement in markets, and rejects innovations for raising total production if the new methods have the potential to decrease peasant dependence. Given these patron strategies, central states sometimes can increase their own revenue by overthrowing patrons and raising total production enough to benefit both themselves and the peasantry. And political and religious movements can gain peasant support by providing peasants incentives to over-throw patrons and enter the market on their own.

The extension of the authority of central states is not necessarily a threat to peasant subsistence. The extension of state authority and the expansion of markets invariably benefits landless peasants be-cause the expanded mobility of labor breaks down some of the coercion used against them by peasants who control land. Whether or not tenants and smallholders benefit from the expansion of states and markets depends on ancillary institutions such as courts, taxa-tion, and titling procedures. These institutions determine entry costs into markets and the distribution of risks and benefits from new commercial opportunities.

Moral economists have viewed peasant political and religious protests as last-gasp, defensive reactions of a dying class. They continually use terms like *decline, crisis, imbalances, decay, loss of legitimacy,* or the *erosion of traditional bonds* to describe the conditions under which protests will occur. On the contrary, I argue that short-term declines or drops are neither necessary nor sufficient for protests, that even without any drop in welfare peasants seek individual or collective means to improve their situation. Protests are collective actions and depend on the ability of a group or class to organize and make demands. Thus, many movements are an ex-pression of "green power," a reflection of the peasants' growing ability to organize and struggle for rights and privileges previously denied them. Peasant struggles are frequently battles to tame mar-kets and bureaucracies, not movements to restore "traditional" systems.

VILLAGES

Corporate villages existed throughout most of Europe until the nineteenth or early twentieth century and are still common in parts of Asia and Latin America.[1] In contrast to the "open" villages

1. Jerome Blum, "The European Village as Community: Origins and Func-tions," and "The Internal Structure and Polity of the European Village Community from the Fifteenth to the Nineteenth Century"; Eric Wolf, "Closed Corporate Communities in Meso America and Java," and "Types of Latin American Peasan-try: A Preliminary Discussion."

more common throughout the world today, members of corporate villages had a well-defined notion of village "citizenship," of who belonged to the village corporation; they regulated the local economy; and they imposed certain forms of discipline on inhabitants, particularly in relation to the decisions and coordination involved in open-field agriculture, where plots are intermingled, scattered, and unfenced.

The degree of involvement of the corporate village in the economic activities of its members varied according to the nature of the supravillage institutions and according to the nature of local agriculture, but the differences were of degree and not of kind. Where there were communal pastures, the village decided how many animals each family could pasture; where the fields belonging to each family were intermingled and unfenced, the village determined the times for planting, harvesting, and grazing; where there was irrigated agriculture, the village decided when the fields would be flooded and apportioned the work of maintaining the common irrigation works. The village invariably collected, and frequently assessed on its inhabitants, land and head taxes and decided which men would meet the village quotas for labor and military drafts. The village headman or chief mediated between a village council and the local lord or bureaucrat, and the headman, together with the council, adjudicated conflicts between members of the village. The village also distributed those portions of farmland owned or managed by the village (communal land) and supervised local religious life. Often the village would even hire and fire priests.

The communal pasturage and farmland, the local collection and distribution of taxes, and the many coordinated activities that were a part of open-field agriculture have always fascinated observers of these corporate villages. The extent of interaction among villagers, in marked contrast to modern open villages, has made it appear as if there were a special mentality and logic to them. As a result, they frequently have served (as Jerome Blum notes) as a launching pad for romantic theories about society. The Russian corporate village or *mir,* Baron Haxthausen wrote in 1847, was the bulwark that would save Russia from the abhorrent changes being wrought in the West by individualism and industrialization; because of the *mir,*

Russia, in contrast to Western Europe, had "naught to fear from pauperism, the proletariat, and the doctrines of communism and socialism."[2] From a markedly different but no less rhapsodic viewpoint, Spanish anarchism was supposed to reflect a tradition of spontaneous mass action that had characterized the corporate world of the Spanish pueblo. Anarchism was viewed as the product of the irreconcilable conflict between capitalism and primitive communalism.[3] In the words of Gerald Brenan, "The pueblo was recognized as being the great repository of the virtues of the race, the source from which everything that was sane and healthy sprang. No act in which it did not take part had its roots in national life."[4]

Nineteenth-century German and Danish scholars saw the corporate village as a vestige of ancient agrarian communism which they claimed could be traced back to Tacitus and Caesar.[5] In France, such villages, Emile de Lavelye argued, had secured for French people "from the most remote times the enjoyment of liberty, equality and order, and as great a degree of happiness as is compatible with human destinies."[6] And in Vietnam, Le Thanh Khoi stated that the Vietnamese village "anchored to the soil at the dawn of history . . . was not touched by the [Chinese] conquerors, and has constituted, behind its bamboo hedge, the anonymous and unseizable retreat where the national spirit is concentrated."[7]

It is directly upon assumptions about the performance of corporate villages that much of moral economy theory rests. While less fulsome in their praise of corporate villages than the writers just cited, moral economists, as noted in the preceding chapter, implicitly perceive the change from closed to open villages, with their free land markets and individualistic production, as the peasantry's fall from grace. The transition to open villages is assumed to entail a loss of protection (welfare and insurance) from the village and a change in peasant mentality from a collective orientation to an individualistic, market orientation.

2. Jerome Blum, *Lord and Peasant,* pp. 508–509.
3. Michael Weisser, *The Peasants of the Montes,* pp. 6, 120.
4. Ibid., p. 7.
5. Blum, "European Village," pp. 157–158.
6. Blum, "Internal Structure and Polity," p. 541.
7. Le Thanh Khoi, *Le Vietnam,* p. 133.

At key points in their analyses, moral economists make direct predictions about village outcomes from their assumptions about shared individual goals. To cite one example, since every peasant is assumed by moral economists to be interested in minimizing risk or maximizing security, it is further assumed from this common individual goal that *villages* also will operate to minimize risk or maximize security. These direct leaps from common interest to collective outcome assume, in effect, a collective rationality among the peasantry. Yet the moral economists' inferences do not follow either from the investment logic that they themselves suggest applies to markets or even from investment logic as amended to take account of long- and short-term investments and gambles.

The validity of moral economy arguments discussed in Chapter 1 rests on the extent to which income floors are provided within corporate villages. These floors depend on the common insurance and welfare that peasants within such villages are able to provide. Insurance and welfare schemes are limited by several factors. (1) Free-rider problems mean there are risks in investing in mutual enterprises at the expense of private investments. (2) Highly visible and defensible standards not open to ambiguity, misinterpretation, or welfare cheating must be used as the means test to determine eligibility for village assistance. (3) Village leaders use village office as a means of securing and protecting individual fortunes, and village insurance schemes are limited to assets with which leaders cannot abscond; indeed, the transaction costs involved in villagewide insurance schemes appear to have been so high that peasants adopted individual means of protection from crop failure which cut total village production by more than 10 percent. In other words, the moral economy predictions about collective security, based on assumptions of collective rationality, are borne out partially at best: village processes are shaped and restricted by individual self-interest, the difficulty of ranking needs, the desire of individual peasants to raise their own subsistence level at the expense of others, aversion to risk, leadership interest in profits, and the free-rider problem. Let us examine some of these processes more closely.

There is substantial agreement between moral and political

economists that peasants are preoccupied with the constant threat of falling below the subsistence level. Thus, the main focus of the comparisons between the two approaches is on the production, consumption, and exchange of material goods. On the production side, organization and financing of both private and public goods are examined; specifically, explanations of taxation, village finance, insurance programs, leadership, and innovation are considered and contrasted. On the consumption side, access to goods as manifested in village citizenship, the distribution of communal resources, and the provision of welfare are compared. Market exchanges, alliances, and patron-client relationships also are examined. A major consequence of these relationships, stratification, is discussed as well.

Taxation

Romantic scholarship to the contrary, corporate villages had their origins not in a primitive communal mentality, but in the problems of taxation confronting both peasants and supravillage authorities—be they feudal or bureaucratic—during (and after) the Middle Ages. Accurate production figures were not easily obtained, and central states (or feudal lords) had difficulty collecting reliable information as a basis for taxing the means of production, such as manpower and land, for each family (costly information). Conversely, peasants often found it difficult to have their tax records adjusted to accurately reflect the number of workers and the amount of land they controlled (costly access). When households lost workers to disease, war, or migration, there often would be land on which the family owed taxes, but which the family could not farm with the available labor. In times of unsteady labor supply, such land could not always be rented to meet the tax bill, nor could it be easily transferred to someone else if transfer (among freemen or serfs) were costly or if long-term sales contracts were difficult to enforce. Both states or lords and peasants were then faced with the problem of stabilizing tax flows. Instead of keeping tax records on the number of adults and the amount of land in each family, records were kept by the corporate village. A number of peasants were responsible for meeting head and land tax bills and for filling labor and military drafts from within the village. In some countries and in some centuries, the lands also were controlled by the village and reallocated periodically; in other cases, the lands were all or partially private.[8]

Although it was generally feudal lords who established corporate villages to supervise their peasants, coordinate agriculture, and exact obligations, there were apparently enough benefits from belonging to a village and paying taxes as a corporate group that peasants were willing to enter corporate villages voluntarily[9] for the benefits of life within a political unit with rights before the state, and often with a constitution.[10]

That these intravillage tax procedures benefit the poor is an explicit claim of moral economists. For example, Scott argues that "since villages and not individuals were taxed, one might expect the better off to pay something more than an equal share."[11] Similarly, Migdal claims that paying taxes as a village aided "not the wealthy who could have paid their taxes on an individual basis just as easily, but the man who did poorly this harvest. The village political leadership could compensate for his inability to pay by making slightly higher demands on others."[12]

If there were widespread agreement that those less able to pay should be helped when tax and labor responsibilities were distributed, and if there were widespread agreement on how to assess the ability to pay, one would expect, at the least, that the rich would pay more in absolute terms; indeed, one might even predict a progressive tax system in which the rich paid not just more money than the poor, or not just the same percentage of their income in tax, but a higher percentage of their income in tax. And certainly the subsistence ethic should at least express itself in a tax "floor," an income below which no taxes would be collected from the villagers as long as the village's total tax bill could be met by other villagers above that "floor."

This, however, raises the same questions posed earlier: How is

8. Blum, *Lord and Peasant*, pp. 506–521, is the best source.
9. Ibid., p. 514.
10. Blum, "European Village," p. 162.
11. James C. Scott, *The Moral Economy of the Peasant*, p. 54.
12. Joel Migdal, *Peasants, Politics and Revolution*, p. 82.

ability to pay—or "needs"—assessed? Arguing from the assumptions of political economy, one would expect that peasants, instead of readily agreeing about need, ability to pay, or standards, would hide their wealth from common scrutiny and thus make it even more difficult to decide who is better off and able to pay a larger share of the load. Indeed, there is commonly a "cult of poverty": "Peasants . . . hide wealth to avoid 'claims of friends,' taxes and contributions."[13]

When peasants seek to maximize long-run welfare through family and savings, rather than relying on the long-run viability of their village institutions or of any particular rules for determining need or ability to pay, they will hide wealth and there will be struggles in which each person attempts to minimize his own tax. In such a situation, the only stable systems for allocating taxes would be those based not on abstract or complex standards of need, but on criteria that are highly visible and easily defensible. Although systems that share the tax equally are regressive, they are, in fact, based on such visible and defensible criteria. The only groups commonly granted tax relief, for example, are the aged, widowed, and orphaned, whose conditions can be easily verified. Both rich and poor can expect to benefit from such rules of exemption during the life cycle. Aside from the aged, widowed, and orphaned, the only other clear case would be when "all is gone," where there is nothing left to conceal. In Vietnam, as we shall see, peasants typically were expected by fellow villagers to pay their own taxes even if it meant selling or mortgaging land, entering into debt-slavery, or breaking up the family. Members of a family might help one another avoid onerous declines due to tax demands in bad years, but village rules in Vietnam (and in the other areas) show no evidence that the village as a village compensated for or eased the burden of individual households in a bad year.[14]

Aside from tax relief for easily identified categories, there is no

13. Oscar Lewis, *Life in a Mexican Village, Tepotzlan Restudied,* p. 54. This is but one of many formulations of the cult of poverty.

14. Sometimes on the precolonial frontier, landless persons with no money and no property had their taxes paid for them by the village (or rich men) in exchange for labor services, but this was more like servitude or debt bondage than the adjustments suggested by the arguments of moral economists.

evidence of the actual use of progressive taxes or of tax floors within precapitalist villages. Head taxes, assessed according to the total number of males in the village, were divided equally among male inhabitants. Land taxes, assessed on the total area of land in each of several quality grades, were paid equally if there was village ownership or by the individual owners in the case of private land. There is no evidence that owners of large tracts of land paid more taxes per acre or hectare than did small landowners. Neither capitation nor land taxes were paid in a way that provided either floors or leveling.[15] Instead, there is a clear pattern of opposition to progressive taxes by village leaders eager to minimize their own share of the taxes and to ensure their short-run welfare at the expense of the poor. Occasionally when colonial governments sought to implement progressive tax methods, the opposition came from within the village. When the colonial government in Indonesia once attempted to rebate taxes to the poor (after village leaders had assessed an equal tax share on everyone in the village), village leaders resisted and "the poor and weak continued to pay the highest taxes."[16]

There are two interpretations possible for this resistance: (1) village officials administer the village for their own private benefit, or (2) it is extremely difficult for villagers with even the best intentions to agree on ability to pay—they therefore tend to rely on easily coordinated strategies to avoid interminable conflict, with the result that taxes tend to be regressive. Although both these possibilities are counterarguments to the moral economy position, both would find support among political economists and both are consistent with the data.

The struggle to minimize individual shares of external demands on the village is even more pronounced with respect to the military draft. Whereas tax systems usually emphasize equal payments by all—without standard deductions, floors, or progressive rules—it is common for labor demands and military drafts to be pushed onto the poorer villagers. In seventeenth-century France, for example,

---

15. If all taxes were land taxes, (in other words, if there were no head taxes at all), then there would have been some floor. Additionally, as we shall see in Chapter 4, the ratio of head taxes to land taxes has important distributional consequences.

16. Clive Day, *The Dutch in Java*, p. 187. "Poor" is defined by landholdings.

rich peasants so consistently managed to manipulate local selection procedures to avoid military service that lotteries were attempted as a means of ending unfair selections. Even then the rich managed to escape the burden.[17] Although this example suggests that states may sometimes intervene to equalize village procedures, there are also times, as in precolonial Vietnam, when a state may support the creation of a privileged class within the village to insure a steady tax return of its own. That is, a progressive tax system may not be in the short-run interests of either the state or the better-off villagers.

Village Citizenship

In their discussions of welfare and insurance in precapitalist villages, moral economists imply that "all villagers" is equivalent to "all persons." The two, however, are not synonymous. Common features of precapitalist society are a stratum of residents known as "insiders," who have full citizenship within the village (although not necessarily with decision-making roles), and a stratum of "outsiders," who are allowed to reside in the geographic confines of the village, but who have fewer rights and benefits than insiders. Some of these "outsiders" are persons who marry into the village and seek to earn a place within it; others are "foreigners" who want to live in a better village. Historically, many "outsiders" have been individuals who were denied full access to village resources by the better-off members of the village. Summarizing the available data for precapitalist villages of Europe, Blum notes,

Nearly everywhere only certain peasants qualified for active membership. Only these people had the right to vote at communal meetings and to make the decisions which affected the lives of all the villagers. They held the communal offices themselves or arranged to have people they wanted in these posts. Often they had either exclusive or superior rights to the use of the common lands and forests of the village. Presumably, all or nearly all

17. Blum, "Internal Structure and Polity," p. 547. See also, Joan Rockwell, "The Danish Peasant Village," passim. But it is possible to divise visible and defensible rules for conscription. Under these rules, one son, either the youngest or the eldest (depending on the country), would be exempt from drafts to ensure family continuity. There would still be potential for conflict any time a family had two sons drafted before all other families had one son drafted. (If a couple with two sons sends one of them to live with a childless relative, do both sons get exemptions?)

the residents of a village once had equal rights, at least ideally, in the use of communal resources and in the conduct of village affairs. When, however, the population of the village grew, pressure on the common lands increased to a point where the more prosperous villagers decided that they had to prohibit or limit the use of communal resources by the poorer peasants of the village. The better-off peasants realized that to ensure their continued control of the village resources they had to restrict the right of active participation in communal decision making, and so they established criteria to determine who should have this privilege.[18]

This serves to emphasize the conflicts of interest inherent in precapitalist villages. It does not follow from individual risk minimization or security maximization that villages will function to minimize risk or maximize security for all. As noted earlier, there are conflicts of interest, in addition to common interests, inherent within the village. Coalitions may be organized for the sharing of resources or contributing to village projects (clearing additional land for the additional peasants, for example), but self-interest can lead also to coalitions organized to drive persons from the village or to deprive them of benefits, in which case the "outsiders" serve as a source of cheap labor for the insiders.

In other words, whereas moral economists predict that better-off villagers will help their less fortunate neighbors when times are bad, the evidence indicates that affluent villagers commonly react by excluding such persons from the village long before everyone is reduced to the cultural minimum or subsistence line.[19] Indeed, it is

18. Blum, "Internal Structure and Polity," p. 549. The evidence from the Cochinchina region of Vietnam, discussed in Chapter 3, is consistent with a hypothesis different from Blum's: access to full participation in the village always may have been limited for the profit of insiders, even when there was no population pressure. However, there are not enough data to test alternate explanations for the origins of outsiders.

19. Similarly, in today's peasant world, castes, families, and villages can redefine their boundaries and make new demarcations between insiders and outsiders. Further, persons of substance can avoid responsibility while maintaining a moral front by adapting the posture that they fulfill obligations to their employees and retainers and should, therefore, not be held responsible for the problems of others. During Jan Breman's fieldwork in India, "a grandfather, a father, and two daughters returned to the village in mid-season. They suffered from typhoid fever and had been sent away from the brickyard so as not to infect the other laborers. Gravely ill and penniless, they had found their way back. . . . Once they were in Chikhilgam, not one of the farmers for whom members of this household sometimes worked gave them any aid. I found these people in their hut, uncared for and without food, lying on jute bags. Two of them died of the fever the next day." Breman, *Patronage and Exploitation*, p. 252.

not unusual for governments to intervene in corporate villages, for the sake of political stability and/or increased tax revenues, to protect the lower strata against expulsion (or landlessness) or to force villagers to clear additional land for laborers or others who are landless.[20]

Such conflicts over village membership serve to emphasize the importance to peasants of control of and access to courts, both within the village and at higher levels of authority. In sixteenth-century Germany, when a class of landless laborers first developed within the villages, it became particularly important for tenants to control the hiring and firing of the priest, for the priest had an important role in adjudicating disputes over village membership.[21] Similarly, in Vietnam access to and the right to use government tribunals and courts was a prized possession, and peasants who lacked the legal status necessary to use these institutions were at a marked disadvantage in local economic and political struggles. In Java, there was a "complex and rigid system of social stratification based primarily on differential ownership of privately held land and/or rights to communal land"; 20 percent of what communal land there was generally went to the village head, and many persons had no right to own private land or receive a share of public land.[22] In the German peasant wars of the early sixteenth century, the general pattern during village uprisings was for the lord's tenants in a village to demand that no common land be given to the landless laborers, even though the latter usually were related to the tenants.[23]

Even among "insiders," it was common for full shares of resources or eligibility for decision-making roles to be restricted to persons of a certain wealth or with a certain amount of land. This again serves to emphasize the risk of contributing to a village wel-

---

20. Blum, *Lord and Peasant,* pp. 516, 519.

21. David Sabean, "Family and Land Tenure: A Case Study of Conflict in the German Peasant's War (1525)," p. 15, fn. 19.

22. Benjamin White, "Production and Reproduction in a Javanese Village," pp. 71–72. White also notes that the notion of work-spreading implied by involution should not be taken to imply that scarce opportunities were relatively evenly distributed (p. 74).

23. David Sabean, "German Agrarian Institutions at the Beginning of the Sixteenth Century: Upper Swabia as an Example," pp. 76–88.

fare system in years when one has a surplus. When a peasant is in need, instead of receiving welfare, he may be excluded from the village.

At the very least, then, all moral economy generalizations about villages as a source of welfare and insurance (and therefore as a source of social stability) must be reexamined in the light of a large population of "outsiders." As Blum concludes, "These restrictions meant that in many places smallholders, cotters, landless laborers, lodgers, servants and hired hands found themselves excluded from active participation in the management of the community, and from the privileges which accompanied active participation."[24]

The metaphor of corporate village as "collectivity" should be replaced by the metaphor of the corporate village as a "corporation." Membership in a corporate village need not bring any special tax breaks or welfare or insurance to be of value; membership itself—like membership in a guild or even in a stock exchange—is a license to do business and a right of access to crucial institutions, both inside the village and in the larger society. The development of institutions for a functioning local economy—courts, festivals, market days, agreements on when to plant—constitutes a valuable patrimony even when there is no communal land owned by the village, and peasants do not share these corporate assets with persons who did not contribute to building the patrimony, especially when denial of access is profitable to the insiders. At times of depopulation, of course, there are reasons to admit persons into the village to help meet the collective tax bills, but there are at other times numerous incentives to keep institutional access restricted and to maintain a stratum of second-class citizens.

Insurance and Welfare

Moral economists stress both insurance and welfare functions of the village. Phrases such as "risk minimization," "life chance equalization," and "community mechanisms to maximize security" all suggest extensive villagewide insurance. Such phrases as "minimum income," "guaranteed minimums," "danger lines," and "communal welfare" predict not only *insurance,* but actual

24. Blum, "Internal Structure and Polity," p. 550.

welfare policies that subsidize the less well-off against drops below the danger point. It is important to distinguish clearly between specific risk-sharing mechanisms—that is, insurance—and subsidies—that is, welfare. From political economy assumptions it follows that villagewide insurance schemes will be highly specific and limited due to problems of trust and consensus, and that welfare schemes will be greatly restricted and restrictive. Further, reciprocity will be strict and limited to relative equals, and the village leaders will help less fortunate villagers only if it does not affect the long-run welfare of the better-off villagers. This is not to say that there will be no welfare available to the insiders of the village. Given the problems of conflicting standards and claims of need, however, very little welfare is available for indigents or persons with bad harvests, and village welfare or subsidies are allocated mainly to the aged, widowed, or orphaned—specific categories with claims that are clear, hard to exaggerate, and clearly not due to laziness or mismanagement. Further, the emphasis is on insurance schemes—not welfare—and the extent of such villagewide schemes depends on (1) whether, and to what extent, past endeavors have been successful; (2) whether cooperation is expected to continue in the future, so that a peasant can be certain that his specific need will be recognized when he makes his claim; and (3) whether someone can be trusted to hold the insurance premiums of all villagers until they are needed. As expected, there are few insurance schemes that require peasants to contribute money to a common fund—since someone can always abscond with the money—and more schemes that are highly specific, based on strict reciprocity, and require labor (which is not so easily stolen), such as a plan whereby everyone helps victims to rebuild after a fire.[25]

Even among the basically solvent insiders, peasants interested in their long-run security usually make exchanges of a fixed nature where it is certain that both (all) parties will be able to maintain a long-run balance. Instead of general welfare or subsidies of the poor by the affluent, long-term risks will be excluded, and there will be strict reciprocity if peasants are cautious about welfare and

25. Although Blum ("Internal Structure and Polity," p. 546) says that the community provided "welfare services," his examples are chiefly of the kinds of insurance discussed here.

personal savings in dealings with one another: ". . . exchanges and contracts are likely to be either highly specific, with an understanding of just what it is each party is expected to do, or they involve people who are in constant contact so that giving and return can be balanced at short intervals and the advantages to each partner easily assessed."[26] In other words, as Potter found in Thailand, if reciprocal obligations are not to be evaded, "records must be kept and sanctions exerted; there is nothing loose or informal about this at all." Therefore, complex interchanges generally take place among small groups of four or five households.[27]

We can begin to identify the critical dimensions of insurance and welfare systems and specify which types are most viable in peasant society. Schemes can have either fixed or variable returns. The insurance systems common in peasant society, such as labor exchanges or burial societies, have fixed returns. In these groups each peasant receives exactly what he has put into the scheme. Such organizations derive their value from utilities of scale in peasant life: eight days of labor at once by many men in a field make a better rice crop than one man working for eight days, and a few coins from many persons when a parent dies are more valuable for meeting religious obligations and avoiding debts than are a few coins on the many occasions when someone else's parent dies. Schemes also can have exact exchange or equivalent exchanges. Peasant exchange groups are generally for exact exchange—labor for labor, part of someone's pig this month for part of someone else's pig next month, or money for money—rather than exchanges where contributions and payouts involve agreeing on a rate of exchange on more than one item. Schemes can require centralized holdings of liquid assets or decentralized holdings by the members. Peasant schemes generally do not concentrate any abscondable funds; contributions are held by the members and given to the bereaved on the death, or the labor is given to the farmer on the agreed upon day. Further, peasant schemes generally tend to involve small groups in which only self-management with little lead-

26. Elizabeth Colson, *Tradition and Contract*, p. 50.
27. Jack Potter, *Thai Peasant Social Structure*, pp. 171, 163.

ership (or actuarial skills) is required.[28] We can also distinguish among schemes where everyone has a chance of benefiting and schemes in which many persons have little or no probability of any return. Old age, widow, and orphan support are likely to have some potential value for all villagers, whereas subsidies for poor households are less likely to be of benefit to all villagers and thus may require coercion to establish and maintain.

Ironically, one of the most frequently cited examples of a conservative, safety-first strategy followed by peasants—namely, scattered fields—is an individual-level strategy for avoiding risk that suggests, as we shall see in Chapter 3, that villagewide insurance schemes are not very comprehensive. It is a clear example of a conflict between individual and group rationality whereby each individual, following a safety-first strategy, ends up with less production than he would if the village as a whole could follow an aggregate safety-first strategy.

Peasants throughout the world farm several plots of land at any one time, and the plots usually are scattered throughout that area of the village under cultivation. The scattering of plots substantially reduces the maximum damage that small local disasters or climatic variations can cause in a given season: mildew or rot in one area of the village, an errant herd, an exceptionally light or heavy rain, and similar minidisasters will be less likely to wipe out a peasant's entire crop when fields are scattered. While scattered plots reduce the variance of yield from year to year and thus reduce the probability of losing the entire crop, scattering also cuts the maximum yield per farmer and for the village as a whole. In a series of ingenious and pathbreaking articles, Donald McCloskey has estimated that the scattered (pre-enclosure) fields in England cut total production by 10 to 13 percent.[29] Why, it must be asked, are peasants close to the danger line willing to throw away 10 percent of their output?

28. There can be large groups with little management required for tasks with large economies of scale, like a bucket brigade, or where only low-quality labor is required. Agricultural development and refinement of techniques often lead to smaller exchange groups because higher quality labor input, and thus more vigilance against slackers, is required.

29. Donald McCloskey, "English Open Fields as Behavior toward Risk," pp. 124–125. See Bibliography for other McCloskey articles.

Consolidated fields with higher average output and higher variance from year to year would be a better strategy for peasants to follow if the village could provide insurance for farmers to compensate for the increased variance of consolidated fields. A village granary or risk pool, if moral economy assumptions were correct, could have prevented the loss in output by providing "interest-free credit rationed in accord with the publicly known incidence of relatively favorable or unfavorable agricultural conditions."[30] But who will hold the grain, and who will decide whether a particular loss is due to nature or sloth?

Village-level, safety-first strategies would be both more productive and more secure (and would be adopted!) if, *and only if,* the moral economy assumptions about villagers were correct. In fact, individual-level, safety-first strategies are followed, and this is one of the most important challenges to moral economy conceptions of the village.

Indeed, plot consolidation is a subject worthy of far more attention than it has received from scholars of all persuasions, for it raises a plethora of important issues about markets, risk, and sharing. Scattered plots are often more desirable than a single plot per family when there is no reliable widespread insurance system. However, centuries of division sometimes lead to scattering in the extreme. In Greece, for example, Kenneth Thompson found that the number and dispersion of plots belonging to the typical family was far greater than that needed for insurance value and that a majority of villagers in eighteen villages favored a program of plot consolidation to increase production, decrease family friction over inheritances, reduce violence over access to inside plots, and put land consumed by paths and boundaries back into production. But this majority of villagers believed that a voluntary program of consolidation would not work because the differences in fertility and soil type as well as the problems of accurately evaluating the yield (and variance) of plots made weighting systems for establishing equivalences difficult to establish, and there was little willingness to

---

30. Stefano Fenoaltea, "Fenoaltea on Open Fields: A Reply," p. 405. Fenoaltea argues that since such insurance was possible, scattering was not due to the absence of insurance. I obviously disagree.

trust any committee of villagers to arrive at an equitable consolidation. For that reason, the general feeling was that compulsory consolidation was the only way to proceed.[31]

The complex problem of trading and consolidating parcels arises whenever an inheritance is shared among more than one offspring. Michael Lipton describes an Indian village where the farmland runs down the side of a long slope. Soil quality varies from top to bottom of the slope, but varies little along a contour of the slope. If plots were divided horizontally along the contours of the hill, plowing would be easier and cheaper, and average output would be higher. Each father, however, avoids the problem of equating contours with different averages and variances by dividing the patrimony into vertical strips: "This saddles each generation of sons with longer, thinner sloping strips, increasingly costly and inconvenient to plough properly, *i.e.,* repeatedly and across the slope."[32] The very lack of insurance and the difficulties of comparing plots mean that for every generation the share of land occupied by partitions increases, as does the gap between actual and potential production.[33]

It is enlightening to examine the procedures used in European medieval villages to govern harvests and gleaning, for they provide valuable insights into the difficulties of developing workable procedures for stabilizing incomes. They also illustrate the conflicts between the tenants of the manor and the cotters, or laborers, who lived in the villages and worked for the tenants—and the mistrust and suspicion of the poor within the village.

There were three basic stages to the harvest. First, the grain was reaped with sickles and bound into sheaves. Then stalks that had not been bundled or somehow had been missed were raked or gathered along with fallen grains. Then the remaining grains that had fallen or had been missed in corners of the field were gleaned. The timing of harvest, and the need for an adequate supply of labor

31. Kenneth Thompson, *Farm Fragmentation in Greece,* pp. 40, 69, 86, 187, 207, 243.
32. Michael Lipton, "The Theory of the Optimizing Peasant," p. 339; this article should be considered must reading for scholars in the field, especially for its critique of the free-market laissez-faire approach to peasant economies.
33. Ibid., p. 339.

at the very moment of harvest, were crucial for the tenants. If the reaping were begun too soon, grain would spoil or sour. If the harvest were begun a few days too late, many kernels would fall from the stalks.[34]

Since not all fields ripened on the same day, there were usually at any one time during the harvest fields already reaped and ready for raking (or even for gleaning) and fields just about to ripen. The by-laws of twelfth- and thirteenth-century English villages provided for enforced cooperation among tenants and laborers to insure that no man's reap would be delayed for the sake of another man's raking or gleaning. Village by-laws stated that no one offered reaping work at a minimum wage set by the village could leave the village to work elsewhere (without substantial fines), and no one offered work as a reaper could work as a raker—tenants could not even rake their own fields if a fellow tenant wanted to hire them to reap.[35]

Village rules, then, insured that everyone had a chance to complete his first stage of harvesting before anyone finished his second stage; they provided some income stabilization for the tenant class as well. An alternate way of sharing labor between reaping and raking would have been via internal bidding for labor through price competition, that is, a labor market. If laborers and tenants were simply allowed to work for whoever paid best, this would also have had the effect of spacing the harvest, for persons with no grain reaped would have been willing to pay more for workers than would persons concerned with the secondary raking. However, the labor-market approach would have benefited the laborers at the expense of tenants, who would have had to pay more for laborers. The rules were consciously designed "in the interests of those hiring labor."[36]

34. Warren O. Ault, *Open Field Farming in Medieval England,* p. 28. The word *gleaning* generally refers to both the secondary gathering of grain and the later picking-over of fields for the last remnants. Here, however, *raking* refers to the secondary gathering, while *gleaning* refers to that collection of grain not shared with the farmer in control of the fields.

35. Ibid., pp. 19, 29–30, 33, and "By-Laws of Gleaning and the Problems of Harvest," pp. 217–219.

36. Ibid., "By-Laws of Gleaning," p. 217. Note that a system of maximum wages (which was tried) would not be as effective because it would be harder to enforce. A tenant who secretly overpaid a laborer would not easily be detected; neither the farmer nor the laborer would have an incentive to disclose an otherwise

Not even in the case of gleaning—picking up of fallen grains after reaping and raking—is there evidence of village procedures to protect the poor and provide them with floors. Blackstone wrote, "By the common law and custom of England the poor are allowed to enter and glean upon another's ground after the harvest without being guilty of trespass." Ault found, however, that there is no mention of such right in *any* medieval English village by-laws or procedures.[37] Further, medieval village rules as well as Roman, Salic, and French law all vested the right to glean solely with the owner of the grain.[38]

People sometimes were given the chance to glean any last bits of grain from the fields before animals were set loose to pasture on the stubble and droppings. Even here, however, a strong distrust and suspicion of the poor and the weakness of village commitment to their welfare is evident. Typically, in France and England it was only when outside authority, such as a lord or priest, intervened that the poor were given any time in the field before the animals. Even with outside intervention, gleaning was limited only to those (again, the old, widowed and orphaned) who had passed inspection by bailiffs or who had a letter from the curé certifying their status.[39]

The extensive use of credit and interest rates in precapitalist village society contradicts moral economy predictions. How credit is rationed and distributed within the village is a clear test of whether or not need-criteria are being used in the allocation of resources.

---

undetectable transgression. Third parties, however, can easily see whether a person is reaping or raking, and laws giving precedence to reaping over raking are, therefore, more effective in the absence of class solidarity among tenants. After the Black Death, limitations on outside work became unenforceable.

37. Ibid., *Open Field Farming*, p. 31.

38. Paul De Gruilly, *Le Droit du glanage,* pp. 35, 50; Ault, *Open Field Farming,* p. 37, and "By-Laws of Gleaning," p. 215.

39. Ault, "By-Laws," p. 214, and *Open Field Farming,* pp. 30–31; De Gruilly, *Le Droit du glanage,* pp. 35–51, 70–71; George Homans, *English Villagers of the Thirteenth Century,* p. 103. In the thirteenth century, French priests apparently demanded and received a share of the glean; this tithing of the glean elicited a strong rebuke from Pope Clement IV (De Gruilly, p. 45). Biblical law enjoins owners to leave something for orphans, widows, and outsiders. While it is not clear how these laws were enforced (or if they were), it would appear that rabbis, like priests and lords, tried to protect the floors for the poorest (De Gruilly, pp. 24, 28), for there are numerous legal opinions and arguments in the Talmud about, for example, forgotten or neglected grain, about grain hidden by harvesters, or even about grain that falls on anthills (De Gruilly, pp. 26–28).

Bidding for credit—that is, the use of market-determined interest rates—is evidence of a system in which persons are concerned with maximizing the productivity of their resources, and it is in conflict with maximizing the welfare of the poor. Yet throughout Vietnamese history, attempts to limit the (legal) interest rates charged within villages always failed. Not only does a system of credit and competitive interest rates allocate resources in an economic and not a welfare fashion, but it also channels most credit to persons with fixed collateral, such as land. It simply was not common in precapitalist society for persons to be extended resources solely on their personal pledge. The general rule was that people without fixed assets could borrow money only if a person was given as collateral. In Thailand, for example, "there was no organized police force, and it was easy for the debtor to abscond. . . . The best security for a loan . . . was to have the debtor or his child or his wife living and serving in the creditor's household."[40]

The problem of credit and the related problem of debt bondage in cases where there is no fixed collateral are worth emphasizing. It is often argued that the existence of a wide-open frontier benefits peasants—they can always flee to new areas if the demands of the lord become too onerous. The obverse, however, is seldom noted: if it is possible for peasants to flee, then lords (and other peasants), unless they are unaware of this possibility, will adapt their credit charges to this risk, and credit for persons with no fixed assets will depend on such practices as debt bondage.[41]

40. Akin Rabibhadana, *The Organization of Thai Society in the Early Bangkok Period, 1782–1873*, p. 110.

41. Practices sometimes assumed by some to be unjust, immoral, and exploitative were thus a common feature of precapitalist society: "A man who surrenders his child for a loan or one who sells his birthright for a mess of pottage are extreme examples. The needs of the weaker party have allowed the stronger to impose an exchange that violates the true value of things; the bargain is unjust and extortionary" (James C. Scott, "Explanation in Rural Class Relations: A Victim's Perspective," p. 499).

As Lucien Hanks has noted of Thailand today, "The departing ones recognize their peripheral position under a given roof, since the most dispensable person had to be chosen from among many, yet leaving for a better opportunity in another area also signifies a parent's concern for a child's well-being. A Bang-Chan rice grower, telling of his childhood, upbraided his parents for refusing to give him into the care of a powerful government official who wished to adopt him. The storyteller commented, 'My parents could not have loved me very much'" (Lucien Hanks, *Rice and Man: Agricultural Ecology in Southeast Asia*, p. 88).

Further, a lack of land may mean not only denial of credit, but second-class citizenship as well. It is clear that in many areas pre-capitalist villages were organized around land and that only land-owners had rights as insiders. Today in open villages, when a village patrimony consists of organization to allocate responsibilities for irrigation canals and dams, the landless may have no role in the central core of village society and therefore be looked down on by other peasants. In an open village in Thailand, for example, Potter found that village organization focused on canal work and that the landless did not participate in this activity; they were therefore "really not full citizens of the community" and were "not considered of much account at village meetings."[42]

Limited and specified reciprocities, low levels of welfare and insurance, outsiders, and the prevalence of market-determined credit rates (usury), all challenge the basis of moral economy claims about village welfare and insurance systems. This also means, as we shall see, that the decay of traditional welfare functions under the stress of capitalism and colonialism does not alone account for the rise of new political and religious movements in Vietnam. The successful movements in that country were able to win much of their following merely by providing leadership to extend and improve the insurance and welfare available in the pre-capitalist village, not by restoring old patterns.

Village Finance

Given the importance of insurance and welfare (or loans) to peasants, given also the need for such village-level projects as irrigation and flood control, there is potential value in a village reserve that will be used for public works or for persons in need. The maintenance of such a reserve is consistent with the moral economy approach to the village and necessary for insurance and welfare: since all peasants would have an interest in such a reserve, the village could be expected to provide reserves for specified needs. However, the conflict between individual and group interests points to the possibility that cash reserves will be maintained only when village officials can be trusted not to abscond, that any system of

42. Potter, *Thai Peasant Social Structure*, p. 55.

community finance may be manipulated to benefit the leaders at the expense of the village, and that villagewide sources of credit may be opposed by persons seeking to maintain some villagers in a dependent position.

In fact, village reserves are seldom maintained, and public works are instead financed on a project-by-project basis. As we shall see, during the colonial period (the only period for which the evidence is clear), the systems for raising money to finance village projects in Vietnam were consistently manipulated by village leaders to make a personal profit for themselves at the expense of the village treasury. Furthermore, attempts to develop village granaries as a source of low-cost credit for the poor floundered on village squabbling over claims of theft, and attempts to extend agricultural credit to the poor were either blocked or captured by village leaders for their own profit.

Distribution of Resources

The fact that villages typically manage considerable agricultural resources—including pastureland, cropland, forests, and irrigation water—that are allocated among villagers on a periodic basis often is taken as *prima facie* evidence of progressive redistribution. Periodically allocating resources, however, is not necessarily equivalent to a leveling or welfare function. If, as moral economists state, there is leveling within villages, or if villages maximize security, minimize risk, or keep persons above a minimum level or danger line, there should be evidence of such considerations at work in the distribution of communal lands, particularly when large amounts of cropland are allocated periodically to individuals by the village leaders. In addition to reserving corners for the widowed, aged, and/or orphaned, there should be evidence of consideration given to households in trouble. If the village is to be progressive, the two areas where progressive principles should be most in evidence are taxation and the distribution of resources.

The alternate, political economy assumptions lead to the prediction that progressive principles will be reflected in the distribution of resources only when there is long-run faith in the institution of the village, when "need" is easily operationalized and measured, and when village leaders believe it to be in their long-run interests to support progressive rules—that is, when they feel that their long-run security is better served by supporting progressive rules than by maximizing their current share of resources and diverting their current surplus into private investments designed to promote future security. Even with long-run faith in the village's survival and viability, and even with agreed on standards of need, it is still possible that village leaders may think it better to maximize current shares of community resources and prepare for the future through private investment of those shares. The uncertain prospect of future community guarantees will be balanced against current wealth converted into private preparations for the future.

As noted, many village inhabitants were "outsiders" excluded from shares of community resources. Moreover, indirect evidence suggests that it was rare, even among "insiders," for resources to be distributed in a progressive fashion. Sabean notes that peasant revolts in early modern Europe had their basis in communal life and in "the desire of one faction in the village to control access to resources within the village."[43] Indeed, it is frequently the state that intervenes to enforce redistribution of village-owned lands when one group in the village has excluded others from access to the resources.[44]

This type of evidence strongly suggests short-run maximization behavior vis-à-vis village resources—that in general peasants struggle for as large an immediate share of village resources as they can get (whether or not they invest or gamble, long run or short run, with their shares). Such short-run maximization behavior, in turn, leads to the expectation that factions and coalitions will be highly unstable and subject to change, and that fixed *ascriptive* rules will be used for the actual allocation process.

Fixed ascriptive rules may be the only way to avoid interminable conflict when dividing the pie. Benjamin Ward has shown that any question of dividing a pie is a voter's (Arrow) paradox.[45] That is,

43. David Sabean, "The Communal Basis of Pre-1880 Peasant Uprisings in Western Europe," p. 355.
44. Blum, *Lord and Peasant*, p. 519; for Vietnam, see Chapter 3, this volume.
45. Benjamin Ward, "Majority Rule and Allocation," pp. 379–389.

no matter what plan is proposed to a group for dividing up a resource, if the decision is to be made by majority rule, there is *always* another plan that can defeat the current plan. This is sometimes called the problem of "cyclical majorities," for plan *A* can get more votes than plan *B*, which can get more votes than plan *C*, but plan *C* may then get more votes than plan *A*. Purely on a majority-vote basis, then, it is impossible to reach a final outcome, to find a plan that will defeat all others. In such situations, control of the agenda becomes crucial because the order in which a fixed set of plans is offered in pair-wise competition will determine the final winners. Indeed, in Vietnamese villages, resources were allocated among insiders by their rank in the village, and rank was determined largely by age, wealth, and education. In other cases, resources are allocated by lottery, by turn, or even by rotation based on the position of the sun.[46] Shares may well have been of equal size in many medieval villages, but this is clearly not a progressive principle. On the contrary, if shares are of equal size, and if every male is given an equal size share, then inequality among families and households is reinforced.

Thus, the ranking systems within villages, so often pictured as rankings of prestige, are also rank orders of access to village resources. We shall observe, however, that although the ascriptive system was regressive, and although the ranking system for allocating resources in Vietnamese villages accentuated inequality, the ascriptive nature of the system helped to stabilize the system of distribution.

Leadership

Moral economy interpretations of village decision making stress consensus and systematic participation in the decision process by all villagers. They also stress the leveling function of the demands for feasts and expenditures placed on villagers who seek the "prestige" of a leadership role. I stress the small size of the decision-making group and interpret the emphasis on consensus as an attempt by the elite to close ranks and keep their disputes from the wider village. Moreover, the main motivation for assuming a leadership role is not

46. Rockwell, "Danish Peasant Village," p. 417.

prestige, but gain. Viewed in this light, the feasts and expenditures required of officials are investments, the costs of which prevent many villagers from assuming any role in village leadership or decision making.

The emphasis on unanimity in decision making is widely noted in the literature on villages; this emphasis often is interpreted as evidence of a strong underlying consensus. It may also mean, however, that the elite decision-making body is trying to iron out all conflict internally in order to avoid splits in its ranks and appeals to less powerful villagers. The emphasis on consensus within the elite also can mean that there is a high degree of distrust and suspicion among its members, and that unit veto rules are the only rules that can maintain a stable peace among them. The distrust interpretation of elite consensus is supported by the fact that actual village decision making is generally limited to councils comprised of no more than twelve to fifteen members (whose deliberations may or may not be presented to all other villagers for approval.)[47]

This distrust is also evident in the frequent concern that the headman or chief, who is the link between village councils and the outside authorities, be a lesser person who can be controlled by the council, who will not bring in powerful outsiders to support him in local disputes, or who will not use outside connections to control village resources.[48]

Members of village councils everywhere can and do collude with one another to their common advantage and at the expense of the village. It is equally clear that village officeholding is also often looked on as a way to make money or at least to protect fortunes. Indeed, it is stressed in accounts of prestige economies that peasants will even go into debt to provide feasts and otherwise purchase higher offices in the village. How and why, it should be asked, would conservative, "safety-first" peasants spend so much money, if they were not going to get it back? How are the loans repaid? As

---

47. F. G. Bailey, "Decisions by Consensus in Councils and Committees," pp. 1–20.

48. There will also be times when the potential for profit in the linkage role is clearly less than the level of demands on the role made by powerful outsiders and/or powerful insiders. (See Blum, "Internal Structure and Polity," pp. 557–560, and *Lord and Peasant,* p. 523.)

Barth has noted, "over a longer period of time, a chief certainly expects to derive material advantage from his state."[49] Furthermore, the requirement that persons must give feasts or sponsor festivals *before* attaining high office sets a high entry cost which precludes from office persons who cannot afford the expense or to whom the rich will not lend money. Thus, in many instances, "to the poor man, the higher offices are not open."[50]

(That peasants value feasts is clear; that they consider the best system for providing feasts one in which the rich pay for them is less clear. During the Viet Minh period in Central Vietnam, 1945–1954, feasts were forbidden in most villages; they represented "feudalism" and the old, superstitious ways. After 1954, when the Viet Minh cadres had left the area, the old notables made an effort to reinstitute the old system of feasts paid for and officiated over by (rich) notables. However, there was widespread opposition from among less well-off peasants at the attempted reinstatement of these privileges. In many villages, the protests prevented the old elite from taking control of the feasts, and rent from a piece of communal land was allocated or a tax was instituted to pay for them. With public finance of the feasts, it was no longer necessary to let the rich officiate at them. Now a man of virtue and prestige could be selected by acclaim to officiate at the feast, regardless of his personal wealth. "In the old days," one peasant recounted, "only the rich could officiate at the feast and have the honor of eating the head of the pig. Now any man of virtue and prestige can eat the head of the pig.")

But ceding village offices to the most well-off villagers may not be objectionable to other villagers. A well-off villager, for example, may be content to maintain his fortune rather than seek additional gain by manipulating village affairs; another might be satisfied with enhancement of reputation for the personal credit that it will bring with others. Indeed, if a stable rotation of high office can be arranged among a small number of villagers, a general balance of power may severely limit the short-run (individual as op-

49. Frederick Barth, "Segmentary Opposition and the Theory of Games: A Study of Pathan Organizations," p. 18.

50. Charles Wagley, "Economics of a Guatemalan Village," p. 76.

posed to class) economic payoffs of office holding. Moreover, a person with fixed collateral is less likely to abscond with the tax money. As Potter found, "villagers prefer to have wealthy men as village leaders on the theory that, since they already have money, they are less likely to run off with funds entrusted to them."[51]

In short, the same considerations of investment and profit govern peasant attitudes about village offices as govern their other decisions about security and investment.

Stratification

If, as moral economists state, villages provided viable insurance and welfare, if there were leveling functions, and if it were easy for peasants to flee to precolonial frontiers and clear new land whenever demands of villages or lords became exorbitant, there would be little or no stratification in precapitalist villages. Stratification among peasants would originate with capitalism and markets. But stratification does exist in precapitalist society: "[In the medieval village, there] was clear social stratification by the time we have written records. . . . The division between rich and middle peasants with land and equipment (especially plough teams) adequate for subsistence and poor or landless peasants without enough land for subsistence is found very early."[52] "Polarization of fortunes," then, "could not simply have resulted from competition in production for the market."[53]

Stratification occurred before production for markets because peasants were interested in individual security and approached villages as sources of gain, just as they did markets. Stratification is inherent in the procedures used in many, if not all, village societies. Village welfare and insurance systems were limited, and the use of credit as an alternative added to stratification. Village procedures were not progressively redistributive, but favored the rich. Village

51. Potter, *Thai Peasant Social Structure,* p. 52. Note that both moral economists and political economists agree that there is value in prestige. What needs more development is when leadership will content itself with prestige and when leaders expect a more direct and immediate payoff.

52. Rodney Hilton, "Medieval Peasants—Any Lesson?" pp. 209–210.

53. Hilton, *Bond Men Made Free: Medieval Peasant Movements and the English Rising of 1381,* pp. 32–33.

power was used to control other peasants, as in Russia, where peasants who complained about village officials were sent to the army or to Siberia.[54] Village leaders, furthermore, could use the power that went with their control of village resources to prevent other peasants from opening new lands, so that a source of cheap labor would be available for the better-off peasants.[55]

As Weisser has noted in his reassessment of the Spanish pueblo, "Even in the primitive, pre-industrial world, economic differentiation was so pronounced as to make absurd the notion that communalism was a dominant mode of economic relations either during or long before the advent of the modern era."[56]

During the colonial period, stratification increased in many parts of the world, including Vietnam, because the richer villagers had increased opportunities for profit. But at the core were the same mechanisms of control and stratification as in precolonial and precapitalist Vietnam: allocation of village resources and charges, control of bottlenecks in the local production process, the manipulation of outside connections. Colonialism and capitalism exacerbate, but they do not create economic competition and stratification. Stratification, as Jay noted in Indonesia, is part of village politics and economics:

The power and prestige that can be derived from village officeholding . . . are considerable. The attached land rights afford control over a relatively substantial amount of land, which in turn permits the establishment of a number of power relationships with sharecroppers. . . . Control over largess of central government gives him opportunities to select friends as agents.[57]

54. Blum, "Internal Structure and Polity," p. 575.
55. Oscar Lewis, *Pedro Martinez: A Mexican Peasant and His Family,* p. 7, is but one example of this.
56. Weisser, *Peasants of the Montes,* p. 48. Surveying the evidence on stratification, Weisser notes that "the division between rich and poor, between those who work and those who are idle, was probably greater in the [sixteenth century] past than in the present" (p. 37).
57. Robert Jay, "Local Government in Rural Central Java," p. 226. Assuming the presence of work-sharing and corporate mechanisms, James C. Scott and B. J. Kerkvliet argue that "the typical Javanese village . . . by having avoiding [sic] glaring income differentials, has greatly tempered the local face of class antagonisms" ("The Politics of Survival: Peasant Response to 'Progress' in Southeast Asia," p. 254). Ann Stoler, in contrast, has noted that the "concept of 'shared poverty' . . . obscures the fact that Javanese society has always been stratified . . . through differ-

Alliances, Markets, and Innovations

Evaluation of such phenomena as the development of alliances between villagers and outsiders; the expansion of land, capital, and commodity markets; the adoption of innovations; and the use of supravillage institutions are largely determined by one's view of the corporate village. The moral economy view implies that these changes are the products of powerful outside forces that penetrate the village. The metaphor of "penetration" overlooks the internal limitations of the corporate framework and underestimates the desire of peasants to raise their income beyond the levels possible within corporate villages. Indeed, if village cooperation worked as well as moral economists claim, why should there be any opposition to outside alliances or to innovations that might raise total village output by increasing the supply of credit, gaining the support of powerful outsiders, or in other ways helping the village as a whole to cope with common crises? Even if villages provided ample protection for the poor and insurance against disasters, why would those preclude an interest in opportunities for advancement beyond the income levels possible in a corporate village or an internal initiative for market development and innovation? Moral economists, however, as I have noted in Chapter 1, see peasants as aiming for an income to meet culturally defined needs or to discharge ceremonial and social obligations. In this view, peasants are striving for a "target income"; when they reach this level (which they achieve within the village), they have no further concern with raising production or acquiring goods unavailable within the village. The peasant does not acquire new wants; he is "pulled from the ideal of self-sufficiency by market forces only to the extent that they permit him to purchase certain 'traditional' goods."[58]

The idealization of the corporate village and the accompanying view of the peasant's wants as fixed and met within the village,

---

ential access to strategic resources. It is surprising, then, that the shared poverty concept remains the most popularly held characterization of Javanese rural society, despite the existence of many studies which document the more relevant theme of class stratification based on differential access to land" ("Class Structure and Female Autonomy in Rural Java," pp. 78–79).

58. Jan DeVries, "Peasant Demand Patterns and Economic Development," p. 206.

thus leads, as I have noted, to a view of commercialization and market development as the peasantry's fall from grace. As Jan De-Vries has so aptly phrased it, "Being content with a caricature . . . can only result in a misspecification of the historic and potential role of peasants in economic development."[59]

There is most certainly internal opposition to innovation, alliances, and markets, but there is also internal initiative for such changes. There are, in fact, serious conflicts among members of the elite about the distribution of benefits from outside opportunities, conflicts between classes about opportunities for laborers, and free-rider problems that must be overcome for innovations to be adopted. The expansion of labor markets, for example, brings clear benefits to poor peasants, and it is the rich who often collude to keep the poor from markets. In medieval villages, as we have seen, labor mobility was controlled, when possible, in order to depress wages. In Morelos, Mexico, the arrival of haciendas was a benefit to peasants in many villages, not a threat to well-running corporate villages with strong subsistence guarantees for all. Before the advent of the hacienda, villagers suffered debt, slavery, and exploitation at the hands of local leaders. The introduction of the hacienda, however, led to a wage spiral between competing demands of the hacienda and the *caciques*.[60]

With its passive connotations, the concept of "penetration" implies that the initiative for alliance comes from powerful outsiders. Although the village resists, it finally is broken down and entered. In both precolonial and colonial periods, however, the initiators of alliances are often local notables looking for external allies to strengthen their hands in village power struggles.

Frequently, there is strong opposition to allowing persons living in adjacent areas to own land in villages when such ownership would threaten the village balance of power and the distribution of resources and charges within the village. To prevent or impede bankers, moneylenders, and bureaucrats from owning land in a village, of course, limits the availability of credit (by making mortgages less valuable) and therefore sometimes limits total productivity. However, small landowners oppose the entrance into their

59. Ibid., p. 234.
60. Oscar Lewis, *Tepotzlan: Village in Mexico*, pp. 18–20.

economies of larger, more powerful persons when institutional realities are such that these persons could manipulate taxes, titles, and village resources to the detriment of the small landowners. In fifteenth- and sixteenth-century Wallachia (Romania), nobles could get rights to use communal lands in villages only when a villager would form an alliance with them and take money to adopt them as "brothers." With their wealth and political weight, the nobles then were able to dominate the entire community.[61]

Opposition to outside alliances, I hypothesize, is tied to the quality of land titles. When there is private land with secure title, the opposition to outside landownership becomes far less pronounced; the attractions of credit begin to outweigh the potential threats to smallholders from the entrance into their village economies of moneylenders, bureaucrats, and other foreign landowners. (Of course, there are also numerous attempts by tenants and laborers to prevent landowners from importing tenants and laborers from outside the village.)

Like alliances with outsiders, the advent of new supravillage institutions also can change the power balance within villages; likewise, while some villagers will want to take advantage of these institutions, others will want to prevent villagers from using them. During the colonial period, the new court systems using the laws and languages of the colonizers often had considerable influence on village affairs. Persons who could afford the costs of entry to these institutions (that is, who could afford lawyers or who could speak the new language) had an advantage over adversaries who could not afford the new, higher costs. But the impact of new institutions is not automatic—alliances require at least two parties, and institutions have to be used if they are to have influence. In Mysore, for example, the modern courts established near the village of Namhalli around 1820 had negligible impact on the political and economic life of the village for over a century. No one used the new courts, and "as long as they were avoided by the villagers," they could have only the smallest effect on village life.[62]

Just as peasants are not necessarily averse to new outside al-

61. Daniel Chirot, *Social Change in a Peripheral Society,* p. 46.
62. Alan Beals, "Interplay among Factors of Change in a Mysore Village," p. 91.

liances or institutions, they are not hostile to innovations from which they expect personal gain. Even the simplest of innovations, however, such as the planting of peas or beans, which might look virtually costless and without risk to an outside observer, can require extensive cooperation within the village if peasants are to be assured of realizing the fruits of their labor. Caution based on concern for reaping the fruits frequently is misinterpreted by social scientists as caution based on a peasant belief in a fixed (that is, a constant pie) social product. In this view, peasants resist innovation because, given fixed total production, the gain of any one family will come at the expense of other families.[63]

But distrust of innovation is not due to a belief that there is a constant pie or that one person's gain is another's loss. Even when there is an obvious increase in the total product, peasants will be suspicious and distrustful because they will be concerned with getting gains commensurate with their efforts. The types of innovations likely to be adopted, therefore, are those that make it possible for peasants to believe that they, rather than someone else, will enjoy the fruits of their labor.

For English peasants of the thirteenth century, for example, supplementary crops of peas and beans were of obvious dietary value. Further, they required no milling, they could be picked and eaten green, and in a few minutes enough could be gathered for an entire family meal. However, field peas grew so tall that persons were able to hide among them; since they were generally planted in an area separate from the great fields, this meant a great potential for theft. For the growing of legumes to be possible, it was therefore necessary to find a way to insure that everyone would reap the benefits of their own investment in legumes and to control suspicion and conflict. The solution to this problem (and other similar problems) was centered on the bell tower. By agreeing that persons could be in the pea and bean fields only at a specified hour of the day—clearly marked for all by the bell, which the priest would

63. These views generally derive from the work of George Foster, particularly "Peasant Society and the Image of Limited Good" and "Interpersonal Relations in Peasant Society"; see also James C. Scott and B. J. Kerkvliet, "The Politics of Survival: Peasant Response to 'Progress' in Southeast Asia," p. 243. These arguments are dealt with in greater length in Chapter 3.

ring—suspicion could be reduced from twenty-four hours a day of worry to one hour. That is, during legume time, someone from every family could watch over the family crop; at all other hours, any person carrying legumes could be presumed by all to be a thief.[64]

Much evidence cited as opposition to innovation is no more than individual economic evaluation, that is, rejection based on cost and risk—particularly cost or risk not obvious to the outside observer.[65] In a village which had no rules for regulating pea fields, for example, it would be easy for a social scientist to ignore potential thefts and to conclude that peasants were not growing beans because they were averse to risk or resistant to innovation. Peas and beans, in fact, require innovations that are relatively easy to make within villages. Once the basic procedures to safeguard legumes from theft have been developed, each family can decide on its own whether or not to grow these crops, with no need to consider the decisions of the other families.

In the village mode of production, however, there are clearly times when individual innovations have serious consequences for others (externalities) and require universal adoption. If there is village irrigation and all fields must be flooded at once, it is impractical to shift to a new crop that requires irrigation at a time different from the crop currently raised by other villagers. If all draft animals are allowed to roam freely in all fields after the harvest, a villager who adopts a new harvest technique may leave behind less stubble in his fields; thus, either he receives a "free ride" unless all shift at once, or he is forced to use the same harvest technique as other villagers. Such shifts in agricultural technique are made

64. Ault, *Open Field Farming,* pp. 39–40; Homans, *English Villagers,* p. 103. The same sorts of rules were used to regulate the removal of grain from the field and to decrease suspicion of laborers; grain could be removed only by cart, only between certain hours, and not by laborers. Ault (p. 40) also suggests that the poor may have some rights to gather the peas of others. This example demonstrates how technology, that is, bell towers, can increase community. It also suggests the value of the political (or, in this case religious) entrepreneur who can increase productivity and build organization around such collective goods as the bell tower. (And even if the priest—before ringing the bell—ate everyone else's peas, how much can one person eat?)

65. Anderson and Niehoff, "Peasant Fatalism," is a wonderful analysis of this common phenomenon.

difficult by distrust and conflict within the village, and would be less time-consuming if there were actually a moral economy.[66]

The problems of coordination and decision making within the village also help explain why there is a shift from communal to private property enabling peasants to respond favorably to land, commodity, and capital markets. Peasants are not always "victims" of markets. When they have secure land titles and therefore outsiders are less able to manipulate the lands and taxes of villagers, peasants respond—without crisis or subsistence threat—to the opportunities for advancement and security afforded them by enlarged land, credit, and commodity markets.

Problems of coordination and investment invariably tend to break down communal rotation systems where they have existed. As agricultural techniques develop and intensify, greater investment in the land is required. To receive maximum benefits from irrigation, for example, countless hours of fine grading of the land is required. If communal coordination could insure that everyone would do the same quality of work, agricultural development and land rotation would not be incompatible. In fact, in Vietnam communal land was generally less productive because peasants did not want to "set a banquet for someone else to eat." And more generally, the development of agricultural techniques and investments (whether due to the "push" of population growth or the "pull" of market opportunity), such as planting long-range crops like coffee, leads to a situation of de facto private, unrotated land.[67] Because of the problems of communal decision making and coordination, private land is more productive and generally can support a larger population at a higher level than can communal land.

As land rotations break down and private property develops, the extension of land markets can occur in at least two ways. Localized, internal village land markets develop among insiders whenever there is private property, or even unrotated communal land. Whenever outside credit becomes available and peasants have individual land titles, a more general land market develops in which outsiders also can buy and sell parcels within the village. Whenever

66. See, for example, Blum, "Internal Structure and Polity," p. 569.
67. Chirot, *Social Change in a Peripheral Society,* p. 21; Jan De Vries, *The Economy of Europe in An Age of Crisis,* pp. 41–42; Blum, *Lord and Peasant,* p. 328; Sutti Ortiz, *Uncertainties in Peasant Farming,* pp. 85–132.

it is assumed that corporate villages successfully provided a culturally defined "target income" and that peasants were content (and not pursuing means to raise production), the development of land markets is assumed to be a disaster to the peasantry and is viewed as a product of outside social forces tearing asunder common property. As noted, there were serious limitations on the productivity of communal land, whether or not it was rotated, and the development of land markets and the related extension of commodity markets generally had support among large segments of the peasantry and, in most cases, increased subsistence floors.

The belief that private property and commercialization are deleterious to the peasants goes back, it would appear, to a view of the English enclosure movement that sees in the conversion of common village fields to private, fenced lands the creation of a reserve army of floating laborers upon whose backs the industrial revolution was built. This view of the English enclosures as "sheep-eating men" is a false model to apply to other countries, and it does not even fit with the evidence from England. The English enclosure movement was neither as deleterious to peasants as often assumed nor directly applicable to commercialization in other countries today.

Instead of making all-encompassing generalizations about commercialization or new market opportunities, attention must be paid to the particular crops being cultivated, the specific demands for labor, the potential economies of scale, access to credit, and control of marketing arrangements, all of which determine the distribution of benefits. There are indeed times when new markets and increased commercialization will be deleterious to a large part of the rural population. When English lands were enclosed in order to change from growing grain to raising sheep, some people were driven off the land, for sheep require less labor than most grains. But the majority, probably 90 percent, of enclosed land was not for permanent pasturage, but for grain to take advantage of rising grain prices, to allow farmers to improve their cattle and plough animals by selective breeding (impossible without fences), and to make investments that led to more intensive use of the land:

Mental habits die hard, and it is still thought—and taught—that as a result of enclosure and the introduction of the turnip (one of the most labour-consuming of all the crops in the farmer's calendar) agricultural output rose while the labour force fell—or, as some would say "fled." Agricultural output certainly rose but there is no reason to think that the labour force engaged in agricultural operations fell; the contribution of the Agricultural Revolution was not to release labour for industry, but to make possible a greater output without making a correspondingly greater demand upon the available labour supply.[68]

There was, to be sure, great rural poverty in England during the time of enclosure. But there was also substantial population growth, and the incidence of rural poverty was correlated not with enclosure, but with the lack of nonagricultural employment. Poverty and the industrial revolution may have risen in the same decades, but they rose in different areas.[69]

Enclosures for wheat, then, were the predominant form in England, and they were labor intensive, increasing the carrying capacity of the land: "There is no doubt that enclosure and the improvements which it made possible roused ambitions in the ordinary farmer for the first time, and that the fresh opportunities, suddenly opened up, brought into action stores of human energy never previously tapped. The psychological effect of change doubled and trebled the force of the original stimulus."[70]

Even if the English enclosure movement had not benefited smallholders, it would be a poor model to apply in other cases. Whereas in most of Asia there are no fences, perhaps half the cost of enclosure in England went into fencing to keep livestock apart. Since small holdings require proportionally more fence per unit of land than do large holdings, the initial cost per acre was higher for smallholders than for farmers with more land and was a major reason why smallholders (as opposed to the landless 40 to 50 percent, who certainly benefited on the whole) did not always gain as much, proportionately, as large landowners.[71]

68. J. D. Chambers and G. E. Mingay, *The Agricultural Revolution*, p. 3.

69. Ibid., p. 103; Andrew Appleby's "Agrarian Capitalism or Seigneurial Reaction" is a valuable introduction to the debates over the reasons for rural poverty during enclosure.

70. Joan Thirsk, *English Peasant Farming*, p. 296. "Nor was it the land alone which underwent improvement, but living conditions also. In Messingham, the wealth which flowed into the village after enclosure and the warping of the land was partly used to convert the mud and straw covered huts into brick and tile cottages" (p. 296).

71. Donald McCloskey, "Economics of Enclosure," pp. 144–146. I am grateful to Donald McCloskey for reminding me (personal communication, April 1978)

Even more to the point, the enclosure movement is a bad paradigm because it was administered so fairly, compared to many colonial or contemporary situations. The key determinant of the fate of peasants in open land markets is not the vagaries of commercial agriculture, but the chances which accrue to better educated villagers, who are able to manipulate colonial institutions by registering the land of other villagers in their own name or by using the courts to claim land belonging to others. What is so remarkable about the English enclosure, to a scholar studying mainly contemporary situations, is how much attention (relatively) was given to protecting the rights of smallholders in England.[72]

Just as persistent a myth as that of the enclosure movement as a giant swindle is the notion that small, local commodity markets provide more certain subsistence for peasants than do national or international markets. Certainly as transportation improves and markets reach into once-remote areas, there is generally an increase

---

that "a smallholder of land benefits from an improvement in technique in the village even if he does not undertake it. The value of his land rises because it can be used by others (the buyers) with the new technique." Thus, even a technique which smallholders cannot afford themselves may still benefit them by making it possible for them to survive a bad year by selling a small corner of their now-more-valuable land instead of selling all of their land or some of their children instead.

72. Chambers and Mingay, *Agricultural Revolution,* pp. 85–90. The impact of views of the enclosure movement on analysis of contemporary situations is clearly demonstrated in Scott's discussion of the green revolution in the Punjab region of India. "*As in England,* the transition has not been peaceful. The lower 20 percent of the labor force is perhaps worse off then before and open conflict between landowners' and laborers' factions is common . . . almost all the new profits have gone to those who control land and capital. . . . A portion of the tenants and smallholders *forced off* the land have been absorbed into the agrarian labor force, another portion into the secondary industries of processing, transport, and marketing created by the agricultural boom, and still another substantial portion into the growing industrial sector of the region. It would seem, thus far at least, that the Punjab has experienced a successful shift to productive, capitalist agriculture. The "success" has eliminated many of the traditional securities for the rural poor and has particularly damaged those at the very bottom of the social structure but it has provided enough economic safety valves to absorb much of the peasantry" (Scott, *Moral Economy,* p. 208; emphasis added). Scott is wrong for the Punjab as well as for England. There has been a large influx of laborers into the Punjab from other provinces because the green revolution has been labor intensive. There has been a "discernible and unparalled improvement in employment opportunities and earnings of the agricultural laborers" and an upward shift in income for almost all the farmers in the state. "There are no facts to support that in Punjab evictions took place due to green revolution technology" (S. S. Johl, "Gains of the Green Revolution: How They Have Been Shared in Punjab," pp. 182–185). The green revolution, however, is by no means the panacea suggested by some of its more ardent enthusiasts.

in stratification. But given the lack of village aid for persons with bad harvests, the tenancy that results from selling land in bad years may not be such a bad alternative to wage slavery, infanticide, or selling of children. When village production can enter a regional or national market, the pool of potential creditors is expanded because the land now has value to outsiders. More important is the fact that, while exposure to international and national markets does subject peasants to new and different kinds of uncertainty, larger markets tend to maintain steadier prices and far more certain supplies of food over time; in England, "improved transportation reduced risk by increasing the varieties of weather and soil represented in a single market area and therefore decreasing the variability of prices for the market as a whole."[73] When markets expand, supplies of grain begin to even out, one area's good year canceling another area's bad year. With expansion, then, the actual "insurance value of money," that is, the probability that money saved in a good year will find food to buy in a bad year, itself increases and peasants have a form of protection which they did not have within smaller market areas.

PATRON-CLIENT RELATIONS

A direct comparison of the moral economy and political economy assumptions reveals important differences in expectations for three aspects of the patron-client relation—the terms of exchange, maintenance of dependency, and distribution of resources.

While moral economists assume a fixed, culturally given subsistence level (target income), I assume that the subsistence level is endogenous and variable. Peasants, that is, will try to raise their share of production, through either individual or group bargaining, according to the risk involved.

If the legitimacy of patron or lord depended on a fixed notion of subsistence, and if precapitalist society generally provided subsistence for all, then a drastic reduction in the man/land ratio would have no effect on tenants or clients. In fact, however, throughout

73. McCloskey, "English Open Fields," p. 129.

the precapitalist and colonial world, whenever plagues have drastically reduced the number of tenants on the great estates or holdings, demands for higher wages and better terms of exchange have followed. In fourteenth-century England, "the immediate impact of the Black Death had been that both agricultural and other workers demanded, *according to the strength of their bargaining power,* up to twice or even three times their previous wages."[74]

Similarly, in Japan during the 1920s, conflict between landlords and tenants was most common in the villages near urban and industrial centers. This was not because the movement of landlords into the cities had left peasants more unprotected and with less favorable terms of exchange than in the past. All generalizations to the contrary, absentee landlords at this time were more forgiving in bad years, rented larger plots, charged lower rents, and evicted tenants less often than resident landlords.[75] Tenancy disputes were centered in these areas not because of negative impacts of absenteeism or commercialization, but because opportunities in factories had drawn laborers out of agriculture, reducing competition for tenancies. Thus, although conditions of tenancy were comparatively good around urban and industrial centers, protest and militancy were widespread, for there was little fear of reprisal.[76] Subsistence, therefore, is not fixed at a culturally given level. Economic shares are based on the terms of exchange, and protest frequently occurs when the balance of exchange is *improving* in favor of the tenant.

Among the many limits on tenant bargaining powers were the feudal laws that required lords to return runaways and antipoaching agreements to prevent bidding among lords for the services of tenants. Such attempts at collusion even extended—when the relative power of the lords vis-à-vis the central authorities was high—to

74. Hilton, *Bond Men Made Free,* p. 154 (emphasis added). See also Elias Tuma, *Twenty-Six Centuries of Agrarian Reform,* p. 42; Jerome Blum, Rondo Cameron, and Thomas Barnes, *The Emergence of the European World,* p. 37; Hamza Alavi, "Peasants and Revolution," p. 266; Sabean, "German Agrarian Institutions," p. 80.

75. Ann Waswo, *Japanese Landlords: The Decline of a Rural Elite,* pp. 88–89. Although absentee landlords in Japan at this time provided more secure floors, they were less likely or able than resident landlords to carry out projects that would raise productivity and increase the shares of both landlords and tenants.

76. Ibid., pp. 102–103; John Gitlitz, "Haciendad, Comunidad and Peasant Protest in Northern Peru," p. 426.

limiting the emergence of cities and market areas because cities and markets would benefit clients at the lord's expense.[77]

Within their own domains or estates, it was common for lords to monopolize crucial bottlenecks in the production process in order to maintain control over tenants. At one time or another, mills, ovens, and bulls were all preserved as monopolies by European lords. By forcibly maintaining such monopolies (killing all other bulls, for example), lords were not only able to provide a service for their tenants, but they were also able to shift the transaction costs to those who must come to the lords for a vital service. Thus, for example, "it is no wonder that in a society where bread was so scarce and uncertain the term 'keeper of the loaves,' *hlaford,* came to mean, in Anglo-Saxon, 'master' or lord."[78]

If lords are an important "functional," "legitimate" part of peasant livelihood, then whenever there is a chance to increase production by upgrading the "human capital" of the tenants, lords logically should do so. In fact, there are many occasions when lords will not risk their position by allowing tenants access to new skills which would raise total output if these skills can also enhance leadership ability and give peasants new options independent of the lord. It is clearly the case that tenants can be forcibly prevented from acquiring skills that increase production but threaten dependency. In Peru, "mestizo overlords regarded the peasants as little better than animals and actively discouraged education or the use of Spanish on the sound assumption that it might create aspirations beyond servile labor."[79] Literacy is particularly threatening because it increases the probability that peasants on estates will be able to take advantage of favorable national political climates to move against lords, and because it undercuts the dependence of peasants on lords. John Gitlitz, discussing the threat of mass literacy to Peruvian haciendas, notes that a literate person

77. Jerome Blum, "The Rise of Serfdom in Eastern Europe," pp. 820–834; Hilton, *Bond Men Made Free,* p. 152; Breman, *Patronage and Exploitation,* pp. 64–65; Mark Elvin, *The Pattern of the Chinese Past,* pp. 71–73.

78. Robert Lopez, *The Commercial Revolution of the Middle Ages 950–1350,* p. 17. G. G. Coulton, *The Medieval Village,* p. 56, discusses common monopolies.

79. Jeffrey Paige, *Agrarian Revolution: Social Movements and Export Agriculture in the Underdeveloped World,* p. 167.

. . . can read the papers, follow national political events, and more readily recognize the availability and relative power of differing potential allies. Finally, on the estate, he can . . . [help] those among his comrades who are illiterate to deal with the outside world. He can read them the directions for the use of pesticides or interpret orders from the sub-prefect. In short, he can to some extent replace the haciendado.[80]

The very process of production, then, can reflect a divergence between providing the best guarantees for clients and maximizing dependence on lords. To maintain control of serfs, a twelfth-century Chinese book advised, "one should not allow them to have fields and gardens of their own, for if one does, they immediately become filled with greedy schemes."[81] Peasants are often forcibly blocked from the market for the same reasons: development of market skills can help the peasant to demand more, or even to do without his patron.

When they were able to do so, large estate owners in colonial Southeast Asia forcibly prevented peasants in their domains from selling paddy, buffalo, or even garden produce on their own.[82] In amassing their estates and maintaining forced dependencies, they relied on the sociological incompetence of most peasants, their lack of the linguistic and legal-political skills needed to work with the colonial power structure.[83]

Although the self-image of the patron was that of a patriarchal, all-encompassing father figure, he himself often lacked the managerial competence to perform such a role for large numbers of tenants concentrated on estates scattered over many villages. The use of intermediaries and agents and the requirements that harvest-

80. Gitlitz, "Haciendad, Comunidad and Peasant Protest," p. 436. He notes also the important role of army veterans in uprisings on the haciendas studied. Veterans home from the Seven Years' War also played an important role in English food riots by "providing a disciplined core of militants able to defy the military, and by giving direction to the disorders" (Walter J. Shelton, *English Hunger and Industrial Disorders,* p. 3).

81. Quoted by Mark Elvin, *Pattern of the Chinese Past,* p. 77. See also Jeffrey Paige, *Agrarian Revolution: Social Movements and Export Agriculture in the Underdeveloped World,* p. 171.

82. For estates on private lands of Java, see Sartono Kartodirdjo, *Protest Movements in Rural Java: A Study of Agrarian Unrest in the Nineteenth and Early Twentieth Centuries,* pp. 24–30. Vietnam is discussed in Chapters 3 and 4, this volume. See also Breman, *Patronage and Exploitation,* pp. 5–6, 10.

83. Michael Adas, *The Burma Delta,* pp. 141–142.

ing be done only in the presence of the owner or agent severely strained relations. Even in the best of circumstances, the patriarch-distant relative analogy often is depicted in an overly positive light. As described in ideal form by a Vietnamese estate owner,

In the past the relationship between the landlord and his tenants was pater-nalistic. The landlord considered the tenant as an inferior member of his extended family. When the tenant's father died, it was the duty of the landlord to give money to the tenant for the funeral; if his wife was preg-nant, the landlord gave money for the birth; if he was in financial ruin, the landlord gave assistance; therefore, the tenant *had* to behave as an inferior member of the extended family.[84]

It is true that landlords preferred multistranded relationships be-cause they allowed them to maintain their monopoly position and the tenant's dependence. Without opportunities to build up reserves of their own, tenants would have to come to the landlord—and be in his good graces—for any unusual expense. Tenants, on the other hand, generally preferred many single-stranded relationships rather than an all-encompassing "feudal" relationship with one lord. Peasants in commercial areas of Burma, for example, preferred not to borrow money from their estate owners if they had jewelry or cattle for security.[85] Dependence also meant subjugation. As Al-exander Woodside has noted, this "inferior member of the extended family" model was "symbolically infantile. . . . The economic value of these positions fluctuated with the prosperity of rural har-vests but their social value had always been monotonously de-graded."[86] And Chinese peasants, both tenants and smallholders, had an expression which emphasized the importance of maintaining some autonomy and maneuvering room in their relations with land-lords: "Embrace Buddha's leg only in time of need" (Look to a benefactor only when one is in difficulty).[87]

Peasants, as we shall see, can overthrow lords and increase their security by changing modes of production and by reorganizing ag-

84. Robert Sansom, *The Economics of Insurgency in the Mekong Delta of Viet-nam*, p. 29. Emphasis in original.
85. Adas, *Burma Delta*, p. 137. Vietnam is discussed in Chapter 4, this volume.
86. Alexander Woodside, *Community and Revolution in Modern Vietnam*, pp. 257–258.
87. Ralph Thaxton, "The World Turned Downside Up," pp. 185–228, 194.

ricultural institutions to remove monopolies and overcome linguistic and legal barriers which put them at a disadvantage in the marketplace. The central state is not automatically a threat to the peasantry; on the contrary, it can be an ally in the process. As Robert Brenner noted for seventeenth-century France, "strong peasant property and [the] absolutist state developed in mutual dependence upon one another. The state increased its power by virtue of its ability to get between the landlord and the peasants, to ensure peasant freedom, hereditability and fixed rents, and thus to use peasant production . . . as the direct source of revenue for royal strength and autonomy."[88] In twentieth-century Japan, landlords became less important to tenant prosperity as state agricultural services provided farming advice, local officials settled disputes, and the government issued disaster relief.[89]

In moral economy terms, lords will strengthen their position and create the highest general level of security by distributing resources equally among all peasants on their lands. I predict unequal distribution. Given political economy assumptions about gain and individual approaches to security, there will be substantial conflicts of interest among peasants, and lords will take advantage of these conflicts to increase their own profits. Lords pursue divide and conquer strategies that capitalize on competition and conflicts among peasants, as can be seen in the unequal treatment of clients and tenants.

The patron-client literature does not deal extensively with the distinction between tenant and client, but the distinction between these two types of relations helps clarify the strategies that landlords use. Successful maintenance of a large estate involves limiting the ability of tenants to engage in collective action. A critical component of a strategy to prevent collective action can be, and very often is, the uneven and unequal distribution of patronage and in-

---

88. Robert Brenner, "Agrarian Class Structure and Economic Development in Pre-Industrial Europe," p. 71. The importance to states—which benefit from increased development—and peasants—who secure their families and are more able to control their offspring—of hereditability should not be overlooked. A major peasant demand in Germany during peasant uprisings was for hereditary tenure. (David Sabean, "Family and Land Tenure," p. 5.)

89. Waswo, *Japanese Landlords,* pp. 92–93.

centives. The clients in reality are usually a small subset of tenants who have curried special position, favor, or treatment from the landlord through special services. These special services often include acting as "strikebreaker" or keeping the landlord informed about the activities of other tenants. In China, the subset of tenants who helped the landlords to control other tenants were referred to by the latter as "dog's leg";[90] in colonial Vietnam, clients were known to other tenants as "basket carriers" and "servile flatterers of the rich."[91]

Within villages or on large estates, lords or notables are usually the arbiters of disputes among peasants. This control of arbitration helps to divide and conquer the peasants, pitting them against one another for future considerations. Notables or lords also control the allocation of scarce resources that put peasants into competition. Indeed, a scarcity of crucial resources can aid the lord by increasing tension among tenants and, therefore, the competition for special treatment.

The very existence of a class of landless laborers in a peasant society suggests that there are critical weaknesses in the moral economy views of the village and of patron-client relations. The concept of common moral expectation and universe appears to conflict with the hostility so often encountered between laborer and tenant. Much of landlord "exploitation" is facilitated by the uneven distribution of resources (which leads to laborers and tenants, instead of a single class of tenants). The lack of common moral solidarity among the peasantry means competition among peasants for land and credit and a waiting source of men willing to help the landlord evict a tenant who makes trouble.[92]

90. William Hinton, *Fanshen*, pp. 112–117.
91. Author's interviews.
92. Alavi's "Peasants and Revolution" is the seminal statement on these class conflicts in agriculture. See also Tuma, *Twenty-Six Centuries*, p. 72; Breman, *Patronage and Exploitation*, p. 56; and Gitlitz, "Hacienda, Comunidad and Peasant Protest," p. 14. At times, however, peasants did maintain solidarity against lords and denied them the power to bring in new tenants. As long as effective boycotts of new tenants were maintained, the newcomers could not survive, particularly when other farmers refused to help extinguish the fires set on unwanted tenants' lands. (Blum, "Internal Structure and Polity," p. 522.) Today, agricultural laborers may boycott or otherwise use collective action against tenants who try to use labor-saving means of harvesting or threshing their crops. Such strategies generally fail, however,

CONCLUSION

I have made assumptions about individual behavior that are different from those of the moral economists. These assumptions have drawn attention to different features of villages and patron-client ties and have led to questions about the quality of welfare and insurance embedded in both villages and vertical patron-client ties. This, in turn, has demonstrated that there is more potential value to markets *relative to the actual performance level* of these other institutions. Commercialization of agriculture and the development of strong central authorities are not wholly deleterious to peasants, although they may dramatically alter peasant society. This is not because capitalism and/or colonialism are necessarily more benevolent than moral economists assume, but because traditional institutions are harsher and work less well than they believe.

Depending on the specific institutional context, commercialization can be good or bad for peasants. In many cases the shift to narrow contractual ties with landlords increases both peasant security and his opportunity to benefit from markets. The protection and material assistance of the past carried an onerous burden, for often it was based on dependencies that resulted in low production plateaus, enforced ignorance, and limited skills. In Latin America, "the patron held life-or-death judicial authority over his dependent serfs, and the murder of peasants or the violation of their wives and daughters was not uncommon."[93] As long ago as the fifth century, a monk described the transformation that overcame freemen who became part of estates: "all these people who settled on the big estates underwent a strange transformation as if they had drunk of Circe's cup, for the rich began to treat as their own property these strangers."[94]

---

because those hiring the labor use divide-and-conquer strategies against the laborers. Divide-and-conquer strategies seldom require more than paying a few laborers higher wages to switch from knives to sickles and to exclude other laborers from the fields, or demanding free preharvest weeding from small numbers of laborers in exchange for giving them rights to do the entire harvest. (William A. Collier et al., "Agricultural Technology and Institutional Change in Java"; Matsao Kikuchi et al., "Evolution of Land Tenure in a Laguna Village," pp. 12–14.) The same focus on visible standards is found in conflicts between laborers and tenants, as discussed earlier.

93. Paige, *Agrarian Revolution,* p. 167.
94. Hilton, *Bond Men Made Free,* quoting J. LeGeof, p. 58.

Single-stranded relationships may be far more secure for the peasant because there may be less coercion, an absence of monopolies, competition among landlords, and less need for submission of self. The development of an independent trading class can give small peasants easy, low-risk access to international markets and a way of escaping the domination of large lords who use coercion to control the economy despite inefficient practices. The growth of independent small traders like the Chinese in Vietnam, for example, is opposed not by peasants but by large landowners. In particular, erosion of the "traditional" terms of exchange between landlord and tenant is not the only way for peasants to turn against large lords. It is not the case that if the patron guarantees the traditional subsistence level, peasants will cede him continuous legitimacy; peasants can and do fight for autonomy when better alternatives exist in the market. There are often better opportunities for peasants in markets than under lords, and markets can reduce the bargaining power of the lords.[95] Indeed, it was not uncommon in Europe for men to buy their way out of clientage for the security and freedom of markets.[96]

One need only note the land rush in the new areas of Cochinchina after the French made it habitable to see that markets can be an enormous opportunity for the poor, a chance to escape onerous dependencies and establish themselves, as well as to develop and rely on a more extensive family network than was possible in dependent subsistence. Throughout the world, peasants have fought for access to markets not as a last gasp when all else has failed them, but when they were secure enough to want to raise their economic level and "redefine" cultural standards! In medieval England, when peasant conditions were comparatively secure,

The essential quarrel between the peasantry and the aristocracy was about access to the market. It was not that the peasants were worried about the impact of the market in a disintegrating sense upon their community; what

95. See, for example, Jerome Blum, "The Rise of Serfdom in Eastern Europe," p. 816; Breman, *Patronage and Exploitation,* p. 75; Hilton, *Bond Men Made Free,* p. 214.

96. Rodney Hilton, "Peasant Society, Peasant Movements and Feudalism in Medieval Europe," in Henry Landsberger, *Rural Protest: Peasant Movements and Social Change,* pp. 67–94, 81; Blum et al., *A History of the Modern World,* p. 23.

they wanted was to be able to put their produce on the market and to have a freer market in land which would enable them to take advantage of the benefits of the market.[97]

The rise of strong central states and the growth of a market economy, then, even in the guise of colonialism (and compradore capitalism), cannot be directly equated with a decline in peasant welfare due to the destruction of traditional villages and/or elite bonds. In the short run, local village elites with the skills to ally themselves with outside powers may reap the greatest benefits from new institutional arrangements, but in the longer run new elites emerge who form alliances with the peasantry against both feudalism and colonialism.[98]

Indirectly, peasants clearly benefit from the growth of law and order and its resulting stability, as well as improvements in communications. The numerous and onerous taxes of the colonial period—as applied by village elites—increased stratification in the majority of countries, but the colonial infrastructure also led to wider systems of trade, credit, and communications that helped keep peasants alive during local famines. As Day has noted of Java, local crop failures were so serious in precolonial times before there was a developed communications and trade network "because it was impossible to supply a deficit in one part of the country by drawing on the surplus which might exist in another."[99] Colonialism was ugly, but the quality of the minimum subsistence floor improved in most countries.[100]

Having specified the assumptions of the moral and political economy approaches, and having developed and contrasted their predictions, I turn now to analysis of the case that prompted my effort to develop this approach—Vietnam. In succeeding chapters I shall apply the analysis to villages and village-state relations in the precolonial era, the impact of colonialism on villages, and the de-

97. Hilton, "Medieval Peasants—Any Lesson?" p. 217.
98. As Weisser notes for Spain, "anarchism sought to sweep away the remnants of that old system by joining with those elements in the outside world that had begun a similar attack" (*Peasants of the Montes*, p. 117).
99. Day, *Dutch in Java*, p. 25.
100. Clifford Geertz, *Agricultural Involution: The Process of Ecological Change in Indonesia*, p. 80; Tom Kessinger, *Vilyatpur 1848–1968*, p. 87; Charles Robequain, *The Economic Development of French Indochina*, p. 328.

velopment of religious and political movements. I shall then conclude with a comparison of the moral and political economy approaches to peasant movements and an amplification of the collective goods paradigm for peasant society.

This work is not intended to be a complete treatment of the emergence of political and religious movements in the Vietnamese countryside. For the purposes of this study, religious and ideological beliefs are givens that will be evaluated in relation to developing bureaucracies, villages, and organizations. Similarly, villages and village organization will be emphasized to the neglect of supravillage differences among the various religious and political activists during the colonial period.

3

Precolonial Vietnam

THE PLACE to begin testing the competing claims of moral and political economists about peasant society is in the precolonial village. The role of the nineteenth-century Vietnamese village in peasant economic life extended far beyond insurance or welfare to include law and order, property rights, courts, and self-defense. Yet village welfare was limited and insurance was provided not by the village, but by small groups governed by rules of strict reciprocity. Individual reliance on private welfare and insurance produced short-run maximization behavior vis-à-vis village land and taxes, while the difficulties of village-level transactions and insurance mechanisms were sufficient to affect overall production patterns and levels. Far from leveling differences in wealth, village procedures helped generate and protect such differences. In general, village procedures did not minimize risks, maximize security, or insure income floors.

There were competing procedures for allocating village charges and resources—such as between policies to raise average income and policies to maximize income floors—and the choice among competing procedures was determined not only by conditions within the villages, but also by the policies of central authorities. While low levels of information limited the involvement of supravillage officials in daily affairs of the villages, the notion of village autonomy is misleading, for there were still many ways for outside actors to shape village life. Limited intrusion did not mean limited impact, and the oft-used concepts of *autonomy* and *penetration* are particularly misleading, for they divert attention from the many incentives used to attract villagers into involvement with the national political system on their own behalf or on behalf of their village.

National influences on village culture and religion were integral parts of state-making in precolonial Vietnam. Controls on literacy and printing were related to efforts to homogenize local beliefs, contain the effects of Buddhism, and promote Confucianism. The successes of Catholic missionaries, and the techniques they used, emphasize the political problems of making Confucianism dominant as well as the potential for alternate forms of local institutions with more widespread and less costly economic, political, and religious participation.

When a thousand years of Chinese rule ended in 939 A.D., the Vietnamese occupied what is today only one of the country's three regions, the Red River delta—also called Tonkin, the northern region, or most properly, Bac Bo. Most of the long thin strip of coastal rice land edged by highland plateaus and mountain ridges—now called Central Vietnam, Annam, or most properly, Trung Bo—was controlled by the great kingdom of Champa and many small highland tribes. The vast Mekong River delta—the southern region, now called Cochinchina, or Nam Bo—was an integral part of the Khmer empire. The Vietnamese slowly inched their way through Annam into Cochinchina, opening new land to colonization and encouraging migration from older areas.[1] First

---

1. For a summary and careful analysis of the little that is known about the rural society of this period, see A. Terry Rambo, "A Comparison of Peasant Social Systems of Northern and Southern Vietnam: A Study of Ecological Adaptation, Social Succession and Cultural Evolution," pp. 297–323.

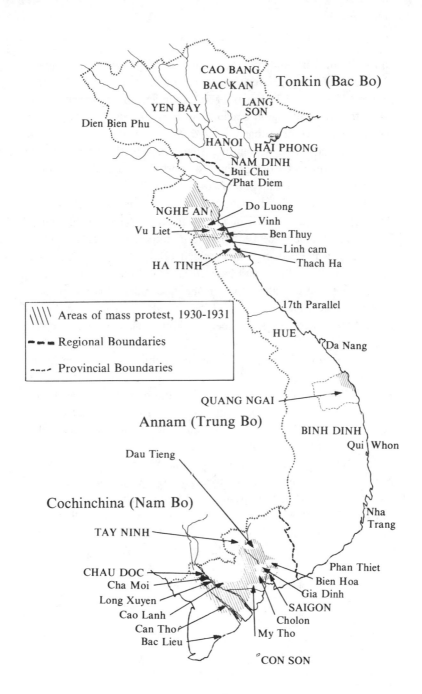

MAP 1. Vietnam

came colonies of soldiers, then colonies of prisoners, and finally offshoots of older, overpopulated villages. The march south reached Hue in 1307, and by 1700 included all of Annam. Soon after, the Mekong region began to fall, but it was really not until the nineteenth century that Cochinchina was part of Vietnam and the country acquired its familiar shape of two rice-basket-shaped deltas, Tonkin and Cochinchina, supported by a pole—the long, thin coastal strip and mountains of Annam.[2]

The late settlement of South Vietnam (Cochinchina and southern Annam) gave a "frontier" quality to much of Vietnam throughout its history of independence, and the country's peculiar, elongated geography was conducive to repeated civil wars. In fact, it was only from 939 to 1527, and later from 1788 until the French conquest in the second half of the nineteenth century, that one dynasty ever ruled the entire nation. And it was only from 1802 until 1860 that all the territory now considered Vietnam was under the control of one ruler.

There is no doubt that peasants in all three regions considered themselves Vietnamese and shared a common identity. Nevertheless, political problems of integrating these three regions into a single political framework firmly controlled by the emperor were severe. These problems of stability and integration were reflected in national policies toward village government.

The Nguyen dynasty gained power in 1802 by defeating the Tay Son. For two centuries the Nguyen had ruled the southern half of the country while another group of lords, the Trinh, had ruled Tonkin and the northern part of Annam. In 1788, the Tay Son overcame both the Nguyen and the Trinh and rode a massive peasant upheaval to power, only to collapse after the death of their most gifted emperor.[3]

From the imperial city of Hue, the Nguyen emperors controlled their empire through an administrative class selected for the most

2. See M. G. Cotter, "Toward a Social History of the Vietnamese Southward Movement," pp. 12–24.

3. Alexander Woodside, *Vietnam and the Chinese Model: A Comparative Study of Vietnamese and Chinese Government in the First Half of the Nineteenth Century*, pp. 2–3.

part by examinations in Confucian doctrine and methods of administration. Under the emperor and his councils, six ministries—appointments, finance, rites, war, justice, and public works—crowned the administrative hierarchy.[4] They supervised and governed through governors who controlled some thirty provinces. In turn, these mandarins supervised 250 district magistrates. Based on the mid-century population estimate of 8 million, provinces averaged about 250,000 and districts about 30,000 people. The district magistrates and their staffs supervised approximately 16,000 villages and villagelike settlements.[5] There was widespread instability in precolonial Vietnam. Indeed, in the four hundred years prior to the French takeover, there were *fifty* emperors and pretenders who exercised (or attempted to exercise) power in the northern half of Vietnam—an average of one every eight years![6]

Furthermore, Tonkin had been threatened with chronic food shortages since at least 1620, and in the eighteenth century as many as 527 villages in the north alone had been deserted in a single year due to exorbitant tax demands (which led to widespread revolt).[7] Even in the moderately stable nineteenth century, the rootless poor and unregistered were a source of instability and a constant concern to the emperor.[8] Indeed, the "Historiographies of the Nguyen Court" and the "Biographies of Rebels against the National Realm" tell of more than 450 local uprisings in the nineteenth century, as well as of countless droughts, floods, epidemics (one cholera epidemic appears to have killed 20 percent of the population),[9] Chinese bandits, jungle bandits, marauders, and plagues of locusts. Nearly everyone, including the notables, were poor and faced constant problems of economic and physical insecurity. Given this poverty and insecurity, it is a serious distortion to picture the Vietnamese world before colonialism as normally Rousseauean with

4. Ibid., pp. 66–74.
5. Ibid., pp. 143–144.
6. Rambo, "Comparison of Peasant Social Systems," p. 262.
7. Vu Quoc Thuc, *L'Economie communaliste du Vietnam*, p. 123.
8. Ibid., p. 33. See also Dennis Duncanson, *Government and Revolution in Vietnam*, p. 59.
9. Ngo Vinh Long, *Before the Revolution: The Vietnamese Peasants under the French*, pp. 31–32; Woodside, *Vietnam and the Chinese Model*, pp. 37, 158.

only occasional small tremors. Colonialism can be attacked without ignoring the Hobbesian nature of the traditional world and inferring a golden past from an ugly present. One should remember, as Lawrence Stone has so aptly said of premodern Europe,

It is now generally admitted that the life of pre-modern man was the very opposite of the life of security and stability depicted by nostalgic romantics. Both groups and individuals were under constant threat, at the mercy of the hands of weather, fire and disease, a prey to famines, epidemics, wars and other wholly unpredictable calamities.[10]

Given the unstable nature of life for peasants and notables alike, the political patterns within the village and between village and state are best understood in terms of the risks and options available to peasants seeking to stabilize and secure their own existence.

THE PRECOLONIAL VILLAGE

Vietnamese villages of the nineteenth century possessed the essential characteristics of what Eric Wolf has termed a "closed corporate community," a village in which there is a common body of rights to possessions, pressures to redistribute surplus in the operation of a religious system, controls which prevent or impede outsiders from becoming members of the community, and limits on outside communications and alliances.[11] The villages generally consisted of three hundred to a thousand persons, with families grouped into several neighborhoods or hamlets. Each village had a chief, a council of notables, and a ranking system or ladder for determining the social hierarchy.

The corporate village community, however, did not consist

10. Lawrence Stone, "The Disenchantment of the World," p. 2.

11. Eric Wolf, "Closed Corporate Communities in Meso-America and Central Java," p. 2. Wolf has hypothesized that this form of village is a product of a dual—usually colonial—society with a "dominant entrepreneurial sector and a dominated sector of native peasants" (p. 8), but the corporate village was a feature of precapitalist and precolonial society in Vietnam and was prevalent throughout much of precapitalist Europe as well. Rambo, "Comparison of Peasant Social Systems," deals at greater length than is possible here with Wolf's criteria for corporate villages and their correspondence with the features of Vietnamese villages. Rambo's work is the best single available compilation and evaluation of ethnographic data on Vietnam. See also Woodside, *Vietnam and the Chinese Model*, pp. 152–158.

nearly of all persons within a geographically defined area. The occupants of a village consisted of *noi tich,* literally, "inside the village."[12] Clearly, the concept of village citizenship was important, for the insider-outsider distinction was sharply drawn, and the outsiders—who included transients, refugees, the poor, and even men who had moved to the village following marriage to an insider—were in a decidedly inferior position.

Pressures to keep outsiders from entering the village were strong and served to keep land in the hands of native villagers. One sanction against outsiders was the tax a groom paid to the village on marrying a local woman, the tax being higher for "foreign" men.[13] Such an outsider was required to change his name if it were the same as that of a village native and thus make his "foreignness" clear to all.[14] Even more important, an "outsider" who was allowed to live in a village had fewer rights to village possessions than did insiders. His descendants, furthermore, might not receive full citizenship—and with it, the right to own property and be notables—for several generations.[15] Such marked distinctions made it exceedingly difficult, if not impossible, for a man to move into a village and take over another man's land. Even well into the period of French rule, a person from another village who tried to farm in a corporate village was likely to have his crops destroyed.[16] Outside moneylenders thus found it difficult to claim a villager's land if he defaulted. If they did manage to seize it, they were often unable either to farm or sell it.[17] The emphasis on village citizenship, therefore, encouraged local ownership and impeded the development of powerful multivillage landed fortunes.

Corporate control over common possessions and the same insider-outsider distinction were found in those villages specializ-

12. Alfred Schreiner, *Les Institutions annamites en Basse Cochinchine avant la lonquête française,* vol. 2, p. 18; Pierre Pasquier, *L'Annam d'autrefois,* p. 48.
13. Nguyen van Khoan, "Essai sur le dinh et le culte du genie tutelaire des villages du Tonkin," p. 131.
14. Paul Ory, *La Commune annamite au Tonkin,* p. 36.
15. Rambo, "Comparison of Peasant Social Systems," p. 37; Gerald C. Hickey, "Social Systems of Northern Vietnam: A Study of Systems in Contact," p. 54; Schreiner, *Les Institutions annamites,* pp. 17–20.
16. Pierre Gourou, *Les Paysans du Delta Tonkinois: Etudé de géographie humaine,* p. 361.
17. Ibid., p. 378.

ing in artisanry, crafts, and cottage industries. The techniques were the property of the village, and so jealously were they guarded that single women were not taught the essential techniques unless they married an "insider."[18] Artisans also dealt with the outside world as villages, not as individuals, for they had especially strong reasons for remaining anonymous—a clever artisan could suffer a fate akin to "labor slavery" if his identity became known to demanding mandarins.[19] (Local industry, as a result, was not a lucrative alternative to agriculture, but a last resort of villages with poor or insufficient land.)[20]

This sense of corporateness, of a community set against the outside world, was expressed in the large, dense hedge that surrounded each village. In an insecure country the hedge was a functional security measure, but beyond its protective value it was also

. . . a kind of sacred boundary of the village community, the sign of its individuality and its independence. When in times of dissension a village has been a party to agitation or has given asylum to rebels, the first punishment inflicted upon it is to cut its bamboo hedge. This is a serious blow to its pride, a stamp of dishonor. The village feels as uncomfortable as a human being would were he undressed and marooned in the middle of a fully dressed crowd.[21]

Wet rice agriculture prevailed throughout the country. The only other common food crops were such less desirable supplements as manioc, sweet potatoes, and maize. In Tonkin and Annam there were extensive systems of seawalls, storage ponds, drainage ditches, and irrigation canals, all maintained in large part by the village. There was also a system of massive river dikes in Tonkin. These latter were supervised by mandarins who called on village authorities for the necessary labor:

An earthen dike needs constant upkeep. One must be on guard lest trees send in their roots, animals burrow in it, or termites build their galleries, for it is essential to avoid undermining infiltrations. This supervision must be intensified when the river is at high water, as putting the dike under

18. Ibid., pp. 528–529.
19. Woodside, *Vietnam and the Chinese Model*, pp. 31–32.
20. Dao Duy Anh, *Vietnam*, p. 64.
21. Gourou, *Les Paysans*, p. 250.

pressure always, in fact, produces some accidents. . . . Indispensible repairs must be done at once, and when the need is apparent, the population of the neighborhood is mobilized. . . .[22]

In both Tonkin and Annam at least one-quarter of all agricultural land was communal land, administered and controlled by the village council and chief, and distributed every three or six years to eligible villagers. Cochinchina, on the other hand, had only small amounts of communal land, as well as less extensive water works.[23] The remaining ricelands were privately owned. The family system was patrilinear, and daughters as well as sons shared equally in inheritance of land.

In addition to such material possessions as land, seawalls, dikes, storage ponds for water, and irrigation and drainage ditches, a crucial part of the village patrimony was the institutional foundation of the village itself—the procedures and rules that had been developed to manage daily life and to provide the law and order and property rights essential to a stable existence. So important was this foundation that as villages developed the rules and institutional procedures, they were written down, so that villages were ruled not by custom, but by written customary. A minimum was therefore left to chance. As the customary of the village stated, "In our village the inhabitants are decent, but, as manners change with the times, and as it is to be feared that some day future generations may lose sight of the decent sentiments with which the inhabitants are inspired today, we are compelled to establish the following set of regulations . . ."[24]

The adjudication procedures, the customary, and the entire corpus of rules by which village life was ordered were regarded as a valuable asset by village insiders as well as a source of profit vis-à-vis persons seeking to join their villages. This is seen in the procedures for allowing persons to join villages as outsiders and to eventually become insiders. The presence of a large floating popula-

22. Pierre Gourou, *Land Utilization in French Indochina*, pp. 331–332.

23. The precise extent of precolonial communal land is difficult to estimate because some communal lands of Annam and Tonkin were stolen from village control during the colonial takeover.

24. Gourou, *Les Paysans*, p. 270.

tion of peasants without a village is a distinctive feature of Vietnamese history.[25] To admit floaters, even as outsiders, to a village
in Tonkin or Annam was to stretch physical resources and decrease
one's own share of land and water. Even in Cochinchina, with virtually no communal land or village waterworks, and with a frontier
and an abundance of unfarmed land, the village patrimony was a
source of stratification. Before a newcomer could be admitted to a
village and allowed to clear land for his own use, it was necessary
for him first to serve as a wage laborer for members of the village.
After awhile, he would be allowed to own a "corner of land," and
later, after performing guard duty, transport work, and corvée as
"insurance against deportation" from the village, the newcomer
would be permitted to own land and eventually become an insider:
"Having contributed nothing to the communal foundation, why
should the newcomer be permitted to participate in the collective
benefits? It was necessary first to earn admission as a benefitting
member . . ."[26]

The prestige and power of notables on the council that administered village affairs were considerable, for they handled relations
with the state, collected taxes, allocated communal land, and conducted the rites of worship and the harvest festivals central to the
folk religion.

The village council was also the village court, the final ad-
judicator of local conflicts between and within families. The arbitration of disputes, sanctified and reinforced by the council's important religious role in the community, added to the council's power.
The traditional legal code also strengthened the power of the notables, for it was designed to discourage any use of supravillage
institutions.[27]

25. Milton Osborne, *The French Presence in Cochinchina and Cambodia: Rule
and Response (1905–1959)*, p. 13.

26. Schreiner, *Les Institutions annamites*, vol. 2., p. 19.

27. The legal code also reinforced the corporate nature of the village. It severely
restricted the use of intermediaries, and mandarins were reluctant to arbitrate interpersonal or intervillage disputes. Even pitched battles could break out between villages without the intervention of any official force. This enforced a relative isolation
between villages, and even economic cooperation was rare. (See C. Fournier-Wailly,
"Les Institutions traditionelles et la justice indigène en Annam et au Tonkin," p.
333; Woodside, *Vietnam and the Chinese Model*, p. 154–155.) On the other hand,
the corporate nature of the village made it possible for the mandarins to use collec-

In addition to the members of the council, there were lower grades of notables. The number of echelons of notables, as well as the criteria for receiving a rank and advancing up the ladder, varied from village to village. Generally there were three criteria: mandarinic achievement or education, wealth, and age.[28] The village "chief" was not a chief in the tribal sense, nor was he a "head man." He was a younger, minor notable who served as a secretary to the council of notables, as intermediary with the district mandarin, and as administrator of village affairs. The senior notables, invariably twelve men, formed the village council and were responsible for conducting the religious rites of the village and supervising administration of its daily affairs. Each village had a collective obligation to the state for the repair and construction of dikes, seawalls, and canals for flood control; the number of men presented for the draft; and land and head taxes. How these obligations were to be met was the affair of the village council, which also administered communal land.

The obligations associated with the position of notable were heavy and forced them to share some of their wealth with the community: "Parties, banquets, subscriptions were so many ways for the rest of the people in the community to share the wealth of whoever had attained eminence."[29] The popular saying, "A mouthful at the *dinh* is better than a basketful in the kitchen," emphasized the common desire to be a notable and eat the choicest pieces at communal banquets. The notables ate the head of the animal (usually pig or dog) and the common villagers ate the body—thus symbolizing that the notables were the head of the village and the common villagers the body.[30]

The council of notables that administered village affairs was also responsible for the religious rites of the village. Symbolizing the

tive punishment to enforce order. A village that was the scene of a riot, that refused to pay its taxes, or that harbored even a single dead body might be completely destroyed. (Duncanson, *Government and Revolution in Vietnam*, p. 57; Thuc, *L'Economie*, p. 61.)

28. Rambo, "Comparison of Peasant Social Systems," p. 33. See also Hickey, "Social Systems of Northern Viet-Nam"; Ory, *La Commune annamite*, pp. 39–44.

29. Paul Mus, "Vietnam: A Nation Off Balance," p. 528.

30. Ory, *La Commune annamite*, p. 54.

importance of these rites, the two Chinese characters joined together in the word *xa* to designate village "give the idea of a place where individuals sacrificing to the spirits come together."[31] The folk religion of Vietnam, as of China, was based on local spirit worship. The *dinh,* or house of worship for the guardian spirit, was the village center:

The dinh, in which the guardian spirit of each village lives, is the focus of the collective life of the community. It is there that the religious ceremonies are performed; and there, to put it briefly, that all acts which are the life of Annamese society take place. The guardian spirit represents in a tangible fashion the sum of common memories, of common hopes. He is the embodiment of law, custom, and morals, and at the same time their sanction. He is the one who punishes or rewards according to whether one breaks or observes his laws. All things taken into account, he is the personification of that superior authority which has its source in and takes its authority from the whole society. Moreover, he is the bond which unites all the members of the community; he constitutes an entity, a kind of moral personality, in which are found all the essential attributes of each individual.[32]

Such religious rites were accompanied by feasts in which the entire village participated. In addition, there were countless small groups that trained members for their own rituals, which also included banqueting. These groups, such as students of a revered teacher, wrestlers, cock fighters, ex-soldiers, kite flyers, those born in the same year, and so on, all had their own feasts at which the young gained the training needed for their eventual roles in village rites.[33] Such feasts and banquets were of the utmost importance. Social well-being and security were seen to come from membership in groups, and the ultimate reaffirmation of a group's ability to provide sustenance came from the ritual of eating together.[34] In fact, village socialization, which was recognized as a specific form of training, was called "learning the art of eating and speaking."[35]

The hedge that secured the village and displayed its sanctity to

31. Ibid., p. 3.
32. Paul Giran, *Magie et religion annamites,* quoted in Nguyen van Khoan, "Essai sur le dinh," p. 113.
33. Gourou, *Les Paysans,* pp. 268–269.
34. See, in a similar vein, Richard H. Solomon, *Mao's Revolution and the Chinese Political Culture,* pp. 44–45, 48–49, 161–162.
35. Thuc, *L'Economie,* p. 43; Gourou, *Les Paysans,* p. 269.

the outside world (markets were always outside the hedge) also symbolized the limits on outside communication. Outside communications could mean outside alliances that would benefit the individual at the expense of the group. In every village there were internal controls over the communications between the chief and the local mandarin. The village chief was always a minor notable who aspired through performance of his duties to be rewarded with promotion to a higher rank and membership in the council of notables.[36] Since the senior notables were the heads of the largest and most prominent families in the village, they could rally great numbers of men against him or anyone else who used outside connections for personal advantage within the village.

Retired mandarins who sat on the council were a source of knowledge of outside affairs and could help prevent the young chief who served as outside link from exploiting his position. Thus, a retired mandarin, still likely to have prestige and contacts within the bureaucracy, was an asset to the village. On the other hand, any family who had a son rising in the mandarinate was a potential source of disruption, because a powerful son could tilt the village power balance. In the words of a village proverb, "The student who has not yet passed his doctoral examinations is already a threat to his village."[37]

Cooperation

An extension and modification of George Foster's article "Interpersonal Relations in Peasant Society"[38] opens the way for an understanding of the relationship between conflict and cooperation

36. Rambo, "Comparison of Peasant Social Systems," p. 33.

37. Alexander Woodside, "Some Features of Vietnamese Bureaucracy under the Early Nguyen Dynasty," pp. 177–178. Helping the council to control the power of a family with a member in the bureaucracy, however, was the fact that no one could take the exam without first receiving certification from the village council. (Woodside, *Vietnam and the Chinese Model*, p. 244.)

38. George Foster, "Interpersonal Relations in Peasant Society," pp. 174–178. See also Foster, "Peasant Society and the Image of Limited Good," pp. 293–315; James M. Acheson, "Limited Good or Limited Goods? Response to Opportunity in a Tarascan Pueblo," pp. 1152–1169. In addition, there are valuable commentaries and exchanges accompanying the original Foster article in *Human Organization* and in *American Anthropologist*, vol. 67, 1974, pp. 47–62.

in peasant society that is consistent with the Vietnamese data for both the traditional and modern periods.

Surveying the modern ethnographic literature, Foster finds peasant society generally characterized by a prevalence of conflict, distrust, and envy—to an extent that "the strains and tensions in interpersonal relations make it difficult to understand how the community continues to function." However, he does not infer a direct causal link between distrust, envy, suspicion, and narrow self-interest, on the one hand, and a lack of cooperation, on the other. Rather, he suggests, the distrust, envy, and suspicion that make cooperation so rare are a "logical correlate of the prevailing economic factors" of peasant life. Foster's prevailing economic factor is that the total economic pie is very small and constant in size. Life for peasants, he concludes, is a zero-sum game (or is perceived as such), and the lack of cooperation among peasants is logical. It is better to do nothing than to risk the possibility that a neighbor will advance at one's own expense. Security in life means eternal vigilance with respect to one's neighbors, and strong leaders thus become a threat. Additionally, "Given a market, a peasant family potentially is the most independent of all social units. One reason, then, that peasants are not very cooperative is that they do not have to be."[39]

The Vietnamese equivalent for "eternal security" was the saying, "Neighbors who are fond of each other should set up a thick fence between their houses." It was not the case, however, that peasants never cooperated, nor that there were no possibilities for increasing the size of the economic pie. Nor was it the case that Vietnamese peasant families, in contrast to many peasants today, were independent social units that could function without leadership. There was, in fact, cooperation among small groups of peasants to stabilize production and provide insurance; there was cooperation among all members of the village to provide the collective goods absolutely essential to survival (such as self-defense and irrigation); and there was cooperation—as well as extreme conflict—among the group of peasants who, as notables, dominated the vil-

39. Foster, "Interpersonal Relations in Peasant Society," p. 178.

lage and controlled the distribution of communal resources and charges. Caution and distrust structures the forms of cooperation but does not prevent cooperative behavior.

Among small groups of villagers there were cooperative labor-exchange pools to stabilize production by assuring a fixed and predictable amount of labor at planting and harvest times; neighborhood associations to share the expense of communal feasts; pig associations to share the cost of buying pigs; lending associations, burial associations, and wedding associations. There was mutual aid and cooperation among the peasants, but all the groups and associations that existed were specific and entailed precise and "well defined" obligations limited to small groups where maximum vigilance could be exercised without need for skilled leadership.[40] Thus, it is not the case that a fixed resource base or a static technology will prevent cooperation among poor peasants; it is rather that the cooperation will be oriented toward insurance (the averaging of expenses over time) and security. These forms may be old, well known, and therefore easily utilized by the peasants, but they emphasize the great extent to which cautious, survival-oriented peasants can cooperate. Without these traditional forms of cooperation, life would have been much more erratic and insecure from year to year, and total productivity would have been, in fact, lower than it was.

Nor was the pie always fixed and strong leadership only a threat to premodern peasants. Throughout Vietnam there was the essential need for self-defense against invaders, pirates, starving men, and wild animals. And in all areas but Cochinchina, where irrigation was solely by rainfall, there were village-level flood controls and village-level irrigation works, without which total productivity would have been much lower. All these aspects of peasant family life, plus the religious observances essential to the agricultural cycle, were collective goods supplied not by the individual, but by the village. With respect to water, for example, Gourou observed that in Tonkin, "irrigation was not a purely individual matter; it concerned the whole village, since the well-being of each person de-

40. Thuc, *L'Economie*, pp. 39–40, 54–55, 108–110.

pended on the care with which the water supply belonging to all has been husbanded."[41] Even in the few periods when the country was pacified and there were no invaders or pirates, village defense—and therefore leadership—was still crucial because conflicts between villages over the utilization of water or the construction or elimination of dams was frequent.[42] Over the years the villages had managed to build up a system of water controls and defenses against invasion that added considerably to the size of the total economic pie. The public works and collective goods provided through peasant cooperation by the village were thus an essential aspect of peasant security and survival.

Stratification

Localized landholding and corporatism did not imply internal equality. The nineteenth-century historian Phan Huy Chu decried the fact that little or nothing had ever been done to prevent people from cornering land.[43] Other mandarins of the same century found that some men had "hundreds and thousands of sections of land," while others had "little more than elbow space."[44] Before the colonial era, then, economic concentration did occur within corporate villages, and "nothing was more normal" than periodic need for redistribution of land.[45]

Nor was the overall system of cooperation either leveling or egalitarian. The men who became notables and the men who could afford to have their sons study for the mandarinate were frequently men of leisure who used extensive hired labor or sharecroppers in their fields. Communal land in Annam and Tonkin ensured that insiders had at least a modest plot of land to farm, but there were many landlords, and the fact that landlords were local did not necessarily mean that landlord-tenant relations were easy. The Emperor Tu Duc (1848–1883) reminded tenants that when they visited the owners of their fields, they did not need to bother with questions of precedence by age, but instead "must observe the formalities of inferiors toward their superiors."[46]

41. Gourou, *Les Paysans,* pp. 103–104, fn.
42. Ibid., pp. 103–104, fn.   43. Thuc, *L'Economie,* pp. 73, 149.
44. Ibid., p. 133.   45. Ibid., p. 73.
46. Ory, *La Commune annamite,* p. 57.

The literature on Vietnamese villages and the theoretical work on corporate villages in other societies (discussed in Chapters 1 and 2) has tended to overemphasize the noblesse oblige of the notables and the welfare provided by the village qua village. The procedures used to pay state exactions and distribute internal resources were regressive, and there was a high level of internal competition for control of the villages. When one man or a group could get control of the village, there was widespread opportunity for gain by these "village-eaters."[47] Often "the commune in its capacity as a private corporation is defrauded by the individuals officially entrusted with protecting its interests."[48]

It does not follow that since each individual was striving to maximize the security of his existence, the corporate village, in its functioning, operated to "equalize life chances and life risks of its members."[49] Everyone was better off with a village than without a village, for man could not survive very easily, if at all, apart from one. But corporate villages need not be leveling or egalitarian.

The system of feasts, far from leveling inequality or exhausting all the wealthy, barred many peasants from high positions and reinforced existing inequalities.[50] As in other societies of corporate villages, it was common for a man to go heavily into debt in order to finance the feasts required of those hoping to rise in the village ranking system.[51] But the benefits of becoming a notable far outweighed the costs for the successful. Buying titles and higher rankings in the hierarchy was an "investment" to improve one's financial status by becoming a senior notable,[52] getting one's name on the mandarin lists (discussed further on), and hence obtaining access to outside authority and control over internal distribution of charges and resources. Such investments were rarely possible for a poor villager. Similarly, only in the most "exceptional cases" did a poor man become a member of the council of notables—generally,

47. Nguyen van Phong, *La Société vietnamienne de 1882 à 1902*, p. 108.
48. Ory, *La Commune annamite*, p. 46.
49. Wolf, "Closed Corporate Peasant Communities," p. 12.
50. Rambo, "Comparison of Peasant Social Systems," p. 35.
51. Vu van Hien, "Les Institutions annamites depuis l'arrivée des français: L'Impôt personnel et les corvées de 1862 à 1936," p. 149.
52. Ory, *La Commune annamite*, p. 115.

such prestige and power were available only to the rich.[53]

An important benefit of serving on the council of notables accrued from control of village rolls and from mandarinic registration. In addition to the village's internal roll *(so-hang-xa),* which listed insiders and outsiders living in the village, the mandarins kept official tax lists *(dinh-bo)* of taxable male inhabitants. The number of names on the mandarin's list determined the size of the village's head-tax bill. It was therefore to the collective advantage of the village that as few names as possible be recorded in the mandarin's official tax register. Indeed, contemporary accounts of the village make it clear that generally only about 25 to 35 percent (and sometimes as few as 5 to 10 percent) of the eligible taxpayers were ever recorded on the mandarin rolls.

Although it was in the collective interest of the village to keep the number of listed names as small as possible, it was in the interest of any individual to be on the mandarin's roll. Only men whose names were on the mandarin's list could serve on the council of notables,[54] and only men who were registered with the mandarin could use his courts, call on him for help, or travel safely outside the village.[55] If apprehended, an unregistered traveler was presumed to be a bandit or a vagabond. Registration on the mandarin's list meant an important advantage over nonregistered persons and was a private benefit distributed by the notables with obvious implications for protecting or reinforcing the existing patterns of stratification.

Generally, village procedures gave important benefits to notables and protected—rather than leveled—wealth. The procedures for paying national taxes, the system for allocating communal lands, and the methods for financing village projects were regressive. In theory, only villagers listed on the mandarin rolls paid taxes,[56] but in practice the village head tax was divided equally among all villagers.[57] By paying the same head tax as a richer villager, the unregistered without rights to communal land and the landless with lower incomes were in fact paying a higher percentage of their income in head taxes. Also serving to make the tax system regressive was the

53. Ibid., p. 13.   54. Ibid., p. 28.
55. Ibid., pp. 38–39.   56. Osborne, *The French Presence,* p. 19.
57. Gourou, *Les Paysans,* pp. 172–173. See also Chapter 4, this volume.

national practice of selling low-level mandarin ranks or titles to villagers as a method of raising money for the national treasury in time of war or trouble. Tax exemptions were extended through the sale of titles to so many villagers that those exempt formed a "veritable privileged class" comprising in some areas of Tonkin from 5 to 10 percent of the registered population.[58] Thus, among the most successful village notables—those who could afford to buy titles—no taxes were paid. This fostered a strong, well-entrenched attitude that to pay the head tax was a "personal abasement" and only for persons without the money to buy outside influence.[59]

Students studying for the mandarinate and persons who had passed the mandarin examinations were exempt from the draft. This meant, of course, that in times of frequent warfare there was a strong incentive toward the accumulation of enough wealth to support a son in his studies, not only to secure the advantages of mandarin connections for the family, but also to avoid the possibility of losing a son in battle. Thus, while warfare may provide an incentive for local cooperation to provide security, it also meant local competition to avoid the draft and a reason to prefer private—over public—accumulation.

Within the villages, exemptions also could be purchased by wealthy villagers seeking to avoid their share of collective labor demands placed on the village as a whole. Such villagers became known as "Mister Exempt."[60] Less well-off villagers, then, paid a heavier share of labor and military demands than did their better-off neighbors.

Some communal lands were especially reserved for widows, orphans, and the aged without children. For "regular" families, however, communal lands were distributed not according to need, but ascriptively, on the basis of rank within the village.[61] Villagers, that is, chose on the basis of rank. The council of notables supervised the distribution and also had first choice of select plots of communal land.

As noted in Chapter 2, a pure distributional issue can be a Pan-

58. Vu van Hien, "Les Institutions annamites," pp. 84–107.
59. Ibid., pp. 96–97.
60. Woodside, *Vietnam and the Chinese Model*, p. 156.
61. Ory, *La Commune annamite*, p. 78.

dora's box, which when opened to inspection begins a never-ending round of squabbles. The customary gave general guidelines for each village; the rankings, along with the rules by which they were determined, gave each man a place in the village and established the order in which he would choose communal land. This meant that instead of a general fight of all against all over distribution, each person could instead jockey for the best possible place on the ladder. Each man, therefore, knew the part he would play in the village, and the unforeseen was reduced to a minimum. Although competition was not eliminated, the competitive ranking system individualized competition and apparently minimized—but did not eliminate—the incentive to form coalitions within the village.

Although one method for financing village projects drew on surplus of the wealthy, the financing of village projects generally involved regressive methods. The progressive method for financing village projects involved "buying posterity." Childless villagers—or rich persons with very large holdings—would donate a sum of money or a piece of land to the village, which in return would guarantee to maintain "incense and fire" sacrificial cults after their death.[62] Neither buying posterity nor other forms of donations or taxes from the better-off villagers were adequate to finance village projects, however. A common finance system utilized the ranking system to raise funds. A villager could purchase a higher rank on the village ladder and thus give himself better shares of communal lands and other resources.[63] This suggests that neither the force of gossip and envy nor the desire for prestige or posterity was sufficient to guarantee adequate donations from wealthy villagers to finance such village projects as emergency repair of the water system. Use of the ranking system—in effect paying off loans with communal land and other village resources—to finance projects decreased the future village resources available to the poor

62. Woodside, *Community and Revolution in Modern Vietnam,* pp. 112–113. The actual amount of such land donated is unknown. If it is later shown to be a major source of village finances, the conclusions about the regressive nature of financing will naturally require modification. The argument that neither donations nor progressive financing were the rule, however, gains support from the fact that, prior to the nineteenth century, villagers sold communal land in order to raise funds. (Vu van Hien, "Les Institutions annamites," p. 40.)

63. Ory, *La Commune annamite,* p. 114.

and was certainly not progressive or leveling, but it did provide the village with a method for raising money and maintaining the patrimony.

Landholding

The systems of both privately owned and communally owned land indicate clearly the limitations of village insurance and welfare systems. As it evolved, the communal land system rewarded the successful and raised the average income, rather than the income floor. The private-landowning patterns in the village suggest that the insurance systems seriously limited total village production.

Before the eighteenth century, central governments had promoted communal landholdings to stabilize village population by guaranteeing land to as many persons as possible.[64] By the eighteenth century, rules were promulgated to put communal land exclusively in the hands of the poorer villagers. Only the landless and persons whose land was in mortgage were to be eligible for any communal land.[65]

There was less than universal support for this practice within the villages. The weakening of central power resulted at times in the seizure of communal lands for private use by the notables.[66] Additionally, the granting of communal lands to all villagers—rich as well as poor—and the distribution by rank to all became the general local procedure. By the nineteenth century the efforts of the central government to keep communal lands for the most needy had been abandoned, and the de facto distribution by rank had been accepted. In 1803, and again in 1840, efforts were made to equalize the value of plots so that the poor, despite the lowest ranks, would receive less inferior plots.[67] If the landless had been given all the communal land (or if they had been given larger shares than others), the

---

64. Le Than Koi, *Le Vietnam: Histoire et civilisation,* pp. 259, 258–259. The emperors were trying to stabilize the population of free corporate villages as part of their campaign against feudal estates.

65. Vu van Hien, *La Propriété communale au Tonkin: Contribution a l'étude historique, juridique et économique des cong-dien et cong-tho en pays d'Annam,* pp. 18, 32. Note that this is but one indication of the widespread use of mortgages in precapitalist Vietnam.

66. Le Thanh Khoi, *Le Vietnam,* p. 359.

67. Vu van Hien, *La Propriété communale au Tonkin,* p. 160.

communal land system would have been directed at maximizing the floor, that is, raising the living standards of the least well-off to the highest possible level. Giving everyone a piece of land was a system aimed at raising the average income at the expense of the floor. This suggests a preference for private insurance and welfare—that is, maximizing shares of village resources in one's good years and converting the surplus into private savings and investments for bad times.

Communal-land ownership was the preferred mode in areas where frequent flooding eradicated property lines and in areas, such as riverbeds, where silting constantly created new lands.[68] These two situations aside, however, there is evidence to suggest that communal-land ownership and rotation meant lower productivity than did private-land ownership, and that, as a consequence, there may have been growing preference over time for private lands. As wet-rice cultivation techniques develop and improve, the number of years it takes to realize the full potential of a piece of land also increases. Rotation of land among villagers would work against maximum investment in and development of a plot's full potential, for peasants do not want to "spread a banquet for someone else to eat."[69] Indeed, many sources have noted that communal land seemed less productive than private land for this reason.[70] The many appropriations of communal land for private use noted through Vietnamese history,[71] therefore, may have had support among many villagers. Even if they received less desirable plots than did the notables, villagers may have preferred permanent (private) control of a mediocre plot to rotating access to good, bad, and average public plots. Such appropriations would reinforce preferences for private instead of public resources and investments.[72]

68. Ibid., p. 105.

69. Vo Nguyen Giap and Truong Chinh, "The Peasant Question (1937–1938)," p. 80.

70. Ory, *La Commune annamite,* pp. 73–74; René Dumont, *Types of Rural Economy: Studies in World Agriculture,* p. 150. It is also possible, however, that the best of the communal lands were those confiscated by notables, who left only the inherently less valuable lands as communal property.

71. See, as one example, Le Thanh Khoi, *Le Vietnam,* p. 359.

72. This is also probably one of the reasons why it is so frequently noted that villages rotated lands only every six years, although the laws required triennial rotation.

Among the private lands in the villages, the pattern of landholdings maximized security at the family level, rather than at the village level. Generations of land division had resulted in a situation where each family's landholdings were scattered throughout the village in many small plots. This was a system that resulted in a level of total village production far lower than would have been possible if each family had owned the same amount of land in only one or two large parcels. There were so many tiny parcels in Tonkin that (by a conservative estimate) if all the parcels owned by each family had been integrated, total village production of rice *with the same labor force* would have increased at least 10 percent.[73] But although integration of holdings would have increased total output, it would also have increased the year-to-year variability in each family's yield, giving a higher average production, but also giving lower lows to any individual family. This is because the climate in Vietnam is extremely harsh, especially in Annam and Tonkin. Flooding, both from breaches of dikes and from excess rainfall, is common, as is, paradoxically, the problem of drought—for there are also many months when the rainfall is insufficient for newly planted rice. In such an environment the customary practice of widely distributed land parcels has "considerable adaptive value in that it would reduce the likelihood of all of a family's land being destroyed at a single stroke of nature."[74]

If there had been widespread trust among all peasants and within the village leadership, and if a reliable, low-cost insurance system had existed at the village level, then an integrated system of holdings could have resulted in a higher yield for everyone, every year. It was clearly more important, however, to assure a guaranteed minimum at the family level than to maximize production for the village. The risks and costs of such a villagewide system apparently outweighed the gains.[75]

73. Dumont (*Types of Rural Economy*, p. 150) found consolidation of holdings resulted in a 15-percent increase in production in Japan, which is slightly higher than McCloskey's estimate that consolidation brought a production increase of 10 to 13 percent in medieval England (discussed in Chapter 2). Given the fragmentation in Tonkin and the land lost to production because of retaining walls and paths (see Chapter 4), it appears that 10 percent is a conservative estimate for Tonkin.

74. Rambo, "Comparison of Peasant Social Systems," pp. 78–79.

75. Village granaries were encouraged by the French during the colonial period but did not prosper due to "abuse." Thuc, *L'Economie*, p. 113.

Decision making

Within the village, the decisions of the village council of notables were made by unanimity and not by majority vote.[76] This "mystique of consensus," where nothing was decided until the entire council agreed, is one of the main sources of romanticizing about the supposedly democratic and harmonious nature of traditional villages, a theme that runs through much of the older anthropological literature. F. G. Bailey, in an important attack on this romanticism, notes that it is almost always assumed that if councils are consensual, the people in the communities "naturally adjusted to work in harmony with one another."[77] Bailey points out, however, that a council operating on a consensus (or unanimity) rule does not necessarily mean a lack of tension or a low level of conflict or a democratic system. It is just as possible, and much more plausible, that consensual decision making is symptomatic not of a united society, but of overriding personal considerations on the part of each council member—that each notable was striving to the utmost to avoid the personal consequences of an unfavorable decision.

Bailey suggests one obvious reason that an elite council might encourage consensus: an elite ruling oligarchy has every reason to dissuade dissident factions from publicizing their grievances.[78] The Vietnamese council of notables was a self-perpetuating elite body, not one that was democratically selected. Within the general criteria of the village ranking system, the council itself selected replacements for vacant seats. A "balance of power" on the council was so important that in the rare instance when a notable's mandate was withdrawn and he was forced off the council, the disgraced notable would nominate his own successor.[79]

There is another, perhaps stronger, reason why the notables might operate on a consensual basis. Most of the notables, although richer than the majority of peasants, were certainly not rich in any

76. Ralph B. Smith, *Viet Nam and the West,* p. 46.
77. F. G. Bailey, "Decisions by Consensus in Councils and Committees with Special Reference to Village and Local Government in India," p. 3.
78. Ibid., p. 6.
79. Ory, *La Commune annamite,* p. 13.

absolute sense. They were cautious and conservative men, as concerned with keeping themselves from falling into worse conditions as with advancement. A consensus rule meant that no project could be approved by the council unless it was favorable to each and every member of that council. Thus, the most conservative, security-conscious, risk-averse notable could block any proposed project if it were of no benefit to him personally, or if the proposed benefit to him were not large enough to overcome the expected risk should the investment fail. Paul Ory, one of the most meticulous observers of the nineteenth-century Vietnamese village, found, for example, that "a word pronounced by an influential notable is enough to thwart the best projects, even though nearly the entire council may admit their usefulness."[80]

The notables were responsible for distributing many charges and resources. In addition to supervising projects to improve the village, they allocated communal land and irrigation water. They also allocated the land taxes and head taxes within the village, decided who would do corvée labor both within the village and for the mandarin, and who would fill the village draft quota. Taxes and corvée charges were not light, and some of the draft calls in the nineteenth century appear to have been almost as heavy as in recent times. Given the stakes involved, then, consensus rule ensured that a majority of the twelve members of the council did not form a sub-coalition and take advantage of the other notables—a possibility present even in a zero-sum game. A consensus rule did not mean that the council of notables, as a group, could not take advantage of the many peasants who did not belong to the families represented on the council. Ory, for example, reported that the council could "drag the commune in a direction contrary to the commune's interest, but favorable to its own."[81]

Although there was a general emphasis on harmony and the suppression of minority opinions and factions, a premium on consensus does not imply that each villager placed his highest priority on consensus at the expense of his own interests. Consensus among self-interested individuals will still occur in bounded communities be-

80. Ibid., p. 46.   81. Ibid., p. 47.

cause of the multiple, overlapping nature of economic, religious, and political relationships; "in such communities disagreements cannot be easily isolated within one realm of social action and tend to cause total paralysis."[82] Thus, villagers may hesitate to introduce conflict within their community, though they are restrained not by an altruistic value they place on unity, but by "the possible consequences *for themselves*."[83] This would apply especially to the poor and powerless villagers, who, with no option of leaving, had to cope within the village. In fact, ordinary villagers were so reluctant to speak out at the open village meetings where the council presented its decisions that anyone daring enough to challenge the notables became known as a *dau-bo* or ox-head. Needing a head "as hard as that of an ox," the *dau-bo* would dare to step forward and challenge unpopular decisions on behalf of the other villagers.[84]

Small, bounded communities tend to develop high levels of distrust and envy. Such distrust, in situations where cooperation is a necessity, creates a felt need for an adjudication process acceptable to all. That is to say, where there are many conflicts and tensions, but where unresolved conflict may lead to a paralysis destructive to all, there is an acknowledged need for a good judge. Without an adjudication process acceptable to all, villagers may not "forgive and forget." A person who will not accept the final decision—at least publicly, if not internally—is a potential threat to everyone, for it is impossible to know when such a person might take revenge or cause further conflicts.

This interpersonal hostility and tension, combined with a universal fear of paralyzing conflict, can make it easy for skilled village leaders to resolve conflict amicably and avoid using force against dissenters, at the same time as they garner political capital for themselves.[85] Officials can rely on the cooperation of other, disinterested villagers, who, eager to be on good terms with them in the

82. Bailey, "Decisions by Consensus," p. 5.
83. Ibid., p. 6.
84. Nguyen Huu Khang, *La Commune annamite: Étude historique, juridique, et économique,* pp. 202–203; and Ory, *La Commune annamite,* p. 26.
85. Marc J. Swartz, "Bases for Political Compliance in Bena Villages," passim.

hope of ensuring favorable rulings for themselves when the occasions arise, apply personal pressure on adversaries reluctant to settle a dispute.

Conflict and internal tensions, then, can be conducive to consensus and to a high degree of compliance with demands and decisions of the notables.

VILLAGE AND STATE

"The law of the emperor stops at the village gate." Although old and often quoted, this adage does not accurately reflect the realities of village linkage to the larger political system. Given the weaknesses of bureaucratic control from the center and the problems of information flow from village to mandarins to emperor, the ability to intervene directly in village affairs or even to monitor village proceedings was indeed limited. Limited ability to compel procedural compliances or to obtain accurate information, however, should not be confused with limited (or insignificant) impact on village proceedings. Emphasizing village autonomy and the *collective incentives* to withhold information and handle village affairs locally leads to undue emphasis on the concept of penetration by the state and the need for force to gain compliance. In fact, the national system in large part gained compliance and made its impact on the village through the use of *incentives* that *induced* villagers to seek connection with the larger system on their own behalf or on behalf of their village.

Indeed, when one compares Vietnam with China or with other Southeast-Asian countries, it is clear that Vietnamese supravillage government was comparatively influential in local affairs. Vietnamese mandarins, for example, had significantly smaller districts than did their Chinese counterparts, and they were able to meddle at least "slightly more" with their villages.[86] Cambodia had no systematic system of land registers, population registers, or corvée labor in the nineteenth century.[87] The Vietnamese registers were often incomplete and inaccurate, but they did not exist without

86. Woodside, *Vietnam and the Chinese Model*, pp. 157–158.
87. Ibid., pp. 145–146.

periodic, direct interventions into the village by teams sent from the capital to count heads and survey land. In addition, there were direct interventions—not always successful—to protect the poor by restoring communal lands appropriated by the rich and powerful.[88] Despite the fragmented nature of the economy, there were still numerous forms of loans, contracts, land sales, and land mortgages. To be ultimately valid and enforceable, all such transactions had to conform to the national statutes governing the mandarinic courts, and they required the official stamp of the village chief before they could be arbitrated in court. Thus, the wooden seal, which the village chief used to witness and "legalize" all transactions, and which was itself handed to him by the mandarin, was a crucial element of the public business conducted within the village.[89]

The village chiefs themselves, although selected within the village, generally served with the approval of the mandarins, and periodically edicts were issued regulating the qualifications for village chiefs.[90]

Outside influences and linkages also affected the selection procedures for village councils and the very basis of village ranking systems. Originally, it seems, village ranking systems were based solely on age and the twelve oldest men served on the village council.[91] Over the centuries, the ranking systems of most villages changed to take account of wealth and education, so that the twelve wealthiest and/or most educated men administered the village. At least one reason that ranking systems evolved to favor wealth and power, rather than age, was the outside support and connections of wealthy villagers. One official code in 1663, for example, warned villagers that in relations with notables, they should not "presume upon their great wealth."[92] When a village dispute over rankings or

88. Roy Jumper and Nguyen thi Hue, *Notes on the Political and Administrative History of Vietnam, 1802–1962*, p. 53. See also Rambo, "Comparison of Peasant Social Systems," p. 24.

89. Woodside, *Vietnam and the Chinese Model*, p. 156, among others.

90. Ibid., p. 154.

91. Etienne Dumouttier, quoted in Gourou, *Les Paysans*, p. 265.

92. Woodside, *Community and Revolution*, pp. 114–115. This same code also warned against placing village administration in the hands of younger members of wealthy families instead of choosing older men "respected by the masses." Although wealth was protected, there was also an attempt to restrain the power of wealthy families.

titles became too acrimonious, villagers—despite their concern to avoid litigation—appealed to the mandarin. Thus, acting as a mediator, outside authorities were able to influence village rankings.[93]

It is more accurate to view the adage "The law of the emperor stops at the village gate" as a reflection of the numerous incentives to keep village-initiated contacts with mandarins to a minimum. That is, many benefits accrued to villages that kept as much village business within their gates as possible, for any internal conflict that reached the mandarin had potentially negative consequences for the village as a whole.

When an internal dispute became too heated to handle locally, any direct involvement by a mandarin produced negative long-term consequences for the village as a whole due to the incomplete nature of population and land registers and the issue of distribution facing the notables. As long as a village maintained a united front of silence before the mandarin, it was difficult, if not impossible, for him to discover how many unregistered men lived in the village and to add their names to his rolls. Since the total number of names on the roll determined the size of the village tax, military draft, and corvée labor quotas, there were clear, long-term costs whenever the mandarin was able to gather new and more accurate information from a dissident faction seeking his support in a local struggle.

There was a similar incentive for the notables, as a group, to keep their conflicts away from the mandarin. By allying himself in a private (patron-client) relationship with a mandarin and helping the latter to achieve an economic foothold in the village, any notable could gain a relative advantage over other notables on important economic issues. He could, for example, gain considerable advantage for himself in terms of local allocation of the land taxes and protection for his family from disruptive drafts and corvées. The number of benefits available to the notables as a group, however, would be consequently diminished.

The incentives facing the village as a group, therefore, strongly pointed to minimizing village contacts with the mandarins and keeping all disputes and conflicts within the village. There were still numerous court suits, despite the costs and sanctions involved,

93. Ory, *La Commune annamite*, p. 43.

but there was a clear resolve to keep notables from allying with mandarins and the unregistered from reaching the mandarins with complaints.

To a great extent, then, the mandarin could deal with the village only through the village chief and the council of notables and he could collect taxes only with their support. This meant, of course, that the notables and chief were buttressed in their dealings with the village by the implicit power of the mandarin. The mandarin's physical forces may have been employed rarely, and the courts also may have been used infrequently to enforce evictions of the poor from mortgaged lands, but the impact of these outside resources was clearly felt within the villages, even though the effects were indirect. Suppose, for example, that a poor man could not redeem a land mortgage *(dien mai)* and that the rich, registered villager who had given him the mortgage demanded that the land be vacated. With a valid mortgage in the hands of the rich mortgager, it would be clear to all what the outside court would find in such a case; hence, it would be in most people's interest to have the eviction performed locally, particularly if the poor man were unregistered. Precedent and law could easily affect the internal workings of the village, then, with little actual use of outside institutions.

Local considerations were by no means the only reasons for the limited linkages between mandarins and villages, however. National policy was also a factor, for it was in the interests of various Nguyen dynasty emperors to strengthen village institutions at the expense of a weakened mandarinate.

One reason for limited use of supravillage courts by villagers was the imperial effort to reduce the volume of formal litigation as a means of reducing both the power of local mandarins and administrative costs.[94] (Indeed, ruinous litigation between villagers was a common occurrence. The story of the Catfish and the Toad, the oldest known Vietnamese rural tale, tells in verse about two families that exhaust their resources in litigation over petty conflict.)[95]

The deliberate strategy of checking mandarin power was evident in the unwillingness to set up provincial granaries to serve as

94. Woodside, *Community and Revolution,* p. 23.
95. Rambo, "Comparison of Peasant Social Systems," p. 202.

emergency food supplies for villages struck by sudden misfortune. In 1821, a year after a cholera pandemic swept Vietnam and killed perhaps millions (20 percent of the names were stricken from the mandarin lists), provincial mandarins suggested the establishment of granaries to provide relief for villages in their jurisdiction. By the 1830s, some mandarins were virtually crusading for such official welfare institutions in order to rescue villages struck by famine. Emperor Minh Mang's response was a brusque veto, for it was his clear conviction that provincial officials were already powerful enough.[96] As a result of the imperial veto, the only official disaster relief came from the capital itself. The official system was so inefficient (and apparently so corrupt) that it was often cheaper for stricken villagers to buy rice on the private market—covertly shipped in by enterprising merchants—than to pay for the official relief supplies. Such provincial granaries as did exist were for soldiers and officials only and were of little use to the populace at large. Throughout the nineteenth century, consequently, whenever there were famines or floods, armed bands of the hungry and dispossessed roamed the afflicted areas. The primary provincial response to disaster was not relief, but the policing of the province and increased action against "bandits."[97]

There were clear tradeoffs at times, then, when the emperor chose policies detrimental to rural prosperity and stability in order to check the power of local mandarins. Given the way Vietnam developed as a nation, the regional and cultural tensions that ensued, and the monumental task of integrating the two halves of Vietnam after two hundred years of separation between warring dynasties, this dilemma was unavoidable.

To discourage local power bases from emerging, constant attempts were made to limit the growth of supravillage economic power. The export trade consisted mainly of products from the highlands, inhabited by the Montagnards, or of rice from Cochin-

96. Woodside, *Vietnam and the Chinese Model*, pp. 162–163.
97. Nguyen The Anh, "Quelques Aspects économiques et sociaux du problème du riz au Vietnam dans la première moitié du XIXe siècle," pp. 5–22, especially pp. 13–15. Official relief aid was apparently less than 1,000 tons per year. Long (*Before the Revolution*, p. 33) says that over a twenty-five-year period, 15 million kilograms were distributed in relief aid. This amounts to an average of 600 tons a year.

china; and the middlemen for such trade were, by imperial design, not Vietnamese but Chinese.[98] So limited was trade that one nineteenth-century traveler found it "difficult to conceive that a population so extensive can exist with trade on such a small scale.[99]

Securing control of the entire country was a problem throughout the nineteenth century for the Nguyen emperors and helps explain why policies were sometimes less than ideal for stabilizing peasant life. Although the population of Tonkin was denser and poorer than in Annam, for example, the abundant lands of Cochinchina were settled primarily by transfers from Annam. Doubtful of Tonkin loyalty, the Nguyen drew heavily for their military drafts from politically safe Annam, their original home. Consequently, most of the military colonies that expanded settlement in Cochinchina came from Annam.

The tax policies of the nineteenth century reflected the serious problem of raising the revenues required for the prodigious task of unifying and stabilizing the nation while at the same time preventing the mandarins from developing regional power bases from which to challenge the throne. This was a particularly serious problem in Tonkin, where many of the mandarins, both active and inactive, came from families with centuries of loyal service to Hanoi-based "Tonkinese" regimes. To create and strengthen loyalties to the new dynasty that would provide a counterbalance to mandarins with a vested interest in the old regime, thousands of low-level titles were sold in villages throughout the country, especially in Tonkin. For centuries students studying for the mandarinate, men with low-ranking degrees, and retired mandarins had been exempt from head and corvée taxes. By the nineteenth century, as already noted, the practice of selling low-level degrees and titles, all of which carried lifetime exemptions from taxes, had become endemic.

Raising money from the sale of titles and creating an entrenched privileged class in the villages not only increased political and economic stratification within villages, but also greatly increased the number of villagers with personal ties to, and vested interests

98. Mus, "Vietnam," p. 528.
99. Woodside, *Vietnam and the Chinese Model*, p. 30.

in, the Nguyen dynasty. As a result, the tax load carried by the nonprivileged villagers was greatly increased. In the short run, however, it was safer for the emperor to increase his revenue flow by building up the authority of the village notables than to increase the power of the local mandarins.

Ensuring mandarin loyalty to the throne was a continuous problem. Given the difficulty of communications between capital and province, the emperors were "starved for information"[100] about the countryside. As a result, the only constraints they could readily impose on the mandarins were for those tasks that were easily verifiable—for example, management of rebellion or flood. In the absence of these, there could be little monitoring of local events. As long as the mandarin met his tax and draft quotas and kept order, few questions could be asked about his profits. There was, in effect, a system of tax farming by which mandarins lived off their collections and not (in general) from a fixed salary.

With such weaknesses of communication and control, the emperors not surprisingly placed considerable emphasis on ideological indoctrination of the mandarins in order to achieve conformity. Slavishly orthodox in their devotion to the Confucian institutional patterns they had borrowed from China, the Vietnamese emperors sought to use these patterns to strengthen their control.

Centuries of political division had resulted in regional differences in interpretation of national history and linguistic usage. Chinese language, law, and history were imposed on the mandarinate to temper the intraelite conflicts and regional partisanship that would have been aroused by the use of local history and language. Chinese was used for all state documents, and examinations for the mandarinate emphasized Chinese law and dynastic history to such an extent that the elite was likely to know more about China than about its own country.[101]

The official use of Chinese had other consequences as well, for it increased the cost of literacy, which, in its turn, increased stratification. Wealthy villagers could gain advantage over their poorer

100. Ibid., p. 125.
101. Nghiem Dang, *Vietnam: Politics and Public Administration,* pp. 38–39.

neighbors because they could afford to master the language of courts, elites, and examinations.

The desire to impose a Chinese, Confucian model on all of Vietnam led to stringent controls on literacy and written matter. Although almost every village had a local teacher (usually supported by contributions from pupils and, perhaps, a wealthy villager) who provided most village youth with at least a year or two of education, this early training was synonymous neither with the extended education of the wealthy nor with widespread, mass literacy. Its purpose was to ensure that all villagers learned the rites and conduct necessary for proper observance of village and family cult rituals—to prepare even the poorest peasants for their adult roles in the rituals[102] and the proper ways to address and approach superiors. In short, education was civic training, not literacy. This early instruction provided a few Chinese characters, but no Vietnamese characters. The use of Chu Nom, the version of Chinese characters developed in the late thirteenth century for transcribing Vietnamese, would have greatly increased literacy, which is precisely why it found so little favor. The official imperial attitude toward literacy was well expressed in 1834 in Emperor Minh Mang's *Ten Moral Maxims,* which "stated quite candidly that no one outside the scholar class had the slightest need for literacy: 'as for soldiers, peasants, artisans and traders, surely they do not all have to be able to read books and recognize characters?'"[103]

In fact, Vietnamese rulers, "more than those of any other East Asian classical society," were determined to keep all engraving and printing under tight central supervision.[104] Discouraging literacy and curtailing the circulation of books other than Chinese classics was assumed to mean that the masses would be ignorant of the laws and therefore more easily controlled. As Emperor Minh Mang said in 1825, "Petty-minded people of [China] all know its laws, hence it is easy for them to cheat those laws. Our people still do not completely understand the laws. So by being punished they will learn fear, consequently our people would appear to be [more] easily civilized."[105]

---

102. Woodside, *Vietnam and the Chinese Model,* p. 192.
103. Ibid., p. 190.   104. Ibid., p. 186.   105. Ibid., p. 26.

The fetish for control and orthodoxy forced mandarins to choose between rigid dogmatism and rebellion. In China, Confucianism, despite its rigid aspects, achieved a certain flexibility as revisionist approaches to the doctrine developed. No such vantage points for reform were ever allowed to develop within the Vietnamese bureaucracy, and outright rebellion became "intellectually less remote" an act than in China.[106]

Another paradox is that the Sinophile courts, due to the fear of heterodoxy, never developed as widespread and open an examination system as China's. Concerned with keeping the bureaucracy as homogeneous as possible, the Court was more concerned with predictable orthodoxy than with using the examination system to integrate new regions and groups into the government. As a result, family traditions of bureaucratic service developed in only a small fraction of the more than fifteen thousand villages.[107] Cochinchina, for example, was almost totally excluded from government in the nineteenth century, while Tonkin was severely underrepresented. (This would have marked effects on the patterns of rebellion and revolution in the twentieth century.) The attempts of the Vietnamese emperors to politically integrate their domain were continually thwarted by their contradictory, short-run interests in preventing the emergence of regional contenders and by the nature of their allegiance to Chinese political and cultural forms. As Alexander Woodside has so aptly noted, "Thanks to its two thousand years of elitist homage to a foreign culture, in no country in the world is differential acculturation more psychologically invidious and politically dangerous than in Vietnam."[108]

RELIGION AND POLITICS

The Nguyen dynasty's concern with orthodoxy, their fear of regional power bases, their efforts to give village notables a vested material interest in the system, their policies designed to prevent mandarins from gaining personal control of villages, and their efforts to control printing all highlight the basic fact that Vietnam,

106. Ibid., p. 231.   107. Ibid., p. 216.   108. Ibid., p. 200.

despite strong ethnic-linguistic identity, was a cultural battleground where a Confucian court and bureaucracy tried incessantly to suppress political-religious diversity. Contrary to some interpretations,[109] cultural integration was not a reality, but a goal.[110] Constant efforts were made to domesticate the country to acceptance of the forms, roles, and structures of a bureaucratic Confucian state and even, when and where it was possible, to promote the internalization and acceptance of Confucian codes.

The Tay Son rebellion at the end of the eighteenth century established a regime that was significantly different from that of its predecessor. Resenting foreign economic domination,[111] the Tay Son attacked the Chinese commercial class and killed more than 10,000 Chinese in Saigon alone.[112] Their policies and institutions, including land reform,[113] were considerably more egalitarian and Vietnam-centered—and demonstrate the possibilities for varied forms of national government within Vietnam.

Coming to power after their defeat of the Tay Son in 1802, the Nguyen's policies to enforce an orthodox religious and political culture within the village were, therefore, formulated with an awareness of the potential for vastly different local and national forms gathering support among the peasantry. Efforts to enforce an orthodox culture in the villages were part of an effort to control information about alternative forms of local and national institutions, to weaken the institutional bases of challenging ideologies, and to enforce respect for one orthodox system of political symbols.[114]

109. To Paul Mus and John McAlister, traditional Vietnamese society was "a harmonious whole to which a person contributed a single note" (Paul Mus and John T. McAlister, Jr., *The Vietnamese and Their Revolution,* p. 38). For Frances Fitzgerald, precolonial Vietnam was a closed society whose "intellectual foundations remained flawless and immobile"; a "whole indivisible culture" where family, village, and state were "congruent" and "derived from a single set of instructions" (Frances Fitzgerald, *Fire in the Lake,* pp. 12, 13, 16). Such interpretations parallel the emphasis of many social scientists on the importance of "democratic" values for democratic political systems. For a critique of this approach, see Barry, *Sociologists, Economists, and Democracy,* chaps. 3, 4, 7, and 8.

110. Woodside, *Vietnam and the Chinese Model,* p. 290.

111. Ibid., pp. 2–4.

112. Joseph Buttinger, *The Smaller Dragon: A Political History of Vietnam,* pp. 264–265.

113. Duncanson, *Government and Revolution in Vietnam,* p. 52.

114. Woodside, *Vietnam and the Chinese Model,* p. 111.

To say that Confucianism was dominant in Vietnam is to make a political, as opposed to a cultural, statement, and the problem of taming religious organizations in order to maintain Confucianism's political dominance is a recurring theme in Vietnam. Although Confucianism was introduced to Vietnam (by Chinese overlords) before Buddhism, the latter was disseminated among the masses much earlier and became more widespread than in China.[115] From the third until the sixth centuries, countless Indian Buddhists visited Vietnam en route to and from China. After that time, numerous Chinese monks, often fleeing persecution in China, began to disseminate Mahayanist doctrines throughout the country. Studying with Chinese monks, local Buddhist monks became one of the first Vietnamese groups to have extensive knowledge of Chinese language and writing. Hence, literate Buddhists were one of the first groups with access to the principles of centralized government as practiced in China.

After the collapse of Chinese hegemony in Vietnam in the tenth century, the Buddhists were an important political force. Due to extensive knowledge of Chinese and their influence over the masses, the support of the Buddhists was essential to the early emergence of a Vietnamese bureaucratic system. The Ly dynasty (1010–1225) was even founded by a monk.

During this early period, Buddhism received great favor and patronage from ruling dynasties. The Court built many temples and sent delegations to China to request Buddhists texts. Buddhist monks often served as important advisors to the emperors and even received official titles. Their linguistic skills kept them dominant in political life until the thirteenth century, when a new dynasty pushed Buddhism into the political background.

Little by little, Confucianism gained a hold on the bureaucracy and reduced Buddhism to a secondary, restricted position in the country. Until 1075, bureaucrats were selected by examination in the Three Religions (*Tam Giao*—Confucianism, Buddhism, Taoism). In that year, however, a separate examination in Confucianism was also instituted, and by 1247 all examinations were

115. Buu Duong, "The Confucian Tradition in the History of Vietnamese Education," pp. 64–75.

based on Confucian doctrine. By the fifteenth century, Confucianism was dominant in the mandarinate, and emperors were examining Buddhist monks as a means of controlling them;[116] from then on, bonzes were seldom, if ever, influential at the Court.[117]

Thus, Vietnamese Buddhism became increasingly subservient to a Confucian court, depending on it for ordination certificates, as well as for Chinese pharmaceutical products and religious artifacts—the former essential to the Buddhist reputation in the countryside as healers, and the latter to religious rites.[118] Even under Court control, however, Buddhism had to be carefully watched, because the religious rites it offered remained attractive, especially to women. Although Vietnamese women were never as subjugated as their Chinese counterparts, there was little role for them in the male-oriented rites of the village *dinh*. Excluded, they tended to drift toward the Buddhist rites. Men officiated at the village temple and old women attended at the *chua,* or Buddhist temple found in every village.[119]

The effort to "Confucianize" Vietnam, then, did not destroy Buddhist religious beliefs and rites among the masses, but concentrated rather on weakening Buddhism structurally so that it would not be a political threat to the emperor. A dual strategy encouraged the power and prestige of more conservative and geographically narrow cults such as those of the village and family, on the one hand, and tied the remnants of Buddhist organization to Court patronage and licensing, on the other. The patronage was especially important, for it made it possible for the Court to select among competing schools of Buddhist thought and to support the most pas-

116. Truong Buu Lam, "Comments and Generalities on Sino-Vietnamese Relations," p. 39.

117. How and why Confucianism came to dominate Buddhism politically in Vietnam is still not entirely clear, but it can be hypothesized that the fall of the Sung dynasty in China during the thirteenth century was a crucial element in the Confucian "takeover." With the fall of the Sung, many hundreds of mandarins sought exile in Vietnam. These mandarins were apparently welcomed warmly at the Vietnamese Court and appear to have been pressed into service, somewhat like a political version of military mercenaries, to strengthen the Court vis-à-vis regional power-holders and feudal contenders. (Hok-Lam Chan, "Chinese Refugees in Annam and Champa at the End of the Sung Dynasty," passim).

118. Alexander Woodside, "Vietnamese Buddhism, the Vietnamese Court and China in the 1880s" in Wickberg, ed., *Historical Interaction,* p. 20.

119. Nguyen van Khoan, *Essai sur le dinh,* p. 111.

sive and nonworldly sects. This strategy worked so well in Annam and Tonkin that by the middle of the nineteenth century foreign observers found that some provinces had very few bonzes, and that there was little hierarchical organization beyond the area around Hue. Severely weakened structurally, the bonzes had little systematic, rigorous political doctrine and little hold on the population.[120]

Suppressing books and stringently controlling the training of village religious leaders are effective ways to slowly dilute a religion and erode its political potential. Without texts to refer to, without training to constantly update local religious leaders, a religion becomes easily absorbed into local folk culture.[121]

As in China, the Three Religions belief system had slowly diffused throughout all of society to merge with local practices of spirit worship, shamanism, occultism, witchcraft, and the elaborate ceremonial rites centered on the cult of the ancestors and the guardian spirit of each village. So indistinguishable did the originally separate beliefs of Mahayana Buddhism, Taoism, and Confucianism become that Leopold Cadière referred to these three religions and their assorted accretions in the singular to emphasize that religion enveloped all of life.[122]

Buddhist and Taoist beliefs were syncretized with elements of Confucianism. Marriages, births, and funerals—the crucial rites of passage in society—were Buddhist; the mysticism was Taoist, the poetry mainly Buddhist. Elite bureaucratic authority relations and laws were Confucian, of course, but even at the Court the Confucian mandarins often escaped the strict dogmas of Vietnamese elite Confucianism by writing their political criticism as Buddhist poetry.

In the sense that much, if not all, of life was believed to be governed by spirits, genii, and supernatural forces, the Vietnamese were fatalistic. At the same time, however, they were nondogmatic about religious practice, and religious symbols were therefore easily manipulated for political purposes. The traditional saying,

120. Nguyen van Phong, *La Société vietnamienne,* pp. 78–86.
121. See Jack Goody, ''Restricted Literacy in Northern Ghana,'' p. 216, in Goody, *Literacy in Traditional Societies.*
122. Leopold Cadière, *Croyances et pratiques religieuses des vietnamiens,* vol. 1; see also Gerald C. Hickey, *Village in Vietnam,* p. iii.

"Worship wherever there is a god,"[123] indicated that a religion rarely commanded the undivided loyalty of its followers and that there was a pragmatic willingness to give any god or spirit—and hence its earthly representative—a chance to offer its help in time of distress. As long as there was a plethora of possible religious or spiritual proscriptions for a situation, religious tolerance among the masses meant political danger for the elite: choosing among beliefs meant choosing among courses of action, and choosing among courses of action could, and often did, mean a political challenge to Confucianism and its representatives.

In Confucian theory only superior men were entitled to worship the gods and act, in effect, as state diviners. Nothing beyond ancestor worship was deemed necessary for the common man.[124] If local Confucian officials were to be accepted as priests of a religious system, then it was necessary to neutralize the political danger of any other beliefs that could not be eliminated. The strategy over the centuries had relied on both carrots and sticks to keep religious organizations under tight control and dependent on the state.

On paper, Confucianism was a materialistic and empirical philosophy, a rational attempt to cultivate the moral sentiments essential to a stable, hierarchical state. The Confucianists tried, without success, to reinterpret ancient village cults to eliminate their supernatural implications: in the end, Confucian doctrine was forced to accept the realities of primitive religion and adapt to the use of "supernatural conceptions as an instrument to enforce social values and to control the masses."[125]

The ancient cult of the ancestors observed by all Vietnamese, on the other hand, meshed easily with Confucianism and formed the core of religious life. In Confucian thought filial piety was a security pact, a social contract, which established patterns of reciprocity between the generations.[126] This concept merged with the ancient cult of ancestors, extending the bonds backward and forward in time, blending all generations. In return, family patriarchs re-

123. Duncanson, *Government and Revolution in Vietnam*, p. 46.
124. Daniel Overemyer, "Folk Buddhist Religion: Dissenting Sects in Late Traditional China," pp. 21–22.
125. C. K. Yang, *Religion in Chinese Society*, p. 254.
126. Solomon, *Mao's Revolution*, p. 75.

ceived important benefits for themselves and their families, for "Confucianizing" the family meant that the well-developed Confucian family code could be used to settle the inevitable property and marriage disputes within a family. Serious conflicts, furthermore, could be adjudicated in the Confucian courts.

In a world filled with spirits, genii, ghosts, demons, and other supernatural creatures, the various emperors who tried to integrate Vietnam into a coherent nation did not attempt the impossible job of denying the existence of these irrational and most un-Confucian forces. Usually believing in these forces themselves, they tried instead to make the legends of the various genii uniform from village to village and to develop cults deifying national heroes.[127]

In addition to deliberately manipulating legends and spirit cults, efforts were made to promote those cults that were least disruptive to the political system. The village cult managed by the notables, for example, received considerable encouragement from the state, which hoped thereby to keep peasants away from competing and potentially threatening political and religious organizations.

Due to such policies, Taoism and Buddhism had been largely tamed in Annam and Tonkin, but constant vigilance was required to keep religious organizations under control. By the nineteenth century only men over the age of sixty were allowed to become bonzes, and village customaries forbade persons between the ages of fifteen and forty from attending Buddhist ceremonies. The customaries, enforced by the notables, also made it a crime to engage in any religion except family and village cults. As one village customary stated,

. . . there must not be any people who believe in sorcerers; it is forbidden to perform in the houses of private citizens, to create nocturnal scenes like those of the mediums, for there will be a gathering and the spectators will profit by them to commit bad acts. . . . Those who form a religious society will also be punished.[128]

Within the villages, then, religious participation for most peasants became limited to passive attendance at religious ceremonies dominated by the notables and to worship at the family altar.

127. See, for example, Gourou, *Les Paysans,* p. 115.
128. Marcel Rouilly, *La Commune annamite,* pp. 110–111.

In Cochinchina, however, peasants had a greater variety of religious options available to them. During the period when Buddhism was being shorn of its secular role in society and pushed into a parasitic and fragmented monasticism under the watchful eye of the mandarins, a second strand of Buddhism arose in reaction to this increasing impotence. This Buddhism, a *ch'an* (Zen) sect called Truc Lam Yen Tu or Bamboo Grove of Yen Tu Mountain, renounced the monastic life of passive withdrawal from society, stressed asceticism and mass involvement, and resisted cooptation by rigidly Sinophile and Confucian courts. Because of their nonpassivity, its monks were banished to Cochinchina, where they settled in the frontier areas.

During the nineteenth century, an adherent of this sect—a farmer named Doan Minh Huyen—attracted followers throughout Cochinchina when he began to preach salvation and use faith healing. Jealous of his success, more traditional monks denounced him as subversive, and he was jailed by the provincial mandarin. This farmer, also known as the Phat Thay Tay An or Buddha of Western Peace, was too popular to be stopped, however, and the mandarin, unable to thwart his growing movement, released him from jail. He established small farming communities based on mutual help and lay devotion throughout remote parts of western Cochinchina, where his followers were relatively safe from political control by the mandarins.[129]

Many other political-religious doctrines spread to Cochinchina directly from China. In addition to the Chinese trading communities that existed in all three regions of the country, tens of thousands of Chinese poured into Cochinchina after the Ming dynasty fell in the seventeenth century. Most of these Ming loyalists became "Minh-Huong," assimilated Chinese who eventually married into the Vietnamese population. These loyalists propagated millenarian political creeds and sects such as the White Lotus, a Buddhist-Taoist millenarian ideology, and the similar Heaven and Earth Society.

As one nineteenth-century mandarin noted, whenever there was a bad harvest in Cochinchina, heterodox creeds flourished through-

129. Hue-Tam Ho Tai, "The Evolution of Millenarianism," passim.

out the region.[130] Peasants had more attractive forms of religious worship available, forms which offered them a more direct and active role than the elitist forms of "Confucian" villages.

More threatening to the Nguyen dynasty—and more challenging to the image of an organic, harmonious past where family, village, and state always fit together neatly and uniquely—is the history of Christianity in Vietnam. By the nineteenth century, dissident Buddhist and Chinese political-religious sects were a problem confined mainly to the frontier; however, Catholicism was flourishing in the older regions of the country, particularly Tonkin. This was not a new problem. For over two hundred years Catholic missionaries, particularly Jesuits, had been a serious threat to Confucian hegemony. So serious was the threat during Nguyen rule that "hundreds of petitions" were addressed to the emperors by loyal mandarins unable to stem the Catholic influence. In 1826, for example, the Grand Mandarin, in charge of the Ministry of Justice, petitioned Emperor Minh Mang to counter Catholicism by building a competing religious structure:

We implore his majesty to establish a true religion in order that the grand and the [common] people could profit from it. . . . [Catholic] religion is false and contrary to true doctrine. . . . It uses the fear of punishment and of hell in order to scare the feeble. . . . *It even has its own courts to judge affairs.* Those who follow that religion assemble, offer sacrifices and make adorations; thousands come and go, to render homage, as if they were assisting one of the premier dignitaries of the kingdom. . . . Those who follow that doctrine are animated with a zeal which transports them.[131]

At least two foreign priests visited Vietnam and converted Vietnamese to Catholicism before 1600.[132] It was when the Jesuits were expelled from Japan, however, and founded the first Vietnamese mission in 1615 that Catholicism began to grow in Vietnam. Reliable statistics are rare, but there is no doubt that these early Catholic fathers "had somehow touched a motor nerve of Vietnamese society."[133] One source, for example, reported 200,000 converts

130. Woodside, *Vietnam and the Chinese Model,* p. 96.
131. George Taboulet, *La Gêste française en Indochine,* p. 323. Emphasis added.
132. Buu Duong, "The Confucian Tradition," p. 75.
133. Duncanson, *Government and Revolution in Vietnam,* p. 75.

in Tonkin alone for 1650, while another estimates 400,000 a decade later.[134] The various estimates suggest that, at least for Tonkin, 10 percent (perhaps even 20 percent) of the population had converted to Catholicism in the seventeenth century, before the beginning of the severe and bloody suppression campaigns that occurred repeatedly over the next two centuries in Vietnam. Despite these periodic purges, in 1840, after a purge that had killed over 100,000 Catholics, between 5 and 10 percent of the nation still followed the Catholic Church.[135]

Vietnam was not the only country where Catholicism was attractive to the masses. In both Japan and China, missionaries met with some success. In those two countries, however, the central governments had sufficient control of the country to clamp down on the missionaries or to expel them when they began to proselytize too successfully. In Vietnam, however, the central leadership was never in firm enough control of either mandarins or the coastlines to isolate and contain the missionaries. During the centuries when Vietnam was divided into rival warring courts, for example, there were many times when the various emperors ordered the banishment of all missionaries. These efforts were always short-lived because of a desire for the knowledge of science and weaponry (particularly cannons) that the missionaries possessed. The most famous of all the missionaries, Alexandre de Rhodes, was even banished from the countryside once because the cannon he had promised arrived late.[136]

As long as one of the warring dynasties was accepting military aid from the missionaries, along with the attendant risk of religious conversions, the other dynasty was also forced into accepting the aid, as well as the risks, from other missionaries. Later, when the country was unified under the Nguyen dynasty, conflict within the aristocracy continued to give the missionaries the opening to the countryside they needed to work among the masses. More than one pretender to the throne allied himself with the missionaries and their

134. Ibid.
135. Piero Gheddo, *The Cross and the Bo-Tree: Catholics and Buddhists in Vietnam*, pp. 13–15.
136. Duncanson, *Government and Revolution in Vietnam*, p. 77.

followers to gain support for his challenge to the ruling emperor.[137]
Try as they would, therefore, no Vietnamese ruler ever had
sufficient control of the country and the mandarins to banish the
missionaries permanently.[138]

One missionary claimed that a single Jesuit in Vietnam was as
effective as an entire college in Europe, while another missionary
leader, slightly less prone to hyperbole, estimated that a single missionary in Vietnam was as effective as fifty missionaries
elsewhere.[139] There were always members of the mandarinate and
the royal family interested in science or political support, and in the
countryside there was not only a great interest in the religion, but
great attraction to the missionaries, who were more skilled in the art
of governance than many of the Vietnamese mandarins with their
imperfect knowledge of the Chinese model they sought to emulate.

In contrast to the devout and organized bonzes the missionaries
found in Siam and Cambodia, in Vietnam, thanks to the continuing
attempts to fragment religious organization, the village monks and
shamans were poorly trained, with little more religious knowledge
than the ordinary peasant. Rarely were they capable of providing
either welfare or leadership.[140]

Most of the Vietnamese bonzes and shamans hated and feared

137. David Joel Steinberg, ed., *In Search of Southeast Asia: A Modern History*,
p. 130.

138. The missionaries (especially the Jesuits) also had access to the elite and the
rural masses in Siam and Cambodia, but every strategem to establish a Catholic
foothold failed. The elites in the two countries were neither so well educated as the
Vietnamese elite, nor did they have the explicit tradition of cultural borrowing. They
were, furthermore, deeply attached to a well-established and well-organized Buddhist faith. In neither of the two countries was there an interest in the knowledge of
science and mathematics possessed by the Jesuits, and no taste for the paintings and
jewels that had given the Jesuits entree to all the other kings of the Orient. Nor were
the Jesuits successful among the masses of Siam and Cambodia, not even on the
frontiers away from any possible government sanction. In both countries "armies of
bonzes" guarded the tradition and with an austerity that the Jesuits, although they
tried for over half a century, could not match. The attachment of the population to
their religious beliefs was so strong that not even elite support could enable an outside religion to gain a following. One Cambodian king, for example, converted to
Islam, which, even with the support of the king, was unable to compete successfully
with the bonzes. Henri Chappoulie, *Rome et les missions d'Indochine au XVIIe
siècle*, pp. 15–16.)

139. Ibid., pp. 40, 192.

140. Ibid., pp. 16–17, 193–194.

the missionaries. The missionaries' cannons and astronomy gave them prestige at the Court, their religious doctrine was well developed compared to the mélange offered by untrained local bonzes, and—because they were willing and able to act as secular leaders—they could provide organizational benefits and material rewards their native competitors could not match.

In spite of their fears, however, local competition was such that some religious leaders were willing to ally with anyone who could strengthen their magic and their following by giving them access to new gods and new technologies. A diary of Alexandre de Rhodes describes his experiences in the early 1600s:

Nothing so astonished me as the ease with which I was able to convert the idolatrous priests, who are usually the most obstinate. I found them marvelously open to reason. I baptized 200 of them, who will be of unbelievable help to us in converting the others. One of them alone brought me 500 of those he had disabused of error by teaching them the trusts of the faith, and they have since become our most fervent catechists. . . . My favorite method was to propose to them the immortality of the soul and the afterlife.[141]

The promise of afterlife had great appeal, as did the holy water: "They have such reverence for holy water they come to fetch it from five or six days journey away. . . . They give it to all the sick to drink, with marvelous results. Every Sunday I was obliged to bless at least 500 large jars of this sacred water to satisfy their pious desires."[142]

Everywhere the missionaries went in the countryside they found Confucius worshipped among the gentry. But Confucianism and the worship of Confucius were no problem for the Jesuits, for among his maxims there was nothing inconsistent with Christianity. Some missionaries simply transferred his maxims to Christ, while others placed his picture alongside the picture of Christ.[143] The missionaries, then, gave all their followers, and not just the rich, access to Confucius.

The Jesuits were as impressed with the family system and

141. *Alexandre de Rhodes of Vietnam: The Travels and Missions of Father Alexandre de Rhodes in China and Other Kingdoms of the Orient*, p. 68.
142. Ibid.
143. Chappoulie, *Rome et les missions d'Indochine*, pp. 15–16.

ancestor worship as they were with Confucianism. They found that the family organization was based on approved virtues and that the authority of the head of the family sufficed to solve all intrafamily conflicts. Such a system in Europe, Rhodes wrote, would eliminate three-quarters of all court suits.[144] Rich men had many wives and the poor sold children to pay debts, but family bonds were strong. Accepting Confucianism and admiring the family system, the early missionaries required only slight legerdemain to adapt ancestor worship. As one missionary explained the Christain style of ancestor worship,

The Christians keep the ceremonies of bereavement over the death of mothers and fathers; but they remove from the ceremonies the superstitions which the pagans are used to blending in their funerals. Pagans prepare tables and invite the souls of the dead to eat. Christians also prepare their tables, as evidence of their recognition towards those who have given their life and the wealth they enjoy; but they guard against inviting souls to eat.[145]

The missionaries offered material, as well as spiritual, benefits to their converts. Great emphasis was placed on the dedication and honesty of their lay assistants, and the money they collected was used to improve welfare for the poor and the orphaned.[146] Perhaps even more important than the welfare benefits was the ability of the Jesuits to provide less expensive but more consistent justice than the mandarins, as well as the leadership necessary to settle and found new lands.

The missionaries, as noted, were effusive in their admiration of Confucianism and the Confucian principles of government and administration. In contrast to China, however, they seem to have found a much lower level of competence and training among the mandarins: "Those who know even a few [Chinese] characters . . . can attain the dignity of mandarins. These poor, having become great in an instant, in order to uphold their state, vex the small people and make them crawl under their feet; they pillage the widowed and orphaned, they trouble the neighborhood and torment the poor."[147]

144. Ibid., p. 20.   145. Ibid., p. 196. fn. 2.   146. Ibid., pp. 197, 235.
147. Taboulet, *La Gêste française,* p. 106.

In a similar vein, because they actually knew more about Chinese principles of government, the missionaries encountered resentment in many mandarins. The former, who had the latest books shipped directly from China, were often more knowledgeable about current Confucian methods, for example, than were the mandarins. Jealous of the missionaries' knowledge, the mandarins would watch for the arriving ships and try to destroy the books before they reached their destination.[148]

In addition to their welfare and their medical knowledge, the missionaries benefited greatly from the demand in the countryside for an efficient and just system of courts. When the missionaries acted as judges, it gave converts an acceptable means of settling disputes without having to submit to the caprice of mandarins, who—according to the missionaries—judged according to their whims as much as to the law, demanded large gifts to hear a case, and then often ruled according to the size of the gift.[149]

It is clear, then, that the attraction of this new religion was as much economic and political as spiritual. The missionaries' contacts with foreign traders afforded them a warm welcome among native traders resentful of the mandarins' anticommerce mentality.[150] In addition to judging disputes, patching marriages, and disciplining bad Christians, the missionaries did what they could to provide credit for the farmers.

The geographic pattern of missionary success supports the thesis that the material benefits were essential to the attractiveness of their religion. During the 250 years of partition, the missionaries always fared better in the northern "Tonkinese" kingdom than they did in the less crowded kingdom to the south.[151] After unification in the nineteenth century, conversions were confined mainly to the overcrowded and poorer areas of Tonkin and Annam, whereas the open frontier of Cochinchina "provided less successful ground for missionary activity."[152] Their system of adjudication was more valuable in the older areas, where resources were few and often in dispute. Similarly, settling new lands in these areas was much more

148. Chappoulie, *Rome et les missions d'Indochine,* p. 203.
149. Ibid., p. 196.
150. Chesneaux, *The Vietnamese Nation,* p. 38.
151. Gheddo, *The Cross and the Bo-Tree,* p. 4.
152. Osborne, *The French Presence,* pp. 25–26.

difficult than on the frontier, for they were mostly marsh or swamp that required drainage and dike-building. Cooperation was essential and, hence, the worldly organizational skills of the missionaries were welcome.

Ultimately, it was neither the power of the emperor nor the appeal of Confucianism that prevented Vietnam from becoming a predominantly Christian country. It was the overwhelming importance to the Vietnamese of ancestor worship.

The intermittent power struggles between the Jesuits and Dominican, Franciscan, and other rivals came to a head in the eighteenth century and resulted in a Papal Bull that took a hard stance against the Jesuits' easy tolerance of local beliefs. Once this edict was in effect, conversion rates decreased, and the missionaries concentrated instead on grouping their followers in even tighter communities where beliefs could be more easily controlled. Were it not for the missionaries' eventual opposition to the traditional rites of ancestor worship, there might well have been total conversion under the first Nguyễn emperor (1802–1820), who came to power after the Tay Son rebellion with the support of the missionaries and their following. In large part because of their opposition to ancestor rites, however, instead of becoming a ruling majority, the Catholics became a powerful minority who finally used the facts of repression and the promise of foreign trade to maneuver France into colonizing Vietnam.

Well before colonialism, it was possible for new forms of local religious and political organization to emerge in Vietnam. That the "new sorcerers,"[153] as the peasants called the missionaries, were able to take advantage of the disorganized state of Buddhist bonzes and Taoist shamans emphasizes the importance of the nonofficial aspects of the society and the incompleteness of Confucian court control.

CONCLUSION

Strong village identities with clear boundaries between insiders and outsiders characterized nineteenth-century Vietnamese villages. Villages had a well-developed public sector, and village citizenship

153. Woodside, *Vietnam and the Chinese Model*, p. 262.

was highly prized. But villages were not egalitarian, leveling, welfare oriented, or necessarily harmonious. There was at once both cooperation and conflict, and individual behavior in the village was governed by considerations of self-interest.

Instead of the (functional) view that the villages overcome and shape individual interests of its members, I have argued that the individual interests of the villagers shape and determine the nature and scope of village-level cooperation. The changes that occurred during the colonial period therefore can be analyzed in terms of structural changes introduced by the French. There is no need to posit a change from village (or altruistic) to individual (or selfish) orientation.

4

Corporatism and Colonialism

FRENCH designs on Vietnam, Laos, and Cambodia were spurred by commercial and industrial interests eager for business opportunities there and in China. Prompted also by a navy anxious to regain lost empire and a Catholic Church zealous to extend its influence, as well as to protect its converts from persecution, France began its imperialist venture in 1859. In 1867, the Imperial Court at Hue ceded Cochinchina to the French. By 1885, further military activity forced the Court to accept protectorate status for Annam and Tonkin.[1]

Abandoned by the mandarins during the years of fighting,

A somewhat different version of this chapter can be found in "Corporatism and Colonialism: Political Economy of Rural Change in Vietnam," *Comparative Politics* 8 (April 1976):431–464.

1. The best sources for the periods of takeover and widespread resistance are Milton Osborne, *The French Presence in Cochinchina and Cambodia: Rule and Response (1859–1905),* and David Marr, *Vietnamese Anti-Colonialism, 1885–1925.*

Cochinchina from the first days of French rule was governed directly by Frenchmen whose administration was patterned on French bureaucratic forms. In Tonkin and Annam, however, French control was indirect, and provinces continued to be administered by the mandarins, the majority of whom actively collaborated with their French advisors.[2] Nonetheless, the mandarinate decayed under the French, due in part to French promotion of unschooled and unprincipled opportunists who had assisted in their takeover and in part to the corruption and confusion resulting from early reliance on interpreters to deal with the populace. By 1920, the traditional mandarinate was so discredited among the population that the French—still preserving the fiction of a protectorate—abandoned the traditional mandarin examinations and began to recruit civil servants with European-style education and qualifications.[3] In Tonkin and Annam, however, Vietnamese courts based on precolonial law continued to be used in the rural areas, while French courts were reserved for urban areas and cases involving French citizens.[4]

Attempting to replace the use of characters with Quoc Ngu, the romanized script, the French found their efforts supported by Vietnamese reformers aware of its potential for mass literacy.[5] Within a few decades they had built 2,000 miles of railroad line and 20,000 miles of highway and had developed a telegraph system. They had also dug nearly 2,500 miles of canals in Cochinchina (as much dredging as the Suez Canal) and increased its rice-producing area from 215,000 hectares to 2.2 million hectares. None of this abundant land was available to peasants from Annam or Tonkin, however. Migration—or even most travel—among regions was circumscribed except for workers impressed in Tonkin to serve on the rubber plantations of Cochinchina.

2. Marr, *Vietnamese Anti-Colonialism*, pp. 82–83.

3. Woodside, *Community and Revolution*, pp. 8 and 9–18. Nguyen van Phong, *La Société vietnamienne de 1882 à 1902*, pp. 232–261, cites numerous contemporary accounts of plundering by the new "mandarins" during the changeover.

4. This prompted many wealthy villagers to have their children born in Hanoi so that they could come under French law. (Pierre Gourou, *Les Paysans*, p. 10.)

5. Marr, *Vietnamese Anti-Colonialism*, pp. 156–184. John Perkins's "The Adoption of Quoc Ngu Romanization in Vietnam: 1860–1925" is a masterly work on this subject. Quoc Ngu flourished outside Catholic circles only when sufficient "Confucian" material was available in the romanized form to ensure a moral dimen-

The Vietnamese paid a heavy price for these projects, particularly for the railroad, which represented nearly half the capital budget of the colonies for years and which was virtually worthless in a country with extensive waterways. Further, as much as half the colonial budget went into salaries of French colonial personnel. In 1925, for example, there were as many French bureaucrats for 30 million Vietnamese, Cambodians, and Laotians as there were British bureaucrats for 325 million Indians.[6]

Although some mining and light industry developed in Tonkin and northern Annam, the urban population of those areas remained under 5 percent of the total population. In Cochinchina, on the other hand, development of riceland and rubber plantations meant a large-scale commercial export trade and a population that was 15 percent urban. The growth in exports also brought a large influx of Chinese to work for the Chinese firms that dominated the milling, transport, and export of rice.[7] The number of French industrialists and planters who came to Vietnam was relatively small—less then 20,000. However, the general instability of leadership of the colonial bureaucracy—twenty-three governors-general for Indochina between 1892 and 1930—gave these colonists a powerful (and reactionary) voice in colonial politics.[8] Native opportunities for political participation were limited to such impotent vehicles as the colonial council, and the possibilities for higher education were so circumscribed as to merit praise from a British governor of India:

Those who view with deep concern the disturbing effects of the over-hasty spread of "education" on European lines, among Asian and African peoples, would probably be inclined to attribute the comparative peace and

---

sion for education and only when the Vietnamese began to separate their attitude toward European ideas and innovations from their hatred of Western imperialism.

6. Paul Isoart, *Le Phénomenène national vietnamien: De l'Independence unitaire à l'independence fractionée,* p. 200. All but a handful of these Frenchmen served in Saigon and Hanoi.

7. Charles Robequain, *The Economic Development of French Indochina,* pp. 34–43.

8. See, for example, André Malraux's sparring with colonists in Walter G. Langlois, *Andre Malraux: The Indochina Adventure.* It is sometimes assumed that there was a large number of French planters because many wealthy Vietnamese landowners had French citizenship.

tranquility which the French administration in Indo-China have enjoyed up to now to the fact that they have steadily declined to allow themselves to be unduly driven in the direction of the higher branches of public instruction. . . . They have determined that, as far as possible, instruction in French and "higher education" in general shall only be given to those who are likely to make proper use of such privileges.[9]

Export taxes on rice, rubber, and coal were comparatively light; the major source of taxes to support the bureaucracy and its projects came from alcohol, opium, and salt monopolies and from vastly increased—and regressive—land and head taxes. The French took a short-run view of their rural administration and relied heavily on these taxes, making no effort to develop either a progressive tax system or one with floors (which could have brought in far more money in the long run).

Thus, the cost of colonial administration fell heavily on the poorest peasants. Nonetheless, demographic data clearly support the argument that the colonial era (until World War II) was one of fewer extreme crisis years for the peasantry than before the advent of the French—that is, there were fewer years in which hunger was not only constant and painful, but actually killing. Indeed, the population increased from 8 million in 1840 to over 21 million in 1943. Tonkin reached a population of 8.4 million, Annam approximately 7 million, and Cochinchina 5.6 million. Growth rates for the twentieth century were about 1 percent for Annam and Tonkin and 1.8 percent for Cochinchina.[10] This steady population growth strongly suggests that despite the stratification, poverty, and misery generated by colonial policies, there were fewer years in which the population experienced disastrous interruptions to the food supply.

Under colonial rule many persons were forced to take desperate measures—selling children, taking the place of draft animals, foraging for food—but under earlier, more unstable conditions many of these persons would not have survived. One source of increased stability was the suppression of large-scale uprisings, banditry, and

9. Sir Hesketh Bell, *Foreign Colonial Administration in the Far East* (London: Edward Arnold, 1928), pp. 193–194.

10. Rambo, "A Comparison of Peasant Social Systems," pp. 174, 180, 393. Duncanson, *Government and Revolution in Vietnam,* p. 104, estimates the three regions in 1873 as under 5, under 4, and 1.5 million.

piracy. The gradual improvement of the dike system in Tonkin, which decreased the incidence and severity of floods, was another. Finally, a decline in both the general mortality rate (especially for infants) and the specific mortality rate for cholera is a good indication that malnutrition was less of a problem.[11] The increase in population density, particularly in Tonkin, meant that people had to work harder to produce the same amount of rice per capita, and the average income was lower for many peasants. Nevertheless, the number of crisis years also decreased.

The explanations most commonly advanced by Vietnam scholars for the changes that took place in the countryside during the colonial period are all quite similar. In summary, French administrative decrees changed the traditional methods for selecting village notables and chiefs. This destroyed the pre-French sense of collective obligation and mutual support and led to abusive village administration. This new form of village government paved the way for economic stratification and inequality: The good notables of the past were driven from public service by French decrees; they were replaced by less worthy men who lacked legitimacy and who profited from their office at the expense of the poor. Eventually, this opened the way for a revolutionary elite to emerge and replace these new "illegitimate" notables.

In the words of Truong Buu Lam, "Changes in the mode of selecting the village council robbed villagers of the control and trust traditionally inherent in their relationship with the notables"; these changes "undermined the cooperative foundations of the village" and led to land expropriations and other abuses because the notables "no longer owed responsibility to their constituents."[12] In virtually the same words, Nghiem Dang states that an "authority of confidence and identification" was lost. Due to French reforms, there was a "gradual elimination of natural local leaders," and "the oligarchy was replaced by a half-hearted democracy."[13]

To John McAlister and Paul Mus, the French reforms that pre-

11. Gourou, *Les Paysans,* p. 188. See also Carter Marshal, "Health, Nutrition and Roots of World Population Growth," pp. 677–690.

12. Truong Buu Lam, "The Vietnamese Village in the Colonial Period."

13. Nghiem Dang, *Vietnam: Politics and Public Administration,* p. 151.

sumably bypassed village institutions of administration and tax collection destroyed any meaningful mutual assistance beyond the family[14] and turned the village into an "empty shell devoid of substance."[15] Others characterize the new procedures for tax collection as a crucial cause of the colonial "decay" of the village. Referring to the supposed change in tax collection procedures, for example, Fitzgerald explains that

. . . the colonial regime usurped the right of the village council to conduct the census and make up the tax rolls. With one stroke of the pen it broke through the traditional anonymity of the villages and shattered their collective responsibility. Left without any binding obligations to the community, many of the village "notables" seized communal land for their own private property and used their judicial powers to terrorize other villagers.[16]

These explanations conform to Herbert Spencer's definition of tragedy—a beautiful hypothesis destroyed by an inconvenient fact. The inconvenient fact is Annam. All the authors just cited clearly imply that if village administration had been left in the hands of the traditional village notables, their collective obligations would have remained in force, there would have been no land-grabbing, and welfare would have been provided to the needy by the traditional elites. Each of the decrees quoted in support of this view is a decree

14. John T. McAlister, Jr., *Vietnam: The Origins of Revolution*, p. 75.
15. John T. McAlister, Jr., and Paul Mus, *The Vietnamese and Their Revolution*, p. 36. According to the analysis developed by Mus (and adopted in toto by McAlister), three French reforms eroded the power of the traditional village elites and thus led to the growth of individualism: (1) the development of accurate and complete tax rolls; (2) tighter tax and budgetary controls on the council of notables; and (3) the substitution of election for cooptation of council members. According to Mus, "The first two of these reforms undermined the patriarchal system by curtailing the considerable administrative—and consequently financial—latitude with which the council had been accustomed to function. The third reform encouraged the taxpayers to look after their own affairs" ("The Role of the Village in Vietnamese Affairs," p. 269).
There are three major problems with these assertions. First, the reforms referred to were enacted in Tonkin but not in Annam, so they cannot account for the changes that took place in the latter. Second, even within Tonkin, the French never developed accurate and complete tax rolls; they never supervised more than a few village budgets; and they never destroyed the fiscal latitude of village notables. Third, individuals were responsible for head and land taxes in the precolonial village well before any French attempts to reform village government by means of electoral innovations.
16. Frances Fitzgerald, *Fire in the Lake: The Vietnamese and the Americans in Vietnam*, p. 54.

enacted in either Tonkin or Cochinchina. In Annam, however, village administration was left to the notables with virtually no change whatsoever until 1942. Yet the processes of rural political and economic change in Annam closely parallel those of Tonkin.

There are more serious flaws in these explanations than the failure to explain what happened in at least one region of the country. In every part of Vietnam, political and economic abuse and increased stratification appeared *before*—not after—changes in the laws governing village administration. In fact, one of the motivations for many of the major French village reforms in every region was to correct abuses and corruption that were already widespread in the Vietnamese countryside.

Moreover, those who concentrate on French administrative and legal changes have difficulty explaining the differences that emerged during the colonial period between Cochinchina, on the one hand, and Annam and Tonkin, on the other. The fact is that village elites in the two areas responded to French policies quite differently because local economic incentives differed. Because of the different economic incentives, the extent and nature of intraelite conflict were different; the collective incentives to block the use of outside institutions by any given member of the elite were different; the conditions under which the peasants had reason to side with the elite against outsiders were different; and the incentives to ally with members of the bureaucracy against other villagers were also different. These regional variations were due to differences in local economics and the local mode of production: in Cochinchina there were large amounts of available underdeveloped land, whereas in Tonkin and Annam there were no large areas that had not been developed. In addition, there was very little communal land and almost no communal irrigation or flood control in Cochinchina.

It is enlightening, then, to reverse these analyses and place the major emphasis on the notables and the peasants, as they individually and collectively decided which French decrees and institutions they would accept, and in what manner they would use them. The traditional Vietnamese village elites, when their essential economic interests were at stake, did not passively acquiesce in French decrees; rather, as we shall see, they manipulated them in order to turn them to their own advantage (and against the peasants, whom the French were sometimes trying to protect). In the colonial period, the old village elite was not driven from office by French racism (although it existed in abundance). The notables, from within the village, turned French policies to their own advantage; they used French laws and bureaucrats in their intravillage power struggles and promoted their own interests, sometimes at the collective expense of the village. The French created new opportunities, options, and institutions; but much of the change in rural life occurred only because the village elites were willing to use these new possibilities in their own local, age-old power struggles.

Throughout the colonial period and until World War II, the villages of Tonkin and Annam remained corporate. A strong sense of village citizenship continued, as did the elaborate system of internal rankings within each village. Each village was still like a separate land market, and the ownership of land by outsiders met local resistance and was impossible without protection from mandarins. Within the village, collective resistance to outside influences persisted. There was a sharp increase in stratification, the rich getting richer *and* the poor getting poorer, as well as a marked increase in intraelite conflict, which led to the continual splitting of villages.

Despite the increase in internal conflicts and stratification, the institutionalized resistance to outsiders continued, and there was a "moral hygiene which demands that everyone do his duty."[17] The pressure to conform was so strong that even after 70,000 men from Annam and Tonkin spent four years in France during World War I, Pierre Gourou could write of their return home that

Indeed, one is struck by the spectacle of ease with which a peasant who has lived outside the delta [Tonkin] resumes his place in the village community: whether he has lived away as a soldier, miner or trader, without trouble, he once more becomes the simple listed person or influential notable. He has acquainted himself with new techniques but his soul has not changed. . . . If the emigrant who has returned to the village has made a little fortune, he will use a portion of it to secure for himself a place in the village hierarchy; if he has returned poor, his compatriots will mock him cruelly and he will have no influence, his failure destroying any authority among them.[18]

17. Gourou, *Les Paysans*, pp. 269–272.   18. Ibid., pp. 219–220.

In contrast, the villages of Cochinchina (and not just the new villages opened on pioneer lands in the colonial period) became what Eric Wolf has called "open villages."[19] There was little or no sense of local citizenship and no elaborate internal ranking system. An open land market permitted anyone to buy land in a village, whether or not he had been born there. There was no collective resistance from the notables to the use of outside institutions; outside ideas and influences were free to permeate the village. While there was a marked increase in political and economic stratification, as in Annam and Tonkin, in Cochinchina the rich got richer *but* so did the poor, although at a much slower rate. So much did Cochinchina change that Gourou observed there little of the "peasant mentality" common in the rest of the country.[20]

So weakened was the sense of individual village identity, and so limited was collective resistance to change, that in Cochinchina the French were even able to consolidate villages. Whereas the number of villages in Tonkin and Annam continuously increased (because intravillage conflict often led to secession), the number in Cochinchina decreased. Furthermore, when elections were held in Cochinchina, the result was an increase in the supply of services and goods made available within the village by the elected officials. In Tonkin, on the contrary, when elections were held to choose village officials, there was a marked increase in instability and conflict, and no improvements in services.

The open, "modern" villages of Cochinchina were noticeably less subject to manipulation by both government bureaucrats and Catholic priests than were the corporate villages of Tonkin and Annam. In Annam and Tonkin, that is, if one notable converted to Catholicism, the entire village would follow, or else the village would split. In Cochinchina, however, where conversion was less common, the conversion of one notable did not invariably lead to the conversion of the entire village.

What needs to be explained, then, is why under colonial rule the villages of Cochinchina were so different, economically and politi-

19. Eric Wolf, "Types of Latin American Peasantry: A Preliminary Discussion," pp. 452–471.
20. Pierre Gourou, *Land Utilization in French Indochina,* pp. 331–332.

cally, from the villages of Tonkin and Annam, as well as how and why those changes that occurred in the older areas of Tonkin and Annam came about. We must look both to French decrees and institutions, and to the dynamics of Vietnamese villages for the answers.

I shall focus my examination on the impact of French taxation and supravillage institutions on stratification and politics within the village, as well as on the regional variations in response to French initiatives. Although a generalized faith in the ability of corporate villages to redistribute pain and promote cooperation has led many scholars to infer from the conflicts of the colonial period that there were major changes in village procedures, I shall demonstrate that there were, in fact, no major discontinuities in village procedures for tax collection. I shall also demonstrate that, within the constraints imposed by the French, many opportunities existed to adapt such procedures in order to protect the poor or limit inequities. In fact, this was not done. The concept of penetration, furthermore, is rather misleading, for much of the impact of supravillage institutions on village affairs resulted from the initiatives of villagers seeking allies for intravillage power struggles. In part as a consequence of village tax procedures and external alliances, stratification increased during the colonial period. Further, as poverty—and therefore the need for insurance and protection at the village level—increased, villages functioned less well.

ANNAM AND TONKIN

Taxes

French taxes were extraordinarily heavy. By 1901, after only a few decades of colonial rule, taxes in Vietnam were already higher than in Indonesia, India, Malaya, or even Japan,[21] and direct and indirect taxes would rise still higher in the coming years. To state, however, that the French tax collection *procedures* "superseded" village institutions is inaccurate.[22] While the crushing total demand for taxes came from the French, the collection procedures within

21. Virginia Thompson, *French Indochina*, pp. 193–194.
22. McAlister, *Vietnam*, p. 75.

the village were of local origin, and there was only a tenuous link between French decrees and village procedures. The precolonial system had already pushed a large share of the tax burden onto the poor, especially the nonregistered, and although the colonial tax system crushed taxpayers with both its formal demands and the added payments exacted by collection agents, the French kept their tinkering to the bare minimum needed to perpetuate the system.[23]

Traditionally, as noted in Chapter 3, the head tax was determined by the number of *registered* males living in the villages. It was then divided by the notables among *all* the male villagers, except those who had purchased or been awarded exemptions from the head tax. Although the unregistered were generally poorer than the registered and had fewer political and economic rights, all the nonexempt paid the same share of the head tax.[24]

With respect to head taxes, then, the French faced a three-class system: the exempt who formed a "veritable privileged class," the ordinary registered, and the unregistered. Accurate estimates are difficult to make, but based on the available data for Annam and Tonkin the exempt comprised about 12 percent of the population; the registered, 33 percent; and the unregistered, 55 percent.[25] It would be decades before the number of exempt was significantly reduced; although many old exemptions were removed, the French were faced with demands from new employees and village officials for the same exemptions that had been granted by the Nguyen dynasty.

During the colonial period, the French made several changes in their methods of tax assessment for the villages. But the weak relationship between their tax decrees and the collection procedures actually used in the villages underscores the problems facing any central government that attempts local reforms without changing the local power structure or organizing the population.

Throughout the entire colonial period in Annam and Tonkin, the French did not alter the principle of collective responsibility for

23. Vu van Hien, "Les Institutions annamites depuis l'arrivée des français: L'Impôt personnel et les corvées de 1862 à 1936," pp. 84–107.
24. Ibid., p. 89.
25. Ibid., pp. 94–95, 89, 106.

village taxes, both head and land. A tax bill was submitted to the notables in each village, and they were responsible for meeting the village quota.[26] At first, the French taxes were calculated for each village in the traditional manner. To calculate the head tax, the number of registered nonexempt was simply multiplied by the tax per person. The village notables then divided the total bill among all nonexempt, the unregistered as well as the registered. This system created serious problems. The continued granting and selling of exemptions resulted in a shrinking base, for one. Moreover, since the proportion of registered differed from village to village,[27] the high taxes threatened to crush villages lacking the connections needed to keep their registration figures low. In 1914, therefore, the French finally put an end to the practice of granting exemptions.

As colonial expenditures mounted, the French had two options for raising more money through the head tax. In addition to "raising" arbitrarily the official count of village population by a fixed percentage every few years, they had the choice either of increasing the levy on each registered person or of assessing the tax on the basis of both registered and unregistered villagers. In 1897–1898, the French chose to keep the tax rate at 2.5 piastres for each registered male inhabitant, but also to assess a tax of 0.4 piastres for each unregistered man.

At the same time that they initiated this dual system of tax calculation, they also introduced a system of tax receipts—giving a village only as many receipts as it had registered men. This tax-card system was instituted to give the French some control over attempts by villages to hide population without having to interfere directly in the villages. Tax cards could be checked whenever men were seen in a public area or on the highways or canals,[28] and those without cards were arrested.

The dual tax system did not operate as the French intended, however, for the poor did not pay less. Presumably, since the tax receipt indicated the amount each villager paid (0.4 or 2.5 piastres), the receipts would serve both as a check against hidden, unreported

26. Nguyen Huu Khang, *La Commune annamite: Étude historique, juridique et economique,* p. 146; Hien, "Les Institutions annamites," p. 107.
27. Gourou, *Les Paysans,* p. 174.
28. Hien, "Les Institutions annamites," p. 93.

population and as a protection against the poor being taxed as heavily as the rich. But the idea that the registered should always pay more than the unregistered was not acceptable to many of the former. Further, since the correspondence between being registered and being a member of a powerful, prestigious family was high, asking the registered to pay more than the unregistered challenged the realities of power. It was an unsuccessful challenge; even with a system of receipts designed to ensure proportional taxation, the rich and the poor paid the same tax. In some instances, taxes forced men to flee their villages; even then the equal-tax principle was enforced by the notables.[29]

There were, of course, complaints about the increased tax burden that this locally modified dual system represented. The consultative chambers in Annam and Tonkin sharply criticized the counting of both registered and unregistered in taxation procedures. These chambers were drawn from the elite population of the countryside, and they preferred to maintain the old system, which left more than half the population unregistered and therefore in a position with limited political and economic rights.[30] The elite did not prefer a system whereby village taxes were based on the number of registered just because it meant a lower total tax to be paid by each village: after all, instead of the dual system, the same amount of additional money could have been raised by increasing the single tax from 2.5 to 3 piastres. The idea of making everyone a legal taxpayer was perceived by the registered as a threat not only because it raised taxes, but also because it opened the possibility that the arbitrary curtailment of the rights of the unregistered might come to an end.

In practice, the use of tax receipts did not decrease the power of the village officials, nor did it force them to tax according to ability to pay. The use of receipts actually enhanced, rather than eroded, the power of village officials. As populations grew, especially in Tonkin, increasing numbers of landless and poor worked part of every year in other villages. These men desperately needed tax cards in order to engage in seasonal migration. As in the pre-French

29. Pham Cao Duong, *Thuc trang cua gioi nong dan Viet Nam duoi thoi Phap thuoc,* p. 148.
30. Hien, "Les Institutions annamites," p. 91.

period, to be without a tax card (that is, unregistered) and outside one's own village was to risk imprisonment.[31] In the earlier period, however, there was much less seasonal migration, so that now the need to have a tax card increased the hold of the notables over those peasants with less than a subsistence landholding. The poor could not complain if their card (receipt) read 0.4 piastres while they actually paid 1 piastre or more, because they were dependent on the card for survival.

The attempt to specify tax payments by decree worked so badly, in fact, that it was finally abandoned (in Tonkin in 1920 and Annam in 1928) for a head-tax system that taxed everyone at the same rate, which is what the notables had done anyway. The French were simply unable to make any impact on the notables' methods of distributing the head tax.[32]

If a poor peasant could not meet his taxes, his "share" was shifted to another member of his family. If no member of the family could pay, the notables still did not ask a larger payment from the rich. Instead, the delinquent taxpayer's possessions were auctioned off, then his family's possessions. If these measures failed, the peasant or one of his children would become enslaved to anyone willing to pay his tax. If there were so many poor that the village could not squeeze the money out of them by any means, then the same forms of brutal redistribution would be carried out by the mandarins. The mandarin would forcibly take possessions from the rich and auction them off; the rich would subsequently extract from the poor, in any way they could, what they considered the value of their lost possessions.

Similar procedures were used by both the French and the notables to collect land taxes. There were three major categories of rice fields in Annam and Tonkin (generally corresponding to two-crop irrigated fields, single-crop irrigated fields with a second dry crop, and single-crop irrigated fields, with no second crop). Total village land taxes were based on the prevailing rates for each type

---

31. Marcel Rouilly, *La Commune annamite*, pp. 69–70.

32. A concerted effort to introduce a graduated head tax was made again in 1937, when a popular front government in France pushed for more humane colonial policies. Even then, however, poor peasants generally paid as much as rich peasants.

of land and the total amount of each type in the village. When the French required more money, land taxes were raised by changing the rates, decreeing an increase in a village's total lands, or arbitrarily reclassifying and upgrading a portion of the third- or second-category land. Within the village, land taxes were then assessed by the notables, who had ample latitude in collecting the land tax. The result of the village procedures was regressive: the smaller a peasant's total holding, the higher, in general, was the tax per hectare that he paid.[33] Rural stratification increased because French changes in the level and form of taxes, in conjunction with village procedures for distributing the taxes, greatly added to the comparative advantage of the richer villagers. Given the lack of village procedures to cushion the burden for the poor, stratification was increased by the shift from taxes in kind to money, by the ratio of head and land taxes, and by the lack of flexibility in bad years (as well as by the total demand for taxes).

The pre-French head tax was a dual tax, approximately one-fifth of which was paid in rice and money (mostly rice) and the other four-fifths in corvée labor. The village elite, of course, never did any corvée labor, but sent poor villagers in their place. Fed while they worked, poor villagers at least got food they would not have received otherwise. When the obligatory corvée was changed to a money tax, there was an immediate increase of 500 percent in the demand for money. As French demands increased, the money portion of the head tax *rose* from 0.165 piastres per person (0.5 piastres on 33 percent of the population) in the 1880s, to 1.125 piastres per person in the 1890s, when corvée was replaced by money tax and exemptions were cut (2.5 piastres on 45 percent of population). It rose again to 1.35 piastres in 1897 (with an additional 0.4 piastre tax on the unregistered) and to 2.5 piastres per person in Tonkin in 1920 and in Annam in 1928.[34]

Stratification is affected not only by the total amount of taxes collected, but also by whether they are collected in kind or in money. This can be demonstrated by looking at examples from two

33. Yves Henry, *Economie agricole,* p. 36.
34. This estimate does not include the numerous local village taxes which were added on to the head tax, such as school taxes.

other countries where taxes were changed from kind to money without increasing the size of the tax. In 1873, the government of Japan ordered all farmers to pay their taxes in money rather than in kind. The household economy of many farm families promptly collapsed and small farmowners quickly became tenants.[35] The same effect was noted in India by a British colonial officer: "Our first act in a newly acquired district was to decree that the land revenue should henceforth be paid in coin. . . . The consequence of our ill-judged and precipitate action was a ruinous derangement of values. A pressing demand for specie glutted the markets with an immense quantity of produce which had to be sold for whatever it would bring."[36]

In Vietnam, as well, the immediate effects of the sudden change to money taxes were a glut of grain on the market and a dramatic fall in grain prices as desperate peasants sought to get the needed cash. Such a drastic change was of great benefit to exporters and well-to-do villagers, who already had sufficient cash to pay their own taxes and who could therefore use their reserves to profit from the cash shortages of their fellow villagers. This new tax system, then, fell heavily on the subsistence-level peasants, who lacked cash reserves.[37] The majority found themselves in a situation where they needed to sell their crops rapidly after each harvest in order to pay their taxes and loans. With millions of poor peasants bidding against one another for the urgently needed cash, prices fell drastically every year at harvest time, to the profit of intermediaries and affluent villagers.[38]

If all the demanded revenues had been collected by increasing only the land tax and leaving the head tax at a negligible level, the effects of the new money taxes on stratification would have been somewhat mitigated. As it was, the head tax became equal, in every region of Vietnam, to the amount of land taxes paid on a

35. Tadashi Fukutake, *Asian Rural Society,* p. 48.
36. Alan Beals, "Interplay among Factors of Change in a Mysore Village," McKim Marriott, ed., *Village India,* p. 85, quoting Major Evans Bell writing in 1885.
37. Pham Cao Duong, *Thuc trang,* p. 154; Hien, "Les Institutions annamites," p. 105.
38. Gregoire Kherian, "Les Méfaits de la surpopulation deltaique," pp. 476–505.

family-sized farm. This increased the comparative margin of richer farmers over their subsistence-level neighbors and gave further impetus to stratification.

French insensitivity to pleas for tax cuts in bad years was another source of stratification. In addition to the uncertainties of production they had always faced—drought, flood, locusts—the peasants were now forced to bear the added uncertainties of local markets and international demand for rice. In the past, an authoritarian but weak state had had to temper (at least some of the time) its tax demands in bad years and curtail its expenses according to whatever money it could collect. But now an authoritarian and powerful central government did not need to be sensitive to local conditions. Foreclosure, malnutrition, and the sale of children would at times be rampant before taxes were ever cut. In one typical case, exceptionally hard rains destroyed all the crops in part of Hung Yen province. To meet tax payments, peasants were forced to sell more than 15 percent of the land in the area at one-tenth its normal market value. Overnight, thousands of landowning peasants were turned into tenants, paying as much every year in rent as they had received for the sale of their land.[39]

Village Governance and Stratification

The development of a strong and rapacious administration in Annam and Tonkin did not *undermine* the village power structure by taking away the fiscal latitude of the villages (and thus precluding intravillage attempts to soften the impact of French taxes on the poor); rather, bureaucratic development *strengthened* the village power structure. Village officials collected all taxes; they issued birth, death, and marriage certificates; they certified loans, contracts, and land sales; and they determined which men would be sent to the army and which to the disease-ridden, low-paying plantations in the highlands.

The French passed numerous laws intended to control local budgets. These laws, however, were never applied to the vast majority of villages, and supervision was confined to villages with very large budgets or with more than 2,000 inhabitants (500 regis-

39. Gourou, *Les Paysans,* p. 363.

tered males).[40] This means that over 85 percent of the village budgets in Tonkin were never checked in other than cursory fashion, and that there was no supervision at all in Annam. In fact, well after budgetary reforms had supposedly brought village budgets under strict control, Dumont found that the effect of the French administration on the affairs of the village was "very feeble." [41] French policies did not preclude village adaptations which would have protected the poor. There was latitude, but the policies adopted within villages did not protect the poor or equalize burdens.

The fiscal latitude of the notables is clearly demonstrated by the communal land practices during the colonial period. In Tonkin, and even more so in Annam, the distribution of communal lands was left entirely to village custom. The notables showed a marked ability (and willingness) to reap personal profit from communal lands and a marked inability (or unwillingness) to adapt to the changed conditions.

Large portions of communal land had always been used to finance village activities, and as much as 60 percent of the communal land was auctioned off by the notables. By parceling the land to be rented in large lots and requiring rental payment in advance, they excluded the majority of villagers from the bidding:

> The rental-fee, which is established at a ridiculously low rate, profits both the notables and the bidders. The price is presented to the notables, who are eager to pocket a large share of it and then turn over a minimal amount to the communal coffer. . . . The result of these practices is that the poor peasant, neither a notable nor of any rank, finds himself reduced to a small allotment that he must put under obligation to a usuror or that he must offer in payment for a debt.[42]

This system was both regressive—helping the rich more than the poor—and inefficient—raising less money for the village than if smaller lots had been auctioned off. As Nguyen Huu Khang noted in Annam, the notables had a great deal of latitude and were not concerned with aiding the poor:

40. Rouilly, *La Commune annamite*, pp. 140–141.
41. René Dumont, *La Culture du riz dansle delta du Tonkin*, pp. 78–81.
42. Gourou, *Les Paysans*, p. 370; Dumont, *La Culture du riz*, pp. 77–81.

The poor people have no possibility whatsoever of expression or point of view in the matter, which is neither fair nor democratic and which can bring on certain social problems resulting from the tendency of land-owning notables to direct communal affairs and carry out the distribution of "Cong Dien" [communal land] favoring the interest of their own social class and its members.[43]

At the same time, the notables were inflexible about adapting the communal land process to changing conditions. Many of the poor were forced to work outside the village, in factories or mines, to help support their families, but women were not allotted communal land in their husband's absence. Even more striking in a period of severe hunger and poverty was the fact that few villages adapted communal rotation to make the communal land more productive. Communal land was less productive than private land because peasants who worked a piece of land on a three-year basis knew that if they developed the land to improve its yield, a notable would take the lot at the next drawing.[44] If everyone in the village had agreed simultaneously to improve his communal share, this problem would have been solved, but the level of trust and the quality of leadership needed for such long-run undertakings were seldom present. Only in a few villages were communal land patterns ever adapted to increase their productivity.[45]

In some villages extensive attempts were made to rectify the inequities of the land tax system. Persons with the most unfair tax burden—such as a man with third-category land in a village where

43. Khang, *La Commune annamite*, p. 54.
44. Dumont, *La Culture du riz*, pp. 77–81.
45. That the uses and abuses of communal lands reported in the corporate villages of Annam and Tonkin indicate more the limits of ascriptive rule by a self-selected group than the toll of colonial decay may be further emphasized by a comparison with the corporate management of communal lands by Chinese clan (corporate family) leaders in the villages of the New Territories of Hong Kong. Studying the rental of clan lands, Potter found that the leaders were usually more interested in the side payments of "black money" they exacted from their tenants than in maximizing group income, and that their accountability was limited; "since the land belongs to everyone, no one pays much attention to its management." There were rigid rules about the use of the clan lands due not to reverence for the traditional way of doing things, but to the fact that individuals and groups within the clan were "so suspicious of each other and so fearful that other members of the group [would] somehow reap advantages from new arrangements, that cooperation and hence innovation [were] not possible" (Jack Potter, *Capitalism and the Chinese Peasant: Social and Economic Change in a Hong Kong Village*, p. 116).

the French had decreed all land to be first-category land—were to be compensated in the communal land distribution. Villagers who paid the most out-of-line land taxes were to choose the best pieces of communal land. This proved, however, to be only a temporary remedy and was ultimately unsuccessful. Disagreements over the allocation forced the villages to revert to the old ranking system.[46] Encouraged by the French, some villages developed village granaries to provide low interest loans of rice. This institution, which required the concentration of rice in the hands of the notables, did not prosper due to widespread "abuse."[47]

In such circumstances, and in the context of heavy and constant taxation, French efforts to protect the small farmer were of marginal value at best. The traditional protections against landlessness worked no better than they had in the past. Peasants still borrowed money through the *dien mai,* a provisional land sale that guaranteed the right of repurchase within thirty years and left the former landowner as the tenant. But peasants forced to pay the prevailing land rentals would never again see the title to their land. In addition, the French laws limiting interest rates were unenforceable. Countless statutes limited the legal interest rate, but they had no more value than did the same statutes in pre-French Vietnam, when the maximum legal interest rate was 3 percent. The ruses for circumventing the earlier laws continued to be used under the French: most simply, for example, a creditor would require the debtor to sign a note for more money than he actually received.[48] The attempts to stop debt slavery were no more successful. Laws forbidding the traditional practice of giving offspring to moneylenders as repayment for debts were unworkable and never enforced; survival of the family often required the giving of daughters as concubines and sons as slaves as the only alternative to the complete breakup of the family.[49]

46. Vo Nguyen Giap and Truong Chinh, *The Peasant Question,* p. 49. Some villages, however, had communal land planted in mulberry trees, which might have been· an adaptation designed to raise the productivity of communal land.

47. Vu Quoc Thuc, *L'Economie communaliste du Vietnam,* pp. 113.

48. Paul Ory, *La Commune annamite au Tonkin,* pp. 119–121. Usury, however, was not the cause of low productivity; it was the result. Peasants paid high interest rates because there was a high seasonal demand for credit and a high default rate on loans, and because small loans had high administrative costs. (See Robert Sansom, *The Economics of Insurgency in the Mekong Delta of Vietnam,* pp. 104–105.)

49. Gourou, *Les Paysans,* p. 379; Dumont, *La Culture du riz,* p. 68.

The French credit programs, some of which were designed to maintain land ownership by small peasants, merely exacerbated the growing inequality. The only men who were ever able to borrow from Crédit Agricole and other programs were large landholders. They, in turn, lent the money to poor peasants who needed it for consumption, not investment. The rich ultimately used all the credit schemes designed to help the poor to turn them into tenants. The collateral loan programs were crucial in helping the French collect a steady flow of taxes; in doing so, they also helped increase the rate at which inequality grew in the countryside.[50]

As previously noted, smallholders paid more taxes per hectare than large landowners. Furthermore, peasants without clear legal title to their lands were at a distinct economic disadvantage when they had to borrow money to survive during bad years—without clear title they could borrow money only through the notables, who were in a position to extract large profits for certifying loans.

Agrarian Relations and Stratification

In spite of increasing poverty, however, there was no mass exodus from their villages, for the peasants could not afford to migrate and hence had to cope as best they could within their native villages.[51] With migration from Tonkin (and Annam) to Cochinchina blocked by the French, there was no place to go: "It is not so much that they [peasants] are attached to the tomb of their dead, to the pagoda and the bamboo hedge of their village or to their share of communal lands. . . . It is simply that their material and physiological poverty does not enable them to go elsewhere."[52] Prevented from migrating permanently, peasants attempted to cope with their declining situation through seasonal, short-term migration, sometimes by laboring in the few mines and mills, but mainly by working in villages in other parts of Tonkin. They developed regular, long-term ties to particular factories or villages in other

50. René Dumont, *Types of Rural Economy: Studies in World Agriculture*, p. 132; Gourou, *Les Paysans*, pp. 364, 380; Vu Quoc Thuc, *L'Economie communaliste du Vietnam*, p. 107.
51. Gourou, *Les Paysans*, p. 200.
52. Tran van Thong, "Memoire sur la colonisation indigène en Indochine," p. 1118.

areas of the delta where planting and harvesting were done at different times.[53]

This regular migration became an institutionalized aspect of peasant families' attempts to subsist in a situation of limited opportunities. In some industrial areas, the workers even lived together by village of origin.[54] In some provinces where the second crop was not rice, peasants abandoned their second crop entirely and migrated annually to areas where additional labor applied to the planting and harvesting of rice was more remunerative than their own dry second crop.[55] Small groups of men and women moving through the delta became an increasingly common sight, and at least 30 percent of the population of some of the older, denser provinces migrated seasonally.[56]

However, all the sources of additional income—factory work, service in the army, work on the disease-ridden rubber plantations in the south, seasonal migration, and cottage industries—could not meet the crush of population growth and tax demands. Although there are no reliable production and land statistics available for pre-French Vietnam, there is no reason to doubt that economic stratification was increasing and, furthermore, that the living standard of most peasants in Tonkin was declining.

With the "emergence of huge landholdings" in Tonkin, particularly in the poorer areas of the delta, there were "increasing contrasts in landed wealth."[57] This concentration of land did not occur because peasants sold their land to move on to better opportunities elsewhere. The majority of land sales were debt settlements by smallholders faced with a bad crop or a family disaster.[58] Indeed, throughout the colonial period there was a steadily increasing pauperism in the countryside, as well as huge, sudden "enslavements" in such periods as 1931–1932, when exports dropped and added market uncertainty to the whims of nature.[59] Colonial rule and development did not simply bring wealth to a few in Tonkin

53. Gourou, *Les Paysans,* pp. 214–223.
54. Ibid., pp. 216–217.
55. Gourou, *Land Utilization,* p. 294.
56. Gourou, *Les Paysans,* pp. 222–223.
57. Charles Robequain, *The Economic Development of French Indochina,* p. 82.
58. Gourou, *Les Paysans,* pp. 396–397.
59. Thuc, *L'Economie communaliste,* pp. 196–197, 201–202.

and Annam; they brought wealth at the expense of the majority of the peasants—the "rich got richer" *and* "the poor got poorer."[60]

French official writings perpetuated the fiction that Tonkin was a land of smallholding peasants, 90 percent of whose landholdings were less than 1.8 hectares, the maximum that could be cultivated without the steady use of hired labor.[61] Although the figures are accurate, the statement implies that Tonkin continued to be a land dominated by small farmers. But when Yves Henry compiled his work in 1931–1932, there was already a large landless class in Tonkin: at least 20 percent of peasant households owned no land whatsoever.[62] Although Henry's work is the basis for all discussion of landholding in Vietnam, it seriously underrepresents the extent of large holdings. Holdings scattered over more than one village (a phenomenon discussed further on) were recorded as holdings of separate individuals.[63] Also serving to keep the large holdings underreported was the fact that peasants who lost their land as a debt settlement were still recorded as legal owners until the terms of their "right of repurchase" had expired. In one province, for example, 253 owners were listed as owning 10,000 hectares; the same 253 also controlled another 15,000 hectares whose former owners had, in fact, become tenants, but who were still listed as owners.[64] In addition, land owned by absentee owners was often registered in the name of a villager who paid the taxes on the land. Henry's figures are therefore a conservative reflection of conditions in Tonkin *before* the huge increase in stratification brought on by the international depression. As a conservative estimate of the predepression situation, at least 70 percent of the households in Tonkin in the 1920s did not have enough land to support a family of five persons. Furthermore, the 93 percent of the peasants who together comprised the landless, the dwarf holdings, and the peasants in the subsistence range owned less than one-third of all land in Tonkin. By 1930, then, less than 7 percent of the families in Tonkin directly

60. Dumont, *La Culture du riz,* p. 45.

61. Yves Henry, *Economie agricole de l'Indochine.*

62. Thuc, *L'Economie communaliste,* p. 72; Nguyen van Vinh, *Les Reformes agraires au Vietnam,* p. 32.

63. Henry, *Economie agricole,* p. 112.

64. Gourou, *Land Utilization,* p. 281; although written much later, this is clearly from Henry's data.

controlled at least half of all land or 60 percent of private land in the region.[65]

The increased stratification in landholdings brought a shift in interclass and intraclass relations. Coupled with a steadily growing population, the growing intraclass competition among the poor greatly increased the bargaining power of landowners. In Tonkin, the landlord was king, and the poor fought among themselves to become his tenants; to be taken on as a tenant was considered a great favor.[66] The landlord's share of the harvest increased and, importantly, sharecropping was superseded by renting.[67]

In the past, sharecropping had been the dominant form of tenancy throughout Tonkin, and renting had been virtually unknown. Under the sharecropping system, landlord and tenant shared production expenses and risks. In a bad year, the landlord would take a share of the crop smaller than his usual 50 percent. The change to renting was a direct result of the large size of holdings and the competition among the landless to be tenants. A renter owed the landlord a fixed amount of rice, regardless of the yield. This system particularly benefited large landlords (those with more than five or ten tenants), who were relieved of the need to personally supervise tenants. Sharecropping required trust and a long-standing relationship between landlord and tenant; it was only for relatives, friends, or people to whom the landlord felt personally obligated.[68]

On large holdings, the introduction of intermediary agents into the landlord-tenant relationship made the situation worse. These

65. By adjusting Nguyen van Vinh's figures (*Les Réformes agraires,* p. 24) to account for the families holding no land, we have the proportion of households as landless, 20 percent; less than 0.36 hectare, 49 percent; 0.36–1.8 hectares, 24 percent; 1.8–5.4 hectares, 5.9 percent; 5.4–18 hectares, 1 percent; 18–36 hectares, 0.64 percent; 36 + hectares, 0.16 percent. (See also Henry, *Economie agricole,* pp. 108–109.) I used Henry's data on the number of holdings having tenants and then used Gourou's observations on what size holdings employed hired labor to make different breaks between categories than did Henry: holdings under 1.8 hectares generally used only family labor; 1.8–5.4 hectares used family labor and hired laborers; above 5.4 hectares employed tenants. While some of the landless households were nonagricultural, it is still certain that these are conservative figures because many of the households in the 0.36–1.8 hectare category would still be under 1 hectare.

66. Dumont, *Types of Rural Economy,* p. 130; Vu Quoc Thuc, *L'Economie communaliste,* p. 77.

67. Gourou, *Les Paysans,* p. 376; Dumont, *La Culture du riz,* pp. 54–57.

68. Nguyen van Vinh, *Les Réformes agraires,* p. 27.

agents, remembered to this day with hatred throughout Vietnam, became an additional source of hardship to the tenants as they used their position to profit at the expense of both tenant and landlord. Tenants had always owed deference, gifts, and labor to landowners; now their agents sought and obtained the same deference and exactions.[69]

Thus, both the shift from sharecropping to renting and the increased size of large holdings worsened the status of the tenants. In fact, since a man consumed only half as much food as a water buffalo, the use of water buffalo continuously declined until buffalo were used only for ploughing, while men in harness did the harrowing.[70]

There were now three distinct classes of laborers identifiable in Tonkin—those hired by the year, the season, or the day—and the intense competition among them and their often desperate straits were reflected in the agricultural practices. Along all the paths through their fields, peasants planted early-maturing rice. They could harvest this rice alone and thus prevent laborers who used their paths at harvest times from grabbing handfuls for themselves.[71] Furthermore, the actual harvest process was divided into several stages, for cutting the entire rice stalk at once meant the exposure of large sheaves at night and inevitable theft when food was scarce. Instead, the ears and tops of the stalks—used for fodder—were cut first with a knife and brought into the house. Later, the bottom half of the stalk was harvested for use as fuel; when fuel was scarce even the tufts were uprooted. Blind people were often hired to do the polishing of the rice—they would work at half the standard rate.[72] At times landowners, in need of adequate fertilizer, would use edible vegetable matter. On such occasions, Dumont even saw cinders mixed with the fertilizer to prevent the laborers from eating it![73]

At times the wage for laborers consisted solely of a day's food. In 1929, Dumont witnessed a fight between a landlord and laborers

69. Dumont, *La Culture du riz,* pp. 54–57.
70. Gourou, *Les Paysans,* p. 241; also, *Land Utilization,* pp. 428–431.
71. Gourou, *Les Paysan,* p. 389.
72. Dumont, *Types of Rural Economy,* pp. 145, 137.
73. Ibid., p. 146.

so paid. The men claimed the right to share their evening meal with their families, whereas the farmer argued that if they did not eat the meal themselves, they would be less able to work the next day. The farmer, however, had to give way, for "custom does not allow a man to be forbidden from denying himself for the sake of his family."[74]

Increasingly, poor peasants supplemented rice with less desirable foods, such as sweet potatoes and manioc. In some areas the entire rice crop went to landlords, while the tenants lived on a dry second crop of these less palatable foods. (While all Tonkin grew two crops, only half the land supported two rice crops.)[75] Rats, pond fish, and bugs accounted for 5 percent of the calories of most peasants and cereal grains, 95 percent; meat was seldom seen.[76] People were in tighter competition with animals for food and work than in China: whereas in China only 85 percent of cereal and grain production went for human consumption, in Tonkin 97 percent of all cereals and grains were consumed by humans.[77] Thus, many had no food reserves. In times of flood or drought, bands of needy wandered the countryside in search of food and often raided other people's lands. Such raids were especially prevalent at the approach of the new year and its incumbent ceremonies.[78]

Village Elections

Although the Tonkin village reforms of 1921 are often blamed for the problems of the peasants, the reforms were attempted after, not before, the existence of abusive practices because the old village system was performing so badly—from the French point of view. Single families or small groups, often in alliance with mandarins, were gaining increasing control of villages and using their power to the detriment of the poor. The population was suffering

74. Ibid., p. 142.
75. Dumont, *La Culture du riz*, p. 57.
76. Dumont, *Types of Rural Economy*, p. 143.
77. Ibid., p. 148.
78. Robequain, *Economic Development of French Indochina*, pp. 327–328; Hickey, *Social Systems of Northern Vietnam*, p. 43; Phan thi Dac, *Situation de la personne au Vietnam*, p. 28.

from the "uncontrollable liberty of notables" who took advantage of new taxes and regulations to exploit the other villagers.[79]

The village reforms of 1921 abolished the legal rights of the council of notables and substituted an administrative council *(toc bieu)* that was responsible for communal land, a regular village budget, taxes, village laws, and selection of the village chief. The selection process for the new council was designed to ensure a balance of power within the village and thus to provide a check against domination by a few families for personal advantage. Instead of an at-large selection process, representatives were selected for every twenty-five adult males (registered). Villagers met in groups of twenty-five (males), and each group, either an extended family or a neighborhood, selected one man to represent it on the council. The council members then allocated the specific positions among themselves.

The introduction of elections, as noted, has been blamed for instability and conflict within the villages. In fact, however, the elections caused no trouble where none had existed earlier. If villagers had either been united in support of the old notables' authority or if they had not been receptive to change, there would have been little instability. Elections were introduced chiefly as an option, to resolve tensions. The colonial administration did not expect that true formal elections would be the rule. It was assumed that most council members would be selected on a conventional, informal basis. Only if agreement could not be reached were elections anticipated. In the very rare cases where even elections could not produce an accepted verdict, the reforms left it up to the mandarins to serve as arbitrators. In practice, however, severe political struggles were so common that elections became the norm, and outside arbitration was sometimes necessary.[80]

Clearly, the traditional senior notables could not deign to sit on

79. Rouilly, *La Commune annamite,* pp. 136, 144–145; Lam Le Trinh, "Village Councils—Yesterday and Today"; Paul Kresser, *La Commune annamite en Cochinchine,* p. 126; H. G., "L'Evolution des institutions communales au Tonkin," pp. 246, 256; by far the most perceptive article is by the anonymous H. G.

80. Kresser, *La Commune annamite,* pp. 127–128; Toan Anh, *Nep cu Lang xom Viet Nam,* pp. 109–112.

this new council. For one thing, it was to be a working administrative council that would handle bureaucratic clerical duties for the central administration: it was not appropriate for older, successful men to perform such work and to be subject to harassment or intimidation by mandarins. For another, their role, which they saw as that of a moral tribune sitting in final judgment on village disputes, was sanctified by their control of the customary and *dinh*. Although there was intense competition for membership on the old council, it was covert and based (in belief, if not in practice) on virtue and prestige, not on promises or mass electioneering. For men who had previously been ratified by elite cooptation, joining the new council meant having to ask for legitimacy from the masses and to risk losing, or debasing, their hard-won rankings.[81] In theory, of course, they could have used their "superior virtue and wisdom" to suggest to families and neighborhoods "appropriate" choices for the new council—after which, they could have proceeded as if nothing had changed. But there was sufficient receptivity to change by enough families in the village to negate this strategy. The notables could control their own families and their tenants, but they could not prevent well-to-do but previously excluded families from organizing among themselves to seek control of the new councils.[82]

Taking any direct part in the new system, then, even placing sons or tenants on the new council, meant accepting these "new" families into the village power circle. It was better to stay completely away from the new council and, by secretly undermining its proceedings, force a return to the old customary. Thus would they preserve the traditional ranking system and their own privileges: "In every village there are richer and poorer families, some with more or less prestige; previously only the big and prestigious families would have members who participated in village affairs. Now every family has its representative and [the notables] have not yet overcome their class prejudice and are afraid of losing face if rich and poor families work together."[83]

Predictably, the new administrative council members squabbled

81. H. G., "L'Evolution des Institutions Communales," p. 248; Dao Duy Anh, *Viet Nam van hoa su cuong*, p. 135.

82. Tran Duy Nhat, "Ban ve huong chinh xu Bac Ky," p. 362.

83. Do Thanh, "Cai luong huong chinh," pp. 219–220.

viciously over titles and prerogatives, misappropriated communal land, created new (and useless) salaried posts within the village, and used the money in the treasury for private business, replacing it only when an official inspection was imminent.[84] The new council was never able to develop new procedures for distributing village resources, and the old customary retained its position. Without careful preparation, suddenly to invite villagers to look anew at their procedures, to give a council the actual power to revise communal procedures, was to invite chaos.

The old notables did not win a complete victory, but they did keep almost all their original powers. Reversing their earlier position, they recouped by placing sons and tenants on the council in the next election. Realizing, however, that there were families who could no longer be dominated, they made room in their calculations for the *nouveau riche* who demanded recognition. The mixture perpetuated the conflict, however, and in 1927 the senior notables were again recognized by law and granted veto power over decisions of the administrative council. Once again, the village was run by the old notables, who used their official veto power and their control of the *dinh* and the customary to force the administrative council to choose between submitting to them or launching an open, villagewide struggle in which all would suffer.[85] The French reforms did give somewhat better representation in the village to the *nouveau riche* families, but the reforms did not succeed in correcting the basic *inequities* within the village, and the two village power centers remained the village chief and the head notable.[86]

Intraelite Conflict

The willingness of so many members of the village elite to use outside connections or colonial laws in village power struggles during the colonial period merely exacerbated existing tensions and cleavages. Only in a context of less than total loyalty to village norms and procedures could the many changes that occurred outside the village have had such great impact on the internal power struggles and procedures of the villages in Tonkin and Annam. If con-

84. Ibid., pp. 220–222.
85. H. G., "L'Evolution des institutions communales," pp. 251–252.
86. Ibid., p. 251.

sensus had truly prevailed within the villages, there would have been far more opportunity for the notables and village chief to deflect the impacts—both official and private—of the colonial bureaucracy.

The village chief was not intended to be an independent source of power, but merely the executor of decisions made by the notables. As the link between the village and the colonial bureaucracy, however, he was given the increased load of duties associated with new and heavier tax collection, military drafts, land registrations, land sales, and the notarization of loans. These added responsibilities and outside contacts put considerable potential power in the hands of any village chief who did not feel bound by respect for the village notables, or who (more commonly) was part of a clique, faction, or family struggling for ascendancy within the council of notables.

Whenever there was a power struggle within the council, serious conflict could arise over the way in which the village chief shared the profits from manipulating the tax rolls and rigging the bidding on communal land. Ideally, the head notable, or *tien chi,* was the most important man in the village. Moderating among the other notables, he was responsible for keeping peace among them and thus avoiding village disruption from intraelite conflicts. To keep peace, I hypothesize, it was necessary for the village chief, with his immediate access to so much power and profit, to give a "fair share" to all the notables. If notables could not agree on how to rig the bidding for communal land, for example, open competitive bidding could result at the expense of the notables' private profits. It is not surprising, given the problems of coordination involved and the vastly increased opportunities to use outside contacts and to invoke outside procedures, that the village chief eventually became a second center of power in the village. In fact, he or the group he represented often became the primary center of power.[87]

Intraelite conflict within the villages, and the willingness of villagers to involve outside courts and bureaucrats in their internal struggles, were the primary means the French had to obtain knowl-

87. Gourou, *Les Paysans,* pp. 266–267; Thuc, *L'Economie communaliste,* pp. 106–107; Dao Duy Anh, *Vietnam van hoa su cuong,* pp. 134–135.

edge about village procedures. As Gourou found, it was not through censuses or official inquiries that the French kept their tax lists updated and their revenues flowing in from the villages. The colonial bureaucracy, swollen and inflated as it was, was concentrated in the cities and almost never penetrated the countryside. After the early, arbitrary raising of village censuses by fiat, what kept the tax lists as accurate as they were, (generally within 10 to 15 percent of the true population figure) were "denunciations," for the colonial government was not strong enough to compel accurate information on a regular basis from the villages. Virtually the only sources of information for the bureaucracy were discordant village factions secretly jockeying for power and willing to denounce a village chief for keeping men off the tax rolls.[88] Denouncing the village chief meant increasing the total tax bill for the village, but it also gave a temporary advantage to any one group.

Such intraelite conflicts, along with the increased powers of the bureaucrats under the colonial regime, were essential to the emergence of large multivillage landholdings, where one man owned land in several villages. Such ownership had been impossible previously.

There was always some opposition to control of land by outsiders, because a powerful outsider was a threat to the collective welfare of a village in two ways. First, since total land taxes were assessed on the village as a whole and then divided up within the village, an influential landowner could exert pressure to have his land taxed at a rate lower than that applied to other smaller holdings. Second, a powerful outsider coming into the village had an advantage in fighting for a share of communal land and water, and in competing for land where it was scarce.

Thus, there were powerful economic reasons for the notables to close ranks and to use all means at their disposal to prevent outside landowners from gaining a foothold in their village. Throughout the colonial period and regardless of loan papers, mortgages, or legal claims, *as long as the notables and village chief were united in their opposition* it was virtually impossible for an outsider to claim the land. If he succeeded in claiming the land, he would be unable

88. Gourou, *Les Paysans*, p. 36.

to profit from it and would soon have to resell it to someone in the village:

A person exposes himself to crude disappointment if he buys land in a commune in which he was not born. The villagers band together to prevent the dispossession of one of their fellow villagers. The buyer will be expected to take the seller as his farmer, and will be obliged to put up with his shortcomings; he will find no other farmer if he wishes to make a change. He has to pay two or three times as much as the inhabitants of the village for protection. If his harvest is pillaged, the communal authorities will exhibit extreme ineptitude in discovering the culprit.[89]

The problem of preventing outsiders from claiming land in a village had all the aspects of a classical "prisoner's dilemma." As long as no one among the elite broke solidarity and allied himself with an outsider, the notables as a group had a larger pie to share among themselves. Any one notable who broke ranks, however, could make a profit for himself at the expense of the village.

In this context, the increased powers of the mandarins under the French became crucial to formation of large landholdings in Annam and Tonkin. Two necessary factors for an outsider to control land in a village were the support of the village chief and the complicity of the mandarin in whose jurisdiction the village lay. Without such complicity, the support of the village chief was not sufficient to overcome the opposition of other villagers; only the mandarin could overrule their complaints or trump up charges against them. In fact, the large landholdings that emerged in Tonkin and Annam were all of mandarin origin. Only a mandarin, his wife, or friends could muster the support necessary to thwart local opposition.[90]

This same dynamic—where group and individual incentives so clearly clash—also explains, incidentally, why corporate villages, by reacting *en masse* to a new situation, can change so suddenly. This characteristic is demonstrated by the conversion of entire villages to Catholicism; it also explains why it was rare for a village in Tonkin or Annam to be only partly Catholic. To Virginia Thompson, it seemed that "whole villages had to turn Catholic to avoid the moral and physical isolation that [an] individual conver-

89. Ibid., pp. 360–361.   90. Ibid., pp. 360–362.

sion entailed.''[91] She was observing the same juxtaposition of individual and group incentives that gave the mandarins their footholds in villages and allowed them to create their vast landholdings. Any notable who converted to Catholicism had access, through the Church, to the priest's support against abuse within the village or the bureaucracy. Although many anticlerical colonists were hostile to the Church (every convert was "a citizen lost to his country and a laborer lost to the colony"),[92] the Church had an organization that could oppose the worst excesses of the mandarins and function as a powerful ally for any notable who would convert. Thus, as soon as a notable converted, he had an advantage over the others in the village. To nullify his advantage, the other notables were likely to follow his example quickly: thus, the chain reaction so common to corporate villages.

The Mandarins

During the colonial period, mandarin greed (or the greed of their bureaucratic successors) flourished as the ability of villagers to achieve any kind of redress diminished. In the past, when a local mandarin sought to manipulate a village for gain or to ally with one group of villagers against another, aggrieved villagers could address memorials to the throne or, more vividly, pile excrement around the mandarin's residence or burn his house.[93] Beyond that, the weak power base of the mandarin often meant that a village could march against him in peaceful protest or attack him in a minirebellion. The changing balance of power in the country made these "avenues of redress" meaningless. Just as the increasing power of the government led to insensitivity to pleas for tax forgiveness in bad harvest years, so the government became less attuned to local complaints about bad mandarins. This made it possible, in the words of Phan Chu Trinh, for corrupt and venal mandarins "to use their public offices as marketplaces, to regard the people as morsels to be eaten.''[94]

91. Thompson, *French Indochina,* p. 472. In villages with more than one hamlet, the conversion was sometimes limited to a single hamlet; this may have reflected power struggles among hamlets.
92. Ibid., p. 275. 93. Dumont, *Types of Rural Economy,* p. 130.
94. Marr, *Vietnamese Anti-Colonialism,* p. 162.

In 1906, Trinh, the most brillant and articulate Vietnamese critic of colonialism and of the weaknesses of traditional Vietnam, wrote a letter to the governor-general highlighting new power relations within the government and indicating how they made possible the mandarins' "terrible parasitism."[95] Before the French arrived, Trinh explained, the Court had been able to establish at least some bounds of discretion within which the local mandarins were forced to operate. The system was not "fair," he pointed out, but at least it had prevented "wide-open pillaging." Now there was an emasculated Court controlled by the French, who had no understanding of what many mandarins and bureaucrats were doing to the villages they controlled. Local notables trying to block abuses by a village faction that was either allied with a mandarin or taking advantage of the mandarins' lack of concern for village affairs could not appeal to the French for aid. The French—no matter what their intentions—demeaned the notables and did not listen to their complaints:

The French have been in Vietnam for some time, have seen the greediness of the mandarins, the ignorance of the people, the corruption of the culture, and have concluded, sneeringly, that the Vietnamese have no sense of national identity. . . . They all show dislike and disdain for Vietnamese, considering them savages . . . unwilling to let them become equals. . . . Local gentry in the villages, walking alone and unexpectedly meeting a Frenchman, be he French official, French soldier, or French merchant, must bow their heads, droop their ears and quicken their pace—simply afraid of being disgraced.[96]

Whenever a group of notables dared to communicate their problems to the French, the local mandarins exploited the French fear of rebellion for their own advantage. Oppressing the peasants and suppressing the notables who tried to preserve a semblance of order and justice, the corrupt mandarins "spoke to French officials in purposefully vague terms about possible uprisings and then managed to frame their enemies or prevent meetings and honest communications on vital issues."[97] Twenty years after Trinh's letter, conditions had not improved. In 1928, another mandarin complained to a French journalist: "There is no more inhibition. In the

95. Ibid., pp. 159–163.   96. Ibid., p. 161.   97. Ibid., p. 162.

past the mandarins kept to themselves on these practices. Now, as soon as they get together, the mandarins discuss the topic openly, priding among themselves on their extortions and exactions with pleasure . . . because they feel that now France must bear the blame."[98]

The incompleteness of official population and land registers was thus a great boon to the mandarins and their bureaucratic successors. Great profits could be made when bargaining with villages to keep their taxes low.[99] With the profits they could accumulate land, and since the registers were inaccurate, they were then able to hide their holdings. Indeed, it is likely that few persons in Tonkin knew that any of the land in their villages had passed into outside ownership. Village chiefs or notables could front for outsiders, and no one in the village could ever be certain of the source of their money.

Annam

Basing their interpretations on the events of Tonkin, many analysts have stressed the effect of colonial administrative decrees on the village.[100] These studies strongly imply that had the village been left to follow its traditional ways, there would have been no problems of rural administration.

But there is reason to suggest that factors other than colonial policy affected village conditions in Tonkin. It might be argued, for example, that the extraordinary increase in land stratification was the result of "demographic exhaustion," rather than of taxes of self-interested notables. Indeed, since the seventeenth century, travelers to Asia had been writing about overcrowded conditions in the Tonkin delta.[101] Although Tonkin appears on the map to be a

98. Paul Monet, *Français et annamites entre deux feux*, pp. 215–216.

99. With respect to the tax rolls, for example, Gourou found that there was "no way of concealing that the French Administration has never made a serious attempt to mount a real census undertaking" (*Les Paysans*, pp. 176–177). He discovered that villages had a cushion of at least 5 to 15 percent due to underregistration, and that notables were able to connive with local bureaucrats at every step of the ladder to reduce the village count (ibid., pp. 174–175).

100. See, for example, McAlister and Mus, *The Vietnamese and Their Revolution;* McAlister, *Vietnam;* Fitzgerald, *Fire in the Lake;* Truong Buu Lam, "The Vietnamese Village"; and Nghiem Dang, *Vietnam.*

101. Gourou, *Land Utilization*, p. 174.

relatively large area, at least 90 percent of it is taken up by the malarial highlands and populated only by Montagnards. The actual delta area of Tonkin is only 15,000 square kilometers (about 6,000 square miles). By the 1930s, the only period for which statistics are reliable, this delta was the home of more than 7.5 million persons. The overall density of this area was 500 per square kilometer; in the oldest settlements there was a density of almost 800 per square kilometer, and in some districts the density reached more than 1,600 per square kilometer. At the time, Tonkin was one of the "most densely populated agricultural areas in the world."[102] Due to centuries of equal partition, there were at least 16 million separate plots of land in the Tonkin delta, averaging 0.075 hectares in size.[103] The lands of Tonkin were so subdivided that the tiny banks between parcels actually accounted for 3 percent of all agricultural land.[104]

Perhaps, then, when we look at Tonkin, we are examining a pathology: a decline and decay of corporatism due to sheer lack of land and resources. Both the administrative argument and the demographic argument can be tested by looking at central Annam, for the Annam experience indicates that the manipulations of village notables—and not French "meddling" alone—were an essential part of the dramatic increase in land stratification that occurred during the colonial period.

Except for northern Annam (particularly Nghe An and Ha Tinh), where climatic, water, and soil conditions had always made life uncertain and where population density was high, life for most peasants was never so harsh in Annam as in Tonkin. For the 250 years of warring dynasties, northern Annam and Tonkin were cut off from easily accessible new lands; the rest of Annam, however, had slowly been able to send population south. Densities, therefore, were not so extreme in Annam, particularly in the center. In most of the region, the marginal riceland, uncultivated in easier times when migration had been a more attractive alternative, was put into production as population grew.

102. Colin Clark and Margaret Haswell, *The Economics of Subsistence Agriculture*, p. 121.
103. Thuc, *L'Economie communaliste*, p. 74.
104. Gourou, *Les Paysans*, p. 351.

The population was divided into small coastal pockets between the Annamite mountain chains and the sea. The mountains provided easy access to wood, medicinal herbs, and rattan, all of which could be sold during times of crop failure, as well as roots, which could be eaten.[105] The mountains and hills provided natural shelter for domestic animals as well as good forage for oxen and water buffalo. The nearby sea was a source of black-market salt, so that the salt monopoly was never so painful in Annam as elsewhere. In Tonkin, intensification of cultivation techniques had reached the point where traditional work exchange relations among peasants, by which small groups of farmers helped one another with all harvesting and transplanting, had given way to the use of hired labor for harvests.[106] In southern Annam, however, mutual aid and work exchange were still prevalent,[107] and farmers had not been forced to new levels of intensity.

Further, in Annam, as I have noted, no changes in the organization of village government were made until 1942. Notables were selected according to the customs of the village; the traditional nature of the village was "almost completely retained."[108] By implication, therefore, local politics and economics should have been smoother and less harsh than in Tonkin, for no colonial reforms altered the village ruling group. Yet by 1930, 60 percent of the land in central Annam was being worked by tenants.[109] Severe stratification could occur, in the absence of colonial reforms, simply as a result of the way taxes were assessed within the villages by the notables and of the opportunities this created for the notables to accumulate and use money to amass land within their own villages. As in Tonkin, the village chief in Annam emerged as a major source of village power. Even though there were no electoral reforms, the selection of village chief was at times so bitterly contested that the defeated faction would seek to form a new village "to avoid the vengeance of the winning party."[110] In Annam, just

105. Henry, *Economie agricole*, p. 46.
106. Gourou, *Les Paysans*, p. 374.
107. Henry, *Economie agricole*, p. 46.
108. Khang, *La Commune annamite*, p. 51.
109. Henry, *Economie agricole*, p. 46.
110. Khang, *La Commune annamite*, p. 91.

as in Tonkin, a striking feature of the colonial period was the constant splitting of villages, brought on by political and economic quarrels.[111] The main defense of villagers against political manipulation was segmentation.

The fact that even southern Annam—where there were no French administrative reforms until 1942 and where, in most areas, there were outlets for demographic pressure—was characterized by increasing social stratification and conflict within villages suggests that much of the change in Vietnamese rural society during the colonial period was due to the internal dynamics of the corporate village. The French did place new demands—especially for the heavy taxes which now had to be paid primarily in money—on the village, and they did give individuals—especially the village chief and the mandarins—new options for personal gain. But the decisions about how those taxes were to be distributed and the choice of which of the options were to be used were made within the village.

COCHINCHINA

Cochinchina was colonized earlier and with far more disruption than Tonkin or Annam, and French administration of that southern region was far more direct than in the other areas. In addition, Cochinchina became a major world exporter of rice, whereas Annam and Tonkin produced very small net surpluses at best. Neither the administrative nor the economic factor is sufficient, however, to explain why the political structure of Cochinchinese villages developed differently from that in the other regions.

Although the French presence was far stronger in Cochinchina than in Tonkin or Annam, it still proved impossible for the colonial authorities to implement their policies by force in the face of strong village opposition. In the 1890s, when for forty years the Cochinchinese villages had been "decaying" and supposedly losing their "collective sense," the French instituted new land registration procedures to regularize all land titles. These procedures were poorly

111. H. G., "L'Evolution des institutions," p. 244; Dao Duy Anh, *Vietnam van hoa su cuong,* p. 137; Thuc, *L'Economie communaliste,* p. 41; Khang, *La Commune annamite,* pp. 91–92.

publicized; they were difficult to use; they required trips to distant registries. Thus, many outside operators filed claims against land recognized within the villages as the property of a villager. When the "outsiders" tried to claim their land, however, they were turned out by the villagers and had to go to French magistrates for hearings. In one four-year period, a regional court administering an area of 469 villages was forced on 448 occasions to admit that while the "outsider's" title was legal under the new procedures, no judgment could be executed. In one case, for example, the provincial administrator wrote to the minister of justice, "Judgments of which you speak are absolutely inexecutable. The province of Cantho would rise en masse. The bailiffs and militia chiefs, sent to apply the law, are on the point of being massacred. Your judgments profoundly upset the laws and customs of the Vietnamese. Send me a battalion of marine infantry and perhaps I can succeed in making the executions. I would not care to comment on the events that would follow."[112.]

Not even in Cochinchina, then, were the French powerful enough to gain control of the political processes of the villages. As elsewhere, their resources were too limited to compel changes in all village procedures or to force linkages from villages to central administrative power. They could collect enormous amounts of taxes, even higher than in other areas, by the use of the stick; but in other respects, they could not compel officials to behave as they wished.

The distinction between commercial agriculture in Cochinchina and subsistence agriculture in Tonkin and Annam is not sufficient to explain the range of political and economic differences that emerged in the two areas during the colonial period. There had been a lively rice trade from Cochinchina *before* the French conquest, when its villages were corporate. Moreover, the driving force in all areas of Vietnam was the extremely heavy taxes, taking nearly 20 percent of the net production of smallholders, and sometimes as much as 35 percent.[113] Because of these heavy taxes, now

112. Guy Gran, "Vietnam and the Capitalist Route to Modernity: Village Cochinchina 1880–1940," p. 207.
113. Robequain, *Economic Development of French Indochina,* pp. 156; Mus, "The Role of the Village in Vietnamese Affairs," p. 269; Thompson, *French Indochina,* p. 197.

paid in money, all Vietnamese—not just the Cochinchinese—were affected by market conditions. But there was "much less of the peasant mentality"[114] in Cochinchina. This was in part because, with more land per capita, there was such a large surplus of rice that a sizeable proportion of the peasants had a surplus even after taxes; in turn, there was a higher consumption standard in Cochinchina. A tenant farmer in the latter region, for example, lived just as well as a peasant in Tonkin who owned his own family farm.[115] In general, every class in Cochinchina was a notch ahead of the corresponding class in the other areas. Neither the differences in living standards nor market sensitivity, however, are enough to explain why village politics were so different in two areas of Vietnam.

Two important factors explain the radically different economic and political patterns of Cochinchinese villages: (1) the existence of enormous quantities of unoccupied land; and (2) a very different "means of production." These two essential differences—not those between commercial agriculture and subsistence agriculture or between colonial administrative styles—explain the divergences between the areas (and later are significant for the different revolutionary developments as well).

The irrigation system necessary for the stable production of rice differed in Cochinchina from that required in the other areas of the country. First, since the Mekong is less violent than the Red river, there is no need for dikes and other elaborate flood controls. Second, and even more important, the rainfall in Cochinchina is more even than in other areas: whereas wet-rice production elsewhere requires local water storage ponds and canals within each village, an acceptable quality of irrigation in Cochinchina comes from rainfall alone. Since there was no village water supply to be divided, there was no set of village rules specifying penalties and orders of usage, as in the customaries of other areas. A major source of conflict between villages was eliminated because of the absence of storage systems. In Tonkin, by contrast, it has been noted that "thefts of water are among the most frequent crimes committed in

114. Gourou, *Land Utilization*, pp. 331–332.
115. Ibid., pp. 552–553.

the delta. [If] some peasants have preserved their fields from the common shortage, men from a neighboring commune will approach silently during the night to the carefully diked water-filled paddies and will, with a few blows from their pickaxes, allow the water to escape to their own profit."[116] Thus, in Cochinchina there was minimal intravillage or intervillage conflict over water. Irrigation was an individual matter, not a group concern requiring village planning and organization, or involving distribution. The only water issues in Cochinchina were small-scale fights over passage rather than distribution. Thus, once the French had drained the unsettled portions of Cochinchina, each field could be cleared and farmed independently of all others.[117]

The other major village resource in precolonial Vietnam was communal land. While 20 to 25 percent of all land in Annam and Tonkin had been communal, distributed by the village officials, there had *never* been more than minimal amounts of such land in Cochinchina. With plentiful areas available for private exploitation and with the emperor exercising only weak control over the villages in this region, communal land usually had existed only because someone had bequeathed a piece of land to maintain a village *dinh,* not because it was established by fiat for the poor.

Control over the Cochinchinese village, then, did not, as it did in other areas, give control over vital resources. In addition, it did not provide effective control of the peasants. Thanks to French drainage projects, which more than quadrupled the amount of available land, there was an easily accessible "exit" option for the peasants throughout the colonial period. Once the French dug the extensive central canal network which turned the marshy interior of Cochinchina into land suitable for the cultivation of rice, the peasants always had somewhere to go. For these reasons, Cochinchinese cor-

116. Edmund Chassigneux, quoted in A. Terry Rambo, "A Comparison of Peasant–Social Systems of Northern and Southern Vietnam: A Study of Ecological Adaptation, Social Succession, and Cultural Evolution," p. 94.

117. Even the need to cooperate for village protection differed: prior to 1940, the incidence of banditry in Cochinchina was comparatively low; in Tonkin, by contrast, "each commune must create its own militia and organize its own defense with a system of moats, walls and watchtowers" (Phan Thi Dac, *Situation de la personne,* p. 28; see also Rambo, "A Comparison of Peasant Social Systems," p. 240).

porate villages became open villages, and village economic and political reactions were different from those in other areas. Whereas in Tonkin and Annam each village was like a separate land market with prices varying according to economic conditions within the village, Cochinchina was a uniform land market with prices depending on productivity and overall demand for land. And whereas persons moved in and out of villages with ease in Cochinchina, the insider-outsider distinction never disappeared in Tonkin and Annam.

In the pre-French period there were three critical distributive issues in Tonkin and Annam: water, communal land, and taxes. Since the notables controlled these resources, anyone who dropped out of the council was taking a big risk. There was, however, only one distributional issue that faced the notables in the south during the precolonial and early colonial periods—taxes. The council of notables enforced the equal division of taxes among all men in the village and made sure that each paid his share; thus, they avoided losing any property to the mandarins because of unpaid village taxes.

Analyzing the early colonial period, Milton Osborne argues that French bureaucratic practices caused the decay of the traditional village in Cochinchina.[118] The early French administrators, he suggests, drove the traditional notables from office by placing increasingly heavier demands and penalties on them. Having abandoned their positions, these notables "now devoted themselves to furthering their fortune."[119] This change led to a growth of the rural proletariat[120] and to erosion of village autonomy: "The autonomy of the commune was constantly eroded by French decisions that linked activities within the commune to the central administration in a direct fashion and as the insistence on individual responsibility destroyed traditional reliance on collective obligation."[121] In fact, the evidence for the notables' behavior—that is, their strategy to cope with new French demands—does not necessarily imply that

118. Milton Osborne, *The French Presence in Cochinchina and Cambodia: Rule and Response,* pp. 144–145.
119. Ibid., pp. 146–147.
120. Ibid., p. 146.
121. Ibid., p. 153. [Sic].

the village decayed. It is more likely that, despite French attempts to control the village, the old notables still held sway, furthering their fortunes as they had always done.

An examination of the evidence offered to support the "resignation and decay" thesis reveals that the notables who resigned were, first of all, not the "true notables" (members of the senior council or "executive branch" of the village), but the junior working notables. These junior notables were in charge of carrying out decisions of their seniors and, increasingly, the many orders and decrees of the French. As increasing numbers of laws were enacted, such as those establishing salt and alcohol monopolies, the French tried to hold the junior notables responsible for infractions in their villages. In addition, these men were frequently summoned by the French to present reports and receive orders. When any infraction was detected or when a man was late for a meeting, his property was confiscated. As a result, the notables began to give the jobs of the junior notables to men without property. A personnel turnover among the holders of working positions, which resulted in the foiling of French attempts to dominate village administrators, is not conclusive evidence that the "true notables" of the villages were no longer in charge, or that French decrees were linked directly to village politics. Nor do the French administrators' perceptions of performance mean that the notables were dissatisfied with the way their villages were being run.

The turnover in personnel indicates not that the old notables had abandoned the village, but that they kept their powers and simply put forward men with no property whom the French could not control. If the notables in Tonkin, in order to control the administrative council without being personally exposed, had put tenants and children into official positions, it is certainly plausible to suppose that the Cochinchinese notables were no less imaginative or determined.

Taxation procedures demonstrate the ability of the traditional elite to circumvent French decrees, and they suggest why the notables would put personal front men with no property on the council. As in the other areas of the country, the French based their original tax demands—again for money, not rice—on the registered population of the villages. And again, as Osborne points out, the notables distributed the tax over all the men in the village, registered or not, even though that was not the French intention.[122] As long as taxes were a live issue in the village, it made sense for the notables to put their personal representatives on decision-making bodies. Because all the notables' interests were at stake, they would be prone to use "front" men when the tax burden was being divided up and collected.

But when the French decreed that each person should pay a head tax—and that everyone should pay the same head tax—governmental power stood behind the notables and guaranteed their rights. In Tonkin and Annam, this concession from the government in the 1920s left other major distributive issues, such as water and communal land, in the hands of the elite; but in Cochinchina the legitimation of the equal tax rule by the French removed the last of the potentially divisive intraelite issues, and changed the nature of political competition.

When the French moved to reform taxation in Cochinchina by legalizing the notables' traditional procedures, they removed the major incentives for a member of the elite to perform the functions of a working notable.[123] In the past, when taxes that could not be squeezed from the poor could be taken from the rich, or when legally the taxes were supposed to be paid only by the registered, it had been important for the notables to protect their interests. But when their tax interests were recognized by the French, the distributing of the tax burden ceased to be an issue of severe intraelite and elite-mass conflict. Given the sanctity of private property, a landowner with a legal right to pay his taxes, who did not need resources from the village, did not have to be tied to the village in the same way as did the elite in other areas.

During most of the colonial period, there were no important recurring distributive issues in Cochinchina, and there was frontier to which peasants could escape. These two facts account for the change from corporate to open villages in that region. They contributed to several other developments as well. In comparison to Annam and Tonkin, the land market was open, and elite opposition

122. Ibid., p. 84.
123. Ibid., p. 147.

to outsiders was insignificant. The wealthy were relatively uncon-
cerned with directly controlling the village chief and contented
themselves with merely setting his policies. More public works
were performed by village government; colonial officials intervened
less (both officially and privately); supravillage institutions, such as
courts, were widely used. Finally, there were fewer Catholics overall in Cochinchina, and there existed heterogeneous villages with
only some Catholics.

The reduction of intraelite conflict over distributive issues was
particularly important both for the nature of local political competition and for the inability of the French to penetrate the local political arena. Political competition for village power in Tonkin and
Annam, for example, was essentially a fight among the elite for the
private gain that could be reaped from control of communal land
and water. Whenever elections were held, therefore, there was no
bidding among contenders to offer services and collective goods for
members of the village. Because competition was in terms of individual shares of the profits, no one appealed for votes by promising
to improve matters for everyone. But in Cochinchina, it was a different competition. The elite had fewer individual concerns about
sharing the spoils and greater collective interest in maintaining their
economic and political power. Thus, any candidate who wanted to
be a village official and "get close" to the senior notables and other
rich landholders would have to provide these men with certain services which as a group they needed—for example, enforcement of
their contracts with peasants, which often meant bullying the tenants. Because all candidates could promise to police the landowner's economic interests, they tended to differentiate themselves
by assuring other collective goods and services such as roads,
schools, and bridges. Because the nature of local political competition was different in Cochinchina, village officials usually provided
more public goods and services for the village elite than did their
counterparts in Annam and Tonkin.

Since there was less intraelite conflict, there was less need for
the elites to form alliances with bureaucrats. It was therefore more
difficult for the French to exert control over Cochinchinese villages.
As Gourou noted, these villages were "paradoxically less strongly

organized and much less subject to control."[124] This is one of the great ironies of the colonial period. While romantic Westerners were decrying the shapelessness and lack of character and soul in the southern villages, many of the reformist or revolutionary Vietnamese like Dao Duy Anh looked at the southern "open" villages and saw much to envy.

Anh admired the southern villages because they were less subject to manipulation by colonial officials.[125] While villages in the other areas were constantly splitting, the French were combining villages in Cochinchina and cutting their number in half. He believed the same policy would work in other areas as well. Anh did not realize, however, that in the other areas the key village political issues were distributive: the resulting instability of coalitions "drove" the system and gave officials an access to many villages which they could use for either private gain or public policy enforcement. With no serious distributional issues dividing the elite in southern villages, the only group with the skills and resources to contact officials when abuses occurred had no incentive to do so. Thus, no divide-and-conquer approach could give the officials their leverage. As long as the rich landowners were happy with the enforcement services provided them, there was no one to bring complaints to the French about treatment of smallholders and tenants. In turn, there was nothing the French could do to force the village chief to administer as they wanted him to.

The comparative lack of intraelite political competition in the villages of Cochinchina, the existence of a frontier, and an increase in incomes among all classes in the south do not mean that there was no serious rigging of the game against peasants. The marketplace in Cochinchina was not impersonal, and political manipulation was still an essential part of the economic struggle.

Political manipulation structured the land market, and it was essential for keeping many peasants dependent on the elite. Besides the frontier of western Cochinchina, there were what might be called "minifrontiers" in and around the villages, which had

124. Gourou, *Land Utilization,* p. 564.
125. Dao Duy Anh, *Vietnam van hoa su cuong,* p. 137.

existed at the time of the French takeover. The village elite used every means at its disposal to keep this land from falling into the hands of small tenants. Given the availability of virgin land, these political manipulations were essential for the elite to provide itself with a supply of tenants for its own estates. If a peasant lost his land, in Annam and Tonkin he had no choice but to become a tenant. In Cochinchina, there was free land around nearly every village; but if peasants were allowed the access to this land accorded by French laws, the landlords would be deprived of a labor force.

By law, men who staked claims in the minifrontier areas had several years to bring the land into production before they were required to pay taxes. This grace period allowed them to clear small plots slowly, while serving as tenants, and thus to win economic independence. The notables, however, often demanded tax payments of the land the first year that the peasants began to develop it. In this way, they could keep the peasants in a position where they had no choice but to serve as tenants,[126] unless they left the village. The notables' signature was essential for any claim to virgin land[127] so that, even if a peasant could meet the tax payments, the notables could claim that someone else had already applied for the land. In cases where the French held auctions to sell land on these minifrontiers, many peasants were still blocked by village notables in collusion with landowning bureaucrats, who had similar interests in keeping land out of the hands of smallholders. Officials could— and did—freeze peasants out of the auctions by failing to publicize them, by keeping secret the fact that payment could be made on credit, and by selling the land only in large tracts.[128]

Similar institutional manipulations were essential for the development of huge landholdings in those vast regions of western Cochinchina that had been unsettled before the French drained the area. Here the French policy was to grant large concessions to anyone who would take the unclaimed land, cultivate it, and pay taxes after a grace period. Robert Sansom has portrayed the great land-

126. Gran, "Vietnam and the Capitalist Route," p. 283.
127. Ibid., p. 259.   128. Ibid., p. 280.

owners who reaped immense fortunes in this area as economic entrepreneurs who possessed the necessary skills to develop this land and who were therefore essential to the opening of this new frontier to settlement: "The development of an extensive canal network . . . had to be followed by intensive land development work requiring large labor inputs before rice could be produced. Men skilled in mobilizing labor and capital were *needed*."[129] If these men were, in fact, "necessary," it was because of their skills as political, not economic, entrepreneurs. Before the French granted the majority of these concessions, there was already in progress a mass exodus to these virgin lands by peasants forced from their old villages by rapacious notables. Before the concessions policy was ever adopted, peasants had achieved "notable success" in opening up large quantities of this land by themselves.[130] Frequently, what distinguished the men who obtained the concessions from the peasants who became their tenants was political skill at manipulating registration procedures. While a peasant was clearing a small holding from virgin land, another person could be arranging in Saigon or the provincial capital to have a large concession—including the small holding—ceded to him. Or a person could hire (or bribe) a surveyor to map the plot, and then he could file a claim with the administration and wait until the plot was developed before suing for control of the land. The concession-holders turned many peasants who had attempted to carve out small holdings of their own into tenants because they had the bureaucratic skills to make their claim stand up. Even on the open frontier, then, where the French were willing to cede huge tracts of *uninhabited* land to anyone who would bring it into productivity, political manipulation was common. The political entrepreneurs had to deprive peasants of access to their own land in order to create a supply of tenants for land development.

Thus, while the population of Cochinchina doubled—perhaps even tripled—between 1880 and 1930, the number of landowners remained constant. Seventy five percent of all households owned no land at all, while 2,000 persons owned between 35 and 45 percent

129. Sansom, *Economics of Insurgency*, p. 23.
130. Rambo, "A Comparison of Peasant Social Systems," p. 65; Gran, "Vietnam and the Capitalist Route," p. 77.

of all the land.[131] Agrarian relations between the large landlords and their tenants were tense, and control of tenants and the maintenance of a dependent relationship was part of the strategy of most great landlords. Opposing the establishment of a government administration in the new areas of Cochinchina, they attempted as long as possible to run the area as great estates in the grand feudal tradition. Often, for example, they paid all the head taxes for their tenants, then kept the cards so that tenants would have difficulty leaving the estates. Although solvent tenants preferred to do without production loans or to obtain them not from the lord but from an independent source of credit, they were often forced to borrow from the lord—and from no one else. The lords, finally, maintained client gangs for use when there were disputes among tenants or between the tenant and the lord.[132]

The French, despite their strong presence in Cochinchina, had no better success there than elsewhere in bringing village administration into alignment with their policies. They attempted major village reforms in 1904 and 1927, but all they accomplished was a reshuffling of titles among the minor working notables of the villages. They did strip all official rights and duties from the senior notables in 1904, but, in contrast to Tonkin, this produced no major outbursts and no determined efforts to reclaim lost powers, for, as we have seen, these men had different, more general interests in village government than did the notables of Annam and Tonkin. With no communal land and no communal water at issue, the main village political interests in Cochinchina were more of a class than of a personal nature. Despite all attempts at reform, the French were unable to curtail the power of the great landowning notables over the villages. As one colonial administrator pointed out in calling for yet another reform, the village administration still represented "only the interests of certain groups, who, in holding nearly all the lands in a country that is exclusively agricultural, constitute a force which no other can counterbalance."[133]

---

131. Gran, "Vietnam and the Capitalist Route," pp. 307–308; Gourou, *Land Utilization,* pp. 340–343.

132. Pierre Brocheux, "Grands Propriétaires et fermiers dans l'ouest de la Cochinchine pendant la période coloniale," pp. 63–66.

133. Kresser, *La Commune annamite,* pp. 112–113.

Due to its large quantities of uncultivated land and a very different means of production, Cochinchina developed differently from Annam and Tonkin. The looser village structure of Cochinchina gave the French less leverage in local politics than they had in the other areas. The standard of living improved, even for the poor. Nevertheless, the frontier was not necessarily the land of opportunity for poor peasants. Although the "game" was played differently in Cochinchina from the way it was played in the corporate villages of Annam and Tonkin, the elite in both areas manipulated the rules politically to maintain an advantage over the peasants.

CONCLUSION

In this chapter I have treated the changes produced by colonial rule, especially those external regulations and authorities penetrating the villages, as dependent rather than independent variables which can be explained by reference to local economic and political concerns. The distribution of communal resources and charges, as well as the patterns of self-interest, that had prevailed in the villages before colonial rule determined local responses to external regulations and extractions. Economics shapes village institutions. But economics should be understood to mean not only land, labor, water, and capital, but also the infrastructure of the economic system, including land titles, taxes, methods of conflict resolution, and the provision of security for persons and property.

In seeking to explain why peasants eventually overthrew notables and reorganized their villages, one should not assume that traditional religious values had lost their meaning, that villages had decayed, or that old moral bonds had withered. One should instead concentrate on the ways that colonial influences increased social stratification by adding to the comparative political advantage of the notables and caused an accumulation of peasant grievances which expressed itself in support of a variety of revolutionary movements.

To be sure, French tax policies and bureaucracy in Vietnam would have been an onerous burden for any peasantry. The load of direct and indirect taxes, the shift to money taxation, and the lack of forgiveness in bad years left scars. The taxes, particularly the "body tax," as peasants call it in memory of the debt slavery it brought about, will not be forgotten for generations. And the powerful French bureaucracy, in whose name so many abuses and outrages were perpetrated, was certainly odious to the peasantry.

It must not be forgotten, however, that during the revolutionary upheavals village notables, who had been manipulating and deflecting French policies to their own ends, were primary targets. There were serious problems within the villages as well as outside them, and these problems came to be well understood by politically conscious Vietnamese intellectuals. Vu van Hien advocated economic change—in particular that communal land be abandoned. Dao Duy Anh wanted political/administrative change and felt that there should be direct intervention in the affairs of the corporate villages in order to curb the "excessive powers of the notables."[134]

In response to such views, Gourou warned against any tampering with the corporate villages. He was well aware of the inequality and venality, but admired the way that Vietnamese peasants were integrated into their villages. There was a "strict tyranny," to be sure, but the village was still a community. To alter the village, he argued, would deprive the peasants of what little happiness they had.[135] Not everyone who worked with Gourou felt that the peasant would be best served by preserving the traditional village. After several years in the villages with Gourou, one of his research assistants became convinced that drastic change, both economic and political, was needed to improve the lot of the peasantry. His name was Vo Nguyen Giap.

134. Anh, *Vietnam van hoa su cuong,* p. 136.
135. Gourou, *Les Paysans,* p. 577.

5

Up from Feudalism

IN PRECEDING chapters, I have argued that the quality and extent of insurance and welfare embedded in precolonial institutions often are overestimated and that two general errors result from an overly benign view of traditional institutions. Such a view (1) glosses over the shortcomings of precolonial villages and patrons, and therefore underrates the value and potential of market mechanisms for peasants; and (2) ignores the *connection* between village procedures of the precolonial period and the many abuses, inequities, and grievances of the colonial period. In this chapter, these points are amplified further by an analysis of organizations that were able to mobilize peasants, administer villages, form armies, and do battle with the French (and one another). These organizations were successful because they were not only anticolonial, but *antifeudal* as well.

Four organizations—the Hoa Hao and Cao Dai religions in

Cochinchina, the Catholic Church and the Communist Party in all three regions—were able to gain control of large sections of the country and to channel significant peasant resources into creating new rural societies. Although there were radical differences among these organizations in ideology, in national organization, in their definitions of the problems of peasant society, and in their attempts to reorganize rural institutions, there is at least one thing they had in common: a determination to struggle against "feudalism" *(phong kien)*. *None of these movements attempted to restore the official Confucian "golden past" (whose actual existence has been questioned in previous chapters)*. When the Hoa Hao and Cao Dai, for example, spoke of the past and called for a return to old ways, they built upon alternative models of social organization which had been a precolonial alternative to Confucianism. (Technically, precolonial Vietnam was not a feudal country, but the term *feudal* was—and is—used among peasants in all four movements to describe their rejection of "traditional" institutions and served as a reference point for the ways in which their lives and villages changed under the impact of these organizations.)

There were important ideological differences about the ultimate shape a new Vietnam should take, and in the end the religious movements broke completely with the Communists, as well as with one another. Only the Communists, of course, had the sophisticated understanding of national and international politics necessary to begin the task of forging a nation by incorporating the diverse groups within Vietnam and doing successful battle against French colonialism. Yet there were similarities in the way these four movements attracted support and developed control in the countryside which would be overlooked in a simple division between religious and political movements.[1] When we examine these movements in detail, the ways in which they attracted peasants and raised the resources to build their organizations, we observe that all four attracted peasants by helping them to break their depen-

1. Indeed, when the Cao Dai religion was first developing in the countryside, many French sought its suppression on the grounds that it was nothing but "communism masquerading as a religion" (Virginia Thompson, *French Indochina*, p. 474).

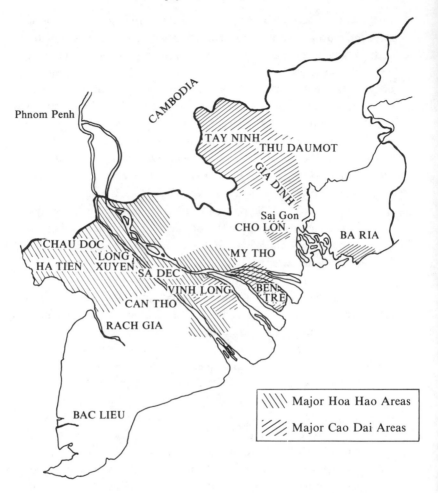

MAP 2. Post-1945 Cochinchina

dence on, and control by, large landowners and/or village officials. This was done by providing the peasants with mutually profitable sources of insurance and welfare, and helping them overcome the institutional manipulations of market and bureaucracy that had reinforced their dependence. These organizations used political skills and bureaucratic connections to give the peasants access to (and leverage against) the institutions that had previously kept them at a disadvantage. By so doing, they helped the peasants to tame markets and enter them on their own.

By undermining the power of village notables, the movements were able to institute village-level insurance and tax, welfare, and communal land procedures that were far more extensive and beneficial than those of either the precolonial or colonial periods. But it must be stressed that village officials and landlords had to be undermined—their powers had not "decayed" during the colonial period, there were no vacuums to be filled. Each of these movements had to build a power base while actively opposed by rural economic and political elites, who had been strengthened, not weakened by colonial policies.[2]

The four case studies presented in this chapter are necessarily limited in detail. Nearly all available documents for this period deal with military and international factors, and most French archives remain sealed. There was no Pierre Gourou to detail the changes in village conditions, no William Hinton to record life in liberated areas. The data available are clearly inadequate to cover all points, but they are *consistent* with my overall arguments.

It must be stressed that the interviews on which the section on Communists is based were conducted some twenty years after the fact; furthermore, they were conducted at a time when certain subjects—such as members in the Communist Party—were highly sensitive. It was possible, nevertheless, to obtain information about village administration, policies, and policy changes and the major conflicts that occurred during this period. Among the informants were persons who had served on village committees or who had participated in village or district Party chapters during the first war of resistance (1945–1954). All data so acquired were then corroborated by interviews with peasants in the same villages. The data for

2. This emphasis necessarily precludes discussion of many other important topics. Among them are the failure of the once-powerful urban Trotskyite movement; the failure of the conservative political parties; the military aspects of the Communist-led Viet Minh—its eventual domination of the anticolonial movement and its war against the French; and the fratricidal conflict that finally ensued when relations between the three religious groups and the Communists broke down. Although of great importance, these subjects are outside the narrow scope of this book.

central Vietnam were collected directly in Binh Dinh and Thua
Thien provinces and were supplemented by interviews with former
residents of Quang Nam province. The data for Cochinchina were
collected in Bien Hoa, Long An, Vinh Long, and An Giang and
were supplemented with data from Rand Corporation interviews in
Dinh Tuong (these are the 1955–1975 province names).

CATHOLICS

Following the Japanese surrender in 1945, the Viet Minh swept
through Vietnam and sought to expand their support. An important
element of their coalition were the Catholics, who at that time comprised about 10 percent of all Vietnamese.[3] Ho Chi Minh himself
attended Christmas mass in 1945, there were Catholics in his
cabinet, and one of his special advisors was a high-ranking member
of the Church hierarchy in Vietnam.[4]

The precolonial, nineteenth-century Catholic hierarchy was dominated by Europeans. In the twentieth century, however, the same
nationalist ferment that was felt throughout Indochina pervaded the
Church. Native priests openly struggled for power, and the
"nationalist insubordination" to foreign domination was so effective that by 1945 the Church had a predominantly Vietnamese
hierarchy, and the foreign missions had lost their grip on the native
Church.[5]

The organizing power of the Church, and its firm hold on
parishioners, lay with the priests, there being approximately one
fully trained priest for every thousand to fifteen hundred parishioners. Above the village priests was the standard Catholic organiza-

3. For the early success of the Church in Vietnam, see Chapters 3 and 4, in
which the incentive system and organizational techniques of the Jesuits are discussed.

4. This is worth noting, for the eventual split between Communist-led forces and
the Catholics has tended to efface from memory the antagonisms that existed between native Catholics and the French. So severe were these animosities that, even
after the split between Catholics and the Viet Minh, no white soldiers were allowed
in the areas controlled by the Catholics! This serves to remind us not only how
complicated were the alliances among Vietnamese groups, but also of the many
bases of opposition to colonialism within Vietnam. (Joseph Buttinger, *Vietnam: A
Dragon Embattled*, pp. 1021–1022.)

5. Thompson, *French Indochina*, pp. 473–475.

tion of bishops and archbishops; there were also the several lay organizations and popular private schools throughout the country. The priest was the quintessential political entrepreneur. Conversions among the elite succeeded, not only because of the appeal of the religion itself, but because of tangible, material benefits— science, cannon, European education—that the priest could offer as proof of the religion's validity. Conversion of the elite gave access to the peasantry and afforded the priests bureaucratic leverage when offering incentives to prospective converts. The priest, moreover, could raise substantial local funds to support his organization by providing more welfare and insurance benefits than could village notables seeking personal profit. Finally, the priest could provide better adjudication, and at less cost, to the faithful. The faith of Catholicism was clearly attractive, but the material benefits were crucial in solidifying the bonds of the faithful. During the colonial period, for example, whenever a wave of anticlericalism swept the administration of Vietnam, and Catholic ability to manipulate the bureaucracy for the benefit of followers was therefore diminished, the Church was threatened by "wholesale defection."[6]

Brutally persecuted in Vietnam during much of the nineteenth century, the Catholics convinced the French government to come to their aid by talking of the great profits to be made in Vietnam from colonial exploitation. However, Catholicism flourished during the colonial period not because the French were sympathetic to Catholic dreams of a Christian Vietnam. Rather, the Church grew because it had an organization that could attract peasants, and because it could further elite ambitions. It is too simple to say that the Catholics succeeded because the colonial government and colonists wanted them to; in large part, they succeeded because the hostile elements in the colonial government and among the colonists could not stop them.

Following the French conquest, the Catholics lobbied for a Catholic monarch, for tax exemption of Church lands, and against the restoration of pagodas and *dinhs* destroyed during the conquest. The colonial government refused their requests. Because of their

6. Ibid., p. 274.

persecution by the mandarins, many native Catholics had supported the French conquest. The gratitude the priests had expected in return, however, was not forthcoming because of the considerable anticlerical sentiment among the colonial administrators and colonists anxious to avoid Church interference with their schemes.[7]

The success of the Catholics during the colonial period, therefore, cannot be explained solely in terms of colonial favoritism or strong official desire to convert the Vietnamese. If success had been due directly to French policy, then Catholicism would have been strongest in Cochinchina, where the French rule was more direct. Catholicism did indeed increase among the urban elite of all three areas of Vietnam, but its major numerical growth was in Tonkin and northern Annam. By 1945, 20 percent of the peasants in these poor and harsh areas were Catholics, in spite of the hostility of so many colonial administrators to Catholicism.[8] The number of Catholic adherents increased because the Church could effectively manipulate economic and political levers. It attracted the upper-class elite in significant numbers by offering them access to modern education in Quoc Ngu and an advantage over non-Catholics in access to jobs within the bureaucracy. Throughout Vietnam, and especially in Cochinchina, the new "modern" elite was disproportionately Catholic.[9] The Church then used its elite contacts for leverage in the countryside.

The spread of Catholicism in the densest and poorest areas of Vietnam, Tonkin and northern Annam, is additional evidence of the declining economic situation of the peasantry in those areas and of the limits of corporate-village rule. Most land not under cultivation in these areas was marginal. Such land was worthless to individual entrepreneurs because the capital and labor inputs necessary to put the land into cultivation made such efforts unattractive as short-run profit ventures. The colonial government's resettlement schemes for

7. Gran, for example, notes the opposition among colonists to the Church's acquiring land in Cochinchina. Guy Gran, "Vietnam and the Capitalist Route to Modernity: Village Cochinchina 1880–1940," p. 291.

8. Dennis Duncanson, *Government and Revolution in Vietnam*, pp. 103–104, 390.

9. Milton Osborne, "Continuity and Motivation in the Vietnamese Revolution: New Light from the 1930s," pp. 100–105, 134, 161–162; Duncanson, *Government and Revolution*, pp. 103–104.

opening new lands to anyone who would develop them failed because peasants could not afford the start-up costs. The Catholic Church, however, turned vast tracts of swamp and wilderness into land that could support starving peasants. Although the peasants were averse to the Church's strictures against ancestor worship, sheer misery created a population receptive to Christianity. Lacking village welfare systems, many peasants abandoned their overburdened villages for the better life the Church was promising on this earth. Dedicated priests provided the moral and social discipline necessary to colonize the new lands; the Church itself provided the necessary financial support while the new villages were developing:

In the last century nothing existed but marshes, a permanent flood where the reddish waters of the estuaries merged imperceptibly with the tidal flow from the sea. But in this region of mud and brine missionaries dug canals, bringing into existence a checker board of green islands and attracting a population. . . . The very landscape was clerical. . . . Each square, with its Church in the middle as a parish; the curé was the lord and the parishioners his serfs.[10]

Catholicism's rural growth came predominantly from the conversion of the poorest peasants, and Catholic villages often were situated on the most marginal land. Yet, when compared with neighboring villages, Catholic villages were "markedly more prosperous."[11] This emphasizes the tremendous economic benefits that stability (even colonial stability) could bring to peasants when coupled with a flexible policy of taxation that forgave in bad years. Additionally, aided by Catholic officials, Catholic coolies obtained a disproportionate share of public-works jobs; for the same reason, Catholic villages were less subject to abuse by mandarins. The village priest was part of an organized hierarchy that could bring wide-ranging power to bear on behalf of claims by the faithful. The Church could blackmail the corrupt, intercede directly with the administration, and dictate to loyal Catholics within the government.[12]

10. Lucien Bodard, *The Quicksand War: Prelude to Vietnam*, p. 211.
11. Thompson, *French Indochina*, pp. 273–274.
12. Ibid., pp. 273–274. Also Pierre Gourou, *Les Paysans du delta tonkinois: Etude de géographie humaine*, pp. 202–203.

The fate of Catholics and Catholic villages during the colonial period, then, contrasts markedly with the fate of non-Catholic corporate villages in Tonkin and Annam. The village priest belonged to an organization that backed up local demands and interests. If a Catholic village chief tried to use his powers for personal gain, the priest could bring enormous moral and political power to bear against him. If an outside landowner tried to take over the lands in a Catholic village by bureaucratic manipulation, or via alliance with a few native landowners, he faced a priest that could call on an organized church, rather than an isolated group of notables with limited legal and political resources.

In addition to opening new lands in Tonkin and Annam, priests often gained access to villages by manipulating power struggles within a village. If a rich man, for example, stole the land of a poor man, and if the poor man converted to Catholicism, the priest would then go to court to plead his case. In some cases, by skillfully utilizing judicial procedures, Catholic villages were even able to appropriate the lands and water of non-Catholic villages. [13]

The failure of the Catholics to win as many adherents in rural Cochinchina as they did in Tonkin and Annam is a caution against assuming that elite influence and the ability to manipulate bureaucratic levers translate directly into influence on the peasantry under all conditions. It serves to point up, moreover, the important economic and social differences between Cochinchina, on the one hand, and Annam and Tonkin, on the other.

The Church, as noted earlier, had always seen westward migration as an obstacle to conversion in Cochinchina. [14] Although power struggles within and between villages in the older parts of Cochinchina led to many conversions, the rate was lower than in Tonkin and Annam because it was so much easier for the peasants of Cochinchina to simply "exit" from their villages for the new lands of the western frontier. Once the canals were dug and the area drained, moreover, emigration to the frontier could proceed at an individual level, without the help of the dedicated and sophisticated

13. Cao Huy Thuan, *Christianisme et colonialisme au Vietnam (1857–1914)*, cited in White, "Revolution and Its Adherents," pp. 47–48.

14. See Chapter 3, pp. 130–31. Also Milton Osborne, *The French Presence in Cochinchina and Cambodia: Rule and Response (1905–1959)*, p. 145.

organizers required by the harsher ecosystems of Annam and Tonkin. On the frontier of Cochinchina there were countless small-scale secret societies with their native entrepreneurs to whom the peasants could turn for assistance and who could successfully compete with the Catholic priests in community formation. Because there were numerous sources of capital available to the peasants of Cochinchina, they were less likely to need the Church for money and credit. The Church, furthermore, was unable to compete directly with large, private landowners in the new territories because it was denied large concessions of new land. It is unclear, however, why more peasants in the new territories failed to turn to the Catholics for help after they were fleeced of their land claims by large landowners, who manipulated both titling procedures and French courts to their own advantage. In part, at least, this can be attributed to hostility from French *colons* (who were concentrated in Cochinchina), as well as to competition from the Cao Dai. Neither condition, however, is sufficient to answer this question completely.

CAO DAI

The Cao Dai have been the least understood of all Vietnamese movements of the twentieth century. The leaders of this esoteric religion revealed only as much to the French as was necessary to win legal recognition and the right to establish oratorics. Contemporary journalists, to whom they revealed nothing, describe the Cao Dai as a syncretic sect combining the beliefs of all the world's major religions and worshipping a pantheon of saints that included Victor Hugo, Joan of Arc, and Charlie Chaplin.[15]

15. Such journalists failed to note, however, the common radical-political streak in the three saints. Given its firm roots in Vietnamese and Chinese culture, and the adherence of hundreds of thousands of followers, it is surprising that only recently have serious academic studies of the Cao Dai been undertaken. The author has relied heavily for this account of Cao Dai organization on the following works: Jayne S. Werner, "Cao Dai: The Politics of a Vietnamese Syncretic Movement"; Ralph Smith, "An Introduction to Caodaism, Part I: Origins and History," pp. 335–349, and "Part II: Party Beliefs and Organization," pp. 573–589; Hue-Tam Ho Tai, "The Political History of Cao Dai 1926–1955," and "The Evolution of Vietnamese Millenarianism 1849–1947: From the Buu Son Ky Huong to the Hoa Hao." The last contains important revelations about Cao Dai.

Despite the paucity of details, scholars have documented the Cao Dai as a syncretism of the Vietnamese Three-Religion system (Tam Giao), which stressed a merger of Confucianism, Buddhism, and Taoism. Most importantly, it combined the vocabulary of religious Taoism and Taoist techniques of spirit mediumship with the essentials of apocalyptic Buddhism, in which the day of judgment—the future epoch—was imminent. Formally organized in 1926, its adherents included Vietnamese from every socioeconomic class and numbered in the hundreds of thousands within a few years.

There were many similarities in organizational form between Cao Dai, with its Pope and Holy See, and the Catholic Church, on which the early Cao Dai consciously relied for a model. Between 1926, when the first group of Cao Dai sought to win legal status from the French (and the concomitant right to open oratories, own property, and receive certain tax protections), and World War II, when nearly a million of the five million-plus Cochinchinese were members, an elaborate hierarchy of over eleven thousand offices (not all of which were filled at one time) developed. Headed by the Pope, the executive branch (Altar of the Nine Spheres) controlled the temporal organization—and eventually the armed forces—of the sect. Laws were promulgated by the Pope and cardinals and were subject to approval by three grand cardinals, all of whom oversaw province-level organizations which guided the affairs of village-level priests and congregations. Nine ministries, including health, agriculture, and education, supplemented the executive branch. There was also a major welfare agency that administered charitable houses for the old, disabled, poor, and orphaned throughout Cao Dai areas. These charitable houses also functioned as recruitment agencies. All members of a local congregation had a role in selecting their leader, who was their link with the higher organization. The moderately heavy local taxes imposed on members financed the welfare activities and supported the hierarchy as it developed and expanded the organization.

Major sources for the Cao Dai base were the previously existing small sects and secret societies introduced into Cochinchina beginning in the seventeenth century by the Chinese. Binding their members with religious oaths and rituals, and offering them self-help and protection, these sects proliferated until, as estimated by the governor-general of Cochinchina in 1916, they comprised perhaps as many as two hundred thousand Vietnamese in Cochinchina.[16] Indeed, it was acknowledged by the French that all rebellions in the region between 1860 and 1916 sprang from one or more of the sects identified with the Tam Giao tradition. Thus, Cao Dai was based on long-standing beliefs and small local organizations that predated the French conquest; it was not, therefore, a wholly new religion. In Cochinchina the French (as they did not in Annam and Tonkin until much later) immediately severed relations between the civil administration and the imperial Court and moved to a purely civil administrative system with no mandarinic overtones or content. Certainly, the resulting absence of Confucian and imperial ideals from administration was an expressed moral concern of the Cao Dai leadership. But all the Vietnamese elite did not satisfy their Confucian longings by forming small, elitist organizations or theological "Confucian studies associations." A new set of beliefs emerged, but more significantly a portion of the Vietnamese elite sought successfully to ally itself with the numerous peasant sects and to use them as a base to gather together in a powerful, if fragmented, organization approximately one fifth of the population of Cochinchina.

Over 60 percent of the original Cao Dai elite were administrative employees of the French, and many of the key founders of the organization were among the highest ranking Vietnamese in the colony.[17] Their goals when founding Cao Dai were twofold: (1) to restore the political and economic influence the French had deprived them of in Cochinchina, and (2) to restore pride in Vietnamese culture. As Pham Cong Tac, an early Pope, stated, the Cao Dai would "no longer accept the spiritual humiliations of before."[18]

How, then, were these men who founded Cao Dai able to further their economic and political interests? Viewing them as political

16. Gran, "Vietnam and the Capitalist Route," p. 517. The Heaven and Earth Society, for example, dropping its emphasis on China and opening separate branches for Vietnamese only, organized eighty branches in 1900–1920 in the region around Saigon (Werner, *Cao Dai,* p. 123).

17. Werner, *Cao Dai,* pp. 9, 95–96. 18. Ibid., p. 296.

entrepreneurs, the question becomes, what were the essential incentives or talents they used to finance and build a mass organization? As previously noted, a major source of the Cao Dai base were the small-scale sects and secret societies already in existence. The refined question, then, is what incentives could the leaders provide to aggregate the previously existing small organizations into one large and powerful organization that could then attract hundreds of thousands of new members?

With their level of administrative and linguistic competence, and with their positions in the French colonial system, the Cao Dai founders were able to provide significant economies of scale and benefits for the small sects simply by being able to legalize the sects and thus offer them protection and security.[19] The scope of the small-scale organizations could easily be increased by legalization, which afforded them considerable protection from local enemies, particular notables and landlords who tried to keep the peasantry fragmented in order to maximize their own profits and power. And indeed the Cao Dai leaders converted droves of monks and their followers to the new legal and open religious-institutional form once they began to win French acceptance of their religion.[20]

With a base in the sects, the Cao Dai were able to attract large numbers of small landowners and tenants. The religion's success can be attributed in large part to the organization's ability to offer peasants protection against the inequities of French courts, marauding notables, and large landlords who manipulated the system to keep their tenants in a state of dependency.

As noted in Chapter 4, there was a great deal of room for structural manipulation of the colonial system by economic entrepreneurs who took advantage of the sociopolitical incompetence of the majority of peasants. It was easy to prevent peasants from becoming landowners—easy even to steal the land of peasants who did not have the legal, linguistic, or sociopolitical skills to understand and use the French titling procedures and courts. Many landed fortunes were built on the wealth and contacts acquired by interpreters for the French, because such jobs provided a Vietnamese with the

19. Hue-Tam Ho Tai, "The Evolution of Millenarianism," p. 131.
20. Werner, *Cao Dai*, p. 58.

knowledge to use the system against less able peasants. The problem in Cochinchina was not that capitalism in its economic dimensions threatened the peasants because they lacked the economic competence to handle markets, risk, and entrepreneurship; rather, the problem was that a colonial dual-language system with extreme inequality of access to courts and property rights provided enormous uncertainty for peasants with economic, but not sociopolitical competence.

In many areas of Cochinchina, there were large landlords whose landholdings and fortunes were gained and/or solidified by using the French courts against their neighbors. Even by merely neutralizing the French administration, they were free to use strong-arm tactics to monopolize control of local land or to bankrupt other landowners and take over the already-cleared land. As a French administrator reported on one such large landowner,

Thefts of fish from the ditches, expulsion by force of smallholders, the burning of harvests belonging to his neighbors, and physical attacks by hired assailants at his command have served in the preceding years to intimidate the population of the region who dread this man. Brought to the tribunal, [he] always succeeded in squashing the affair by buying witnesses and intimidating his adversaries . . .[21]

In addition to such extreme examples, however, there was general and pervasive manipulation of the institutional system of capitalism to the systematic disadvantage of most smallholders and tenants. Village officials often attempted to block surveyors and thereby maintain peasant dependency and insecurity. Peasants complained to journalists that surveying was to their advantage, that if their lands were surveyed, then village chiefs could not take them. The courts, of course, were always available to peasants seeking redress of grievance against such manipulations, but the expenses of a dual-language system gave considerable advantage to the more affluent and sociopolitically competent. As one newspaper noted, a court suit is "all that is necessary to worry an adversary for long years, force him to onerous expense, and even ruin him completely unless the latter, better advised, decides to come to terms."[22] This

21. Gran, "Vietnam and the Capitalist Route," p. 332.
22. Ibid., p. 199.

was no minor problem: at least 30 percent of all land in Cochinchina is estimated to have been subject to title contest![23] And the success of many of the small sects that preceded the Cao Dai was directly linked to struggles between small owner-occupiers and large concessionaires trying to claim their lands via legal manipulations and deed juggling.[24]

With so many adherents in high-level administrative positions, the Cao Dai were able to protect their members against many manipulations of the rural landholding elite, whose initial opposition to the movement was strong.[25] In 1928, two years after Cao Dai was founded, and when membership was already over two hundred thousand, a French inspector toured many of the frontier areas of western Cochinchina, areas where labor shortages meant that supposedly legitimate "feudal"-type (patriarchal) patron-client relations were still in effect: He found Cao Dai successful among only the poor tenants and small landholders and actively opposed by the rich landowners.[26]

The emphasis on protection for the members had considerable appeal to the peasantry. They were also given to feel a sense of equality and brotherhood by the easy communication among all levels of the organization. Cao Dai leaders, for example, were selected with far wider participation than were the leaders of village political or religious bodies. Cao Dai's branches throughout Cochinchina enabled peasants to travel and expand their contacts within a context of familiarity and security far broader than that of family or village. "Don't call me a great mandarin," one high-ranking, civil-servant Cao Dai told the peasants, "Let's be brothers."[27] In another instance cited in French reports, a retired administrative deputy, recruiting for the Cao Dai, moved among the peasants addressing them as "brother" (rather than as the usual "child" or "boy") and preaching equality and a future without maldistribution of wealth. The contrast between the Cao Dai official's emphasis on equality and protection and the patriarchal def-

23. Ibid., pp. 172, 318.
24. Hue-Tam Ho Tai, "The Evolution of Millenarianism, pp. 143–144.
25. Werner, *Cao Dai*, pp. 68, 162.
26. Gran, "Vietnam and the Capitalist Route," p. 545.
27. Werner, *Cao Dai*, pp. 115–116.

erence demanded by the notables and large landholders was not lost on the peasants. Needless to say, the former administrator's egalitarian approach undermined the current admininistrator's status and prestige.[28] The success of the Cao Dai among peasants also led to the recruitment of educated Vietnamese. Many village schoolteachers, who were generally hostile to, and in rivalry with, landlords and notables seeking to control access to literacy, aided or joined Cao Dai.[29] Indeed, the Cao Dai saw themselves as a modernization of and improvement on past sects; they boasted of being the religion of the educated.[30]

The Cao Dai represented a fundamental change in the dyadic patron-client type of landlord-tenant system. Its emphasis on local communities with local collective *welfare* systems contrasted directly with the dyadic *charity* of the landlords. Cao Dai communities restrained the ability of large landlords to forcibly maintain the dyadic pattern of landlord-tenant relationships whereby landlords played tenants off against one another—distributing resources unequally and developing close relations with some tenants in order to control still others and prevent collective bargaining. Using taxes and dues to build an important system of crisis aid for its adherents, Cao Dai weakened tenants' dependence on landlords, as well as the ability of large landowners, through control of notables, to dominate small landowners. This mediation of agrarian relations through the local Cao Dai community with its graduated hierarchy was a distinct change from dyadic, unmediated relations and prompted beneficial changes in the way landlords treated their tenants. When landlords followed their tenants into Cao Dai, a French report noted,

The poor classes of the population who practice this religion are flattered to number among their coreligionists their own bosses—members of the bourgeoisie and high functionaries—who treat them with more humanity, benevolence and generosity than in the past. Indeed, one witnesses everyday a rather remarkable change in the attitude of landowners towards their share-croppers and tenants, for instance, when they all belong to Cao Dai.[31]

28. Ibid.
29. Author's field work. See also Werner, *Cao Dai,* pp. 114–115.
30. Hue-Tam Ho Tai, "The Evolution of Millenarianism," p. 138.
31. Ibid., p. 135.

As the religion developed, some landlords joined the religion for purely instrumental reasons, as a way to stabilize their estates by establishing a religious and social community. A French report noted, for example, of the conversion of Cao Trieu Phat, a Cao Dai leader in the remote southern peninsula, that

His conversion seems to have been dictated by considerations of personal interests rather than by sincere religious conviction. It consolidates his position as landowner in Ca Mau by assuring him of an incontestable moral authority over the population of the region, which is partly a floating population without strong familial and communal traditions.[32]

Clearly, Cao Dai leaders were searching for forms and methods that would grant them equivalence with Western organizations.[33] The Cao Dai was inspired by the forms of the Catholic Church and competed with it for membership and influence. Its welfare activities—granting persons aid as a matter of right and not as a matter of charity or dependence—were attractive, and in a period when the Catholic Church had not yet Vietnamized its hierarchy, the overtly nationalist, cultural content of the Cao Dai program was an important source of satisfaction and attraction to its membership. Whereas both the Cao Dai and the Catholics could offer welfare and protection against the divide-and-conquer tactics of landlords and notables, only the Cao Dai could immediately offer positions of power and influence to local bonzes, administrators, and teachers; the Catholics could offer such positions only after a decade or more of special training, at best.

32. Ibid., pp. 135–136. These Cao Dai allied with the Viet Minh in 1945 and retained control of their area against all opposition throughout the resistance. Although Cao Dai is sometimes called a patron-client system, it has more in common with corporate systems. The value to large landlords of using Cao Daism, rather than a pure dyadic patron-client system to rule estates, is indicative of the management problems involved in trying to extend agrarian management techniques used with a handful of tenants to large estates involving intermediary agents, contracts, and and clienteles. The example of Cau Trieu Phat deserves extended comment. Despite the French cynicism about him, Phat was both the entrepreneur par excellence and a left-wing activist who was influential in earlier political parties before joining the Cao Dai, reminding us that not all landlords were conservative. The example of Phat also reminds us that while I have emphasized the political manipulations of large landowners and their attempts to structure their relations with their tenants so as to keep tenants at a decided disadvantage, there were indeed many landlords who were true economic entrepreneurs and popular leaders of their tenants, men who mobilized land, labor, and capital to benefit landowner and tenant alike.

33. Woodside, *Community and Revolution,* pp. 186–187.

Significantly, just as peasants in the seventeenth century searched out Jesuits to hear their court cases and dispense a more equitable and economical justice than the native mandarins were dispensing, so the Cao Dai leadership often was sought by its adherents to hear cases and dispense justice.[34] For not only did the Cao Dai build elaborate religious and welfare hierarchies from the local village level to their Holy See in Tay Ninh, but they also built a court system copied from the French. This is a clear example of how an entrepreneur can increase profit for himself and for all the members of his religion, while simultaneously strengthening the bonds of the religion by increasing the frequency of contact among members. Along with better justice for commercial transactions than could be obtained from the French, there was also less uncertainty and risk in dealings among members of the Cao Dai, as well as some profit to the religion from court fees (whether in gratitude or in actual payment). This was an incentive for Cao Dai adherents to deal only with one another and thus was an economic benefit for the organization, as well as for its peasant supporters.[35] It is, therefore, no coincidence that in time many rural businessmen and large landowners, seeing the advantage to themselves of being part of a more stable administrative system than the French provided, joined the Cao Dai. The Cao Dai may not have directly attacked large fortunes, but through their welfare and judicial institutions they were able to improve the lot of their adherents.

In some areas, Cao Dai membership was so widespread as to threaten a breakdown of the French administrative system. So successful were they at recruiting and/or controlling the administrative elite that in some districts the French found that the Cao Dai hierarchy and the provincial administration were almost one and the same.[36] One report to the Minister of Colonies complained that in areas where Cao Dai was growing in strength the idea of noncollaboration was spreading—administrative contact was becoming

34. Werner, *Cao Dai*, p. 125.
35. This point is made by Max Weber in his discussion of Protestant sects. See "The Protestant Sects and the Spirit of Capitalism" in *From Max Weber*, translated and edited by H. H. Gerth and C. Wright Mills (New York: Oxford University Press, 1958), pp. 320–322.
36. Werner, *Cao Dai*, p. 113.

most difficult, notables were turning indifferent, and bailiffs were even being threatened.[37]

The success of Cao Dai challenges the popular belief that the growth and expansion of the modern state strips away and destroys traditional organizations—leaving the peasant naked and defenseless in the face of capitalism and colonialism. On the contrary, Cao Dai is an example of how the skill and resources of the modern administrative system can be a stimulus to the expansion and improvement of traditional organizations. The robes and ceremonies, the spiritualism of the Cao Dai, should not obscure the political importance of the institutional framework that the religion developed to deal with peasant problems, nor the improvement it represented over dependence on village landlords and notables. Most certainly, Cao Dai was a religious movement, but it served other interests as well. Some of the Cao Dai elite were interested in a political base for the long-run battle against colonialism and political dependence; others were interested only in the profits to be made from operating a large-scale religious/insurance/protection system. In either case, there was a nonzero-sum situation in which sufficient resources were generated to grant benefits to both the elite and the members. As Tran Van Giau, one of Vietnam's most prominent Marxist historians, summed it up for Jayne Werner, the Cao Dai "had a bit of something for everybody."[38]

HOA HAO

The Hoa Hao religion takes its name from the Cochinchinese village Hoa Hao, birthplace of Huynh Phu So, who founded a peasant-oriented religious movement that combined a "Calvinistic," this-wordly Buddhism with virulent anticolonialism. It is a far more explicitly millenarian, anticolonial, and egalitarian religion than Cao Dai.[39] One of the most intriguing of all twentieth-century Southeast-Asian religious and political figures, So built his movement on the teachings of Phat Thay Tay An, the Buddha of Western Peace and the founder of a religious organization called the Buu

---

37. Ibid., pp. 130–131.
38. Ibid., p. 52, fn. 87.
39. Francis Hill, *Millenarian Machines*, p. 331.

Son Ky Huong.[40] During the uncertainty and disorder of World War II and the Japanese occupation, So used his writings and personal magnetism to transform a small religious organization based on long-standing ideas into a fervid following of more than a million adherents (mostly in the newer, "pioneer" areas of western Cochinchina) in less than five years.

The Hoa Hao never developed more than a rudimentary national structure, in large part because So was assassinated by the Communists in 1947. The heart of the organization was the Hoa Hao council in every village of converts. Above these men was a civil-religious hierarchy concerned with social welfare and propagation of the faith, as well as a military "self-defense" organization. After So's death the military forces split into four groups led by his four main military lieutenants, so that the basic organizational units for the sect were the village and province for welfare activities and the military region for political affairs. In contrast to the Cao Dai's elaborate system of titles and ranks, the Hoa Hao functioned with only village and provincial committees, a small national committee for the propagation of faith, and the four armies.

Huynh Phu So, the "mad bonze," was born in 1919 and appears to have exhibited no particular ambition or talent in his youth.[41] Son of a village notable, he failed the French-oriented primary

40. See Chapter 3, p. 124. Phat Thay Tay An founded Buu Son Ky Huong in 1849. The Buu Son Ky Huong advocated remaining within society (*nhap the*) rather than withdrawing into monastic life. Its heroes were Buddhist emperors who could make the transition from monk to warrior as the nation's problems demanded. Tay Son ideology was also an influence, in large part because many Tay Son soldiers from Annam had been demobilized in western Cochinchina, where the religion was based. (See Chapter 3, p. 118; also Hue-Tam Ho Tai, "The Evolution of Millenarianism," *passim*.) The religion stressed the accumulation of merit for future life, but its definition of merit was revolutionary: merit was acquired by performing good deeds, not by supporting the monastic order. Followers were not to be guided by monks, but were to guide themselves. The traditional Buddhist indebtedness to an emperor, moreover, was changed to indebtedness to one's country. Opposition to French rule was an article of faith. (Hue-Tam Ho Tai, "The Evolution of Millenarianism," p. 126.)

Many of the most violent uprisings against the French at the time of their initial takeover (as well as the twentieth-century uprisings of Phan Xich Long) were led by organizations based on the Phat Thay An's teachings. (Hue-Tam Ho Tai, "The Evolution of Millenarianism.") By the 1930s, however, the Buu Son Ky Huong was but a series of small, local prayer and self-help organizations scattered throughout the western parts of Cochinchina.

41. A. M. Savani, *Notes sur le Phat Giao Hoa Hao*. Major Savani was the key source of data on the Cao Dai and Hoa Hao for the French. As head of French intelligence in Cochinchina, he collected and translated much valuable material. (See

school and spent his days aimlessly wandering through the village, his nights catching crickets. So fell ill and was treated at length by doctors, soothsayers, and mediums—none of whom was successful. His illness was apparently a dual disease of malaria and spermatorrhoea, a combination that left him frail and in a constant state of nervous exhaustion. Villagers assigned various causes to the disease, and one belief common at the time was that a goddess was in love with So and wanted his death in order to have him to herself. Later, it was decided that this three-year illness was a series of trials to mortify his fleshly body—purify it, sanctify it, and enable it to receive and spread communications from the beyond. Whatever the cause, the disease left So pale, emaciated, and with the intense, illuminated stare of a visionary.

When all other cures failed, So's father sent him to a monk who lived in a remote mountain area. There So learned acupuncture, hypnotism, folk medicine, and the history and philosophy of Buu Son Ky Huong. When the monk died in 1939, So returned to his family; still uncured, he projected "light" and a "holy spirit." Soon thereafter, So was miraculously cured, whereupon he established next to his family altar a second altar dedicated to Buu Son Ky Huong and began to spread his message.

Word of this supernatural man and his new preaching spread quickly throughout the area, and people flocked to hear So speak. His preaching was a poetic, vernacular form of the Buu Son Ky Huong teachings of Phat Thay Tay An. Spreading everywhere by word of mouth, it almost immediately brought tens of thousands of persons to follow So's teachings.

So appears to have been aware of the political impact of his actions and of the social significance of his religious appeal. His aim was to create a Buddhist society of this world and not of the next:

According to my observations the Buddhist teaching founded by the Sakyamuni Buddha has as its foundations the doctrines of compassion, altruism and universalism with regard to all living creatures. I see him as a radical ideological revolutionary because of the following sentences:

Werner, *Cao Dai,* p. 33, fn. 52.) Unless otherwise specified, Major Savani's work is the source for this summary of So's life.

"All living creatures are endowed with a Buddha nature,"
and
"Buddha is the same and equal to all living creatures."
Being equal in nature, the reason living creatures are not equal with
Buddha is due to their level of enlightenment and not that they cannot
advance on the same level of the Buddha. If in this world the advanced
peoples still oppress backward peoples, this is contrary to Buddha's teachings. The Sakyamuni Buddha could not practically apply his teachings during his lifetime due to the unfavorable environment in India at that time.
Thus, he just elucidated the spirit of his teachings. Presently the development of mankind has reached a satisfactory level. Along with scientific
advances, we can put into practice those teachings and realize an equal and
humane society. Thus I will coordinate the altruistic, compassionate heart I
have absorbed with a method to organize a new society to practically serve
my compatriots and mankind.[42]

So began with attacks on the waste, ritual, and superstition in the
daily life of the peasant. The stress was on interior faith rather than
impressive appearance. Offerings were to consist only of water,
flowers, and incense, and were to be made only to ancestors, national heroes, and Buddha—it was not necessary to make offerings
to other spirits or to monks. Sacrifices to gods were not necessary,
he explained, for "gods are not like the functionaries here below,
corrupt, dishonest, and extortionary, distributing their favors for re-
compense."[43] As for monks who try to convince people that the
way to earn merit and prepare for the millenium is through gifts to
them, rather than through good deeds,

> The monk is like a lacquer tree,
> Outside it looks very solid, inside it's eaten by a termite.
> How sad that the bad bonzes
> Cheat the world and ruin the religion.[44]

Simplicity and sincerity were central to So's preachings. His religion was also called Buddhism of the Home, because of its emphasis on persons who had obligations to fatherland or family and
who, therefore, could not become monks. There were four prayers
a day to be said at home—for family, for nation, for Buddha, and

---

42. Huynh Phu So, *Sam Giang cua Duc Huynh Giao Chu,* p. 450. The author is
deeply grateful to Hue-Tam Ho Tai for translations from So's works.
43. Savani, *Notes,* pp. 64, 72.
44. So, *Sam Giang,* p. 9.

for the little people "to free themselves from profound ignorance."[45] Funerals were to be simple, for "what use is the expenditure of much money on the pretext of materializing feelings of filial piety, fidelity, and friendship toward the dead, when it would have been better to express these same feelings when they were living?"[46] Similarly, there was to be no haggling or bargaining over marriage; the emphasis, rather, was on free choice. Alcohol, opium, and gambling were to be abjured.

So clearly was interested in liberation and social change, and there is a vaguely veiled anticolonialism in his preachings:

> When one lives in servitude and without energy,
> One must not say one is noble and civilized
> Because all civilized peoples must be able to
> Govern themselves
> And not live all their lives in slavery.[47]

Much of his hostility was directed at what he derisively called "civilization":

> In the cities, people rush to produce bad habits
> For boys and girls.
> People smoke opium, drink liquor,
> Prostitutes and pimps pump away your blood.
> Whoever takes a careful look at society
> Cannot help but wail for the decadent nation.[48]

> Civilized people change their faces [makeup],
> Wearing bright clothes they enjoy themselves day after day.
> They display voluptuous figures
> And in the streets say amorous words.
> In their hearts are evil things,
> Their words, their speeches are too tricky.[49]

> Our ancestors were ignorant
> But they were more honest and sincere than people today.[50]

45. Savani, *Notes*, p. 65.
46. Ibid., p. 64.
47. Ibid., p. 79.
48. Huynh Phu So, *Suu Tap Thi Van Giao Ly cua Duc Huynh Giao Chu,* p. 81.
49. So, *Sam Giang*, p. 65.
50. Ibid., p. 66.

So made his sympathy for the poor and his derision of the rich abundantly clear in his vernacular style. His poems ridiculing the rich and their adoption of French ways were particularly popular:

> As for the rich, they are busy competing with others
> To fill up their coffers and their safes.
> They amass worldly goods and try to hold on to them,
> Afraid that they will be stolen away by thieves.
> They worry about becoming famous and powerful,
> They fear that the poor will not be able to pay them
> Back their money.[51]

Although So decried the callousness of the rich and favored ending class distinctions by treating all alike and abolishing special privileges, he did not preach the class struggle or attack religion. His opposition to Marxist ideology, however, was explicit:

> In this twentieth century,
> People try to get rid of religion.
> Credulous people think that
> One must compete through force.
> Thus one can get power and fame
> By preventing religious people from doing good.
> People are welcoming this new wave in great numbers.
> Their spirits are aroused,
> They despise the old national customs
> And say that religion is an opiate
> And that whoever tastes it becomes addicted to it
> And no longer cares to struggle.[52]

Because So "did not submit to the politically strong or scorn people in difficulties," and because he rejected class distinctions and treated everyone equally, he was called "the general of the common people."[53] So effective were his teachings at winning converts and so frantic and devoted were his followers, that urban Communist orators, "impressed and annoyed by his power and ability to hypnotize peasant audiences by 'speaking volubly without end,'" made "shameless pilgrimages" to ask So for his secrets and to study his techniques.[54]

51. Ibid., p. 108.
52. Ibid., p. 99.
53. Toan Anh, *Tin Nguong Viet-Nam*, p. 386.
54. Woodside, *Community and Revolution*, p. 189.

The rapid success of the Hoa Hao must be understood within the context in which it flourished. Western Cochinchina was an area where the problems of sociopolitical competence to deal with capitalism, violence, and stability were far more apparent than in other parts of Cochinchina, particularly during World War II.

Most of the rice exported from Cochinchina came from the western part of the colony, where there had been only scattered settlements before the French drained the area. Vast concessions had been granted in this area, and the landowners, some with as many as three thousand tenants, expended considerable effort to keep the peasants in a state of dependency and prevent them from buying themselves out of tenancy into small ownership. The scarcity of labor (relative to the rest of the colony) made population control essential to profit maximization for the landlords; as in the older areas of the colony, peasant access to new lands or minifrontiers was often blocked. Provincial officials were sympathetic to the landowners who tried to keep lands either in their own hands or in wasteland. Peasants who occupied and sought to cultivate new lands were constantly harassed; often the lands were seized from them and given to large landowners.[55] The fight to control tenants and maintain landlord domination also meant an active opposition to the development of any communal land sources.

The grand landowners also discouraged any peasant action likely to increase their personal sociopolitical competence to deal with collective action or markets. Peasants were usually forbidden to sell any excess paddy themselves; they were required to have the landlord sell it for them.[56] Tenants were provided with buffalo, tools, and food; their taxes were paid for them by the landlords.[57] Tenants who preferred to obtain these resources on their own in the market were sent away. The large lords clearly did not want tenants to develop their own contacts and skills.[58] In addition, tenants were

55. Gran, ''Vietnam and the Capitalist Route,'' pp. 325–328. In addition to the sources cited, much of this material was developed in interviews conducted by the author with the Hoa Hao in 1966, 1967, 1969, and 1970.

56. Pierre Gourou, *Land Utilization in French Indochina,* p. 353.

57. Pierre Melin, *L'Endettement agraire et la liquidation des dettes agricoles en Cochinchine,* p. 23. The landlords then retained the identity cards to restrict peasant mobility. (Personal research.).

58. Gourou, *Land Utilization,* pp. 352–354, and author's research.

not allowed to organize themselves to provide additional drainage or irrigation ditches for the large estates. Although additional drainage and irrigation often would have been of great profit to the landowners, there was clear aversion to any development of horizontal organization among the tenants. There was, furthermore, a general pattern of opposition and hostility by these large owners to the establishment of schools. Finally, peasants often were forbidden even to make improvements in their own tenancies if these improvements could be interpreted as a long-term, secure claim to the tenancy. In many cases, peasants could recall being forbidden to plant fruit trees: the trees were of value only after many years, and many landlords refused to guarantee the long-term tenancy—dependence was to be wholly upon the estate owner. In short, landlords would not make long-term commitments to tenants even for the prospect of increased profits.

In this western area, furthermore, there were always transients and drifters. Except for the early years of the Depression, there was always money to be made in the frontier areas. Coolies and tenants from the Saigon area, for example, could slip away for five or six years, earn some money, and then return to pay their debts and rejoin their families.[59] In addition, there was a steady stream of men heading west to escape criminal charges and orphans with nothing to lose by migrating.

Regardless of the fluctuation in international prices, the general level of subsistence in western Cochinchina was comparatively high, as the movement from the older areas throughout the colonial period would suggest. But many people, although secure against a true subsistence crisis of the kind so often faced in Annam or Tonkin, found themselves with a surplus, but with few or no ways to slowly or marginally increase their standard of living by investment. It is not surprising, therefore, that Gourou found a passion for high-stakes gambling: a very big stake was needed to buy one's way through the system. Similarly, losses could be easily tolerated because basic subsistence was fairly certain.

The area had a decidedly rough-and-tumble, "wild-west" atmosphere. This unsettled air was most prominent near the Cambodian

59. Ibid., p. 521.

border, where the vast wilderness area was dominated by gangs of smugglers and bandits fighting for control of smuggling routes and the protection money extorted from residents of the area.

The violence and instability were exacerbated by the Japanese occupation of Vietnam in 1940. As administrative controls collapsed, the area became increasingly disorganized. As the credit and market system fell apart, and as production ceased on vast tracts of land, the Japanese tried to extract rice and jute from the area by force of arms. By 1943, bands of smugglers and pirates kept entire villages in a state of constant terror. These were not rebels who robbed only the rich: if they robbed only the rich, it was because the poor had nothing left to give. In such an atmosphere, fortune-tellers, small sects, and "prophets" sprouted everywhere. Huynh Phu So was but one of the many prophets to whom the peasants turned for advice, and his was but one of many "messages" that abounded. But the other prophets to whom peasants turned generally held only small followings, no more than a few hundred faithful, attracted over a long period. So, however, was able to expand his following because he had a message that was credible in the abstract and did not require transmission by him personally to win adherents. He had a message, and its dissemination was facilitated by his talent for organization. "Squads" of peasants were taught So's sayings and poems; then, they fanned throughout the area to spread his message. Thus, So differed from other prophets because he knew how to "mass merchandise" his message—and how to build a powerful organization from a mass following.

Despite its emphasis on individual, home-centered religious practices, and despite its origins among peasants lacking the skills of the Jesuits, Cao Dai elite, or Communist cadres, the Hoa Hao developed a strong village-centered organization. Its leadership accomplished this by offering peasants resources which lessened their dependence on and control by the large landowners; guaranteeing and adjudicating local property rights and disputes; and collecting substantial local taxes, which were then used to provide both insurance and welfare benefits. Moreover the movement's non-Communist and anti-French position interested the Japanese and allowed for expanded operations and continued growth of the movement during the occupation.

So's early aides seem to have come from two sources. In most villages at least a few of the Buu So Ky Huong faithful were willing to take part in a peasant-oriented movement with patriotic and radical overtones. Throughout the area, furthermore, So attracted numerous outsiders—orphans, retainers of the rich, and others with no place in any village.[60] Many of these followers were directed to become friendly with the Japanese or to work for them, and they later provided the Hoa Hao with many weapons.

With the Buu Son Ky Huong and others as a core, So organized village congregations that everywhere charged exceptionally high taxes.[61] In return, the illiterate adherents received instruction in the teachings of the Hoa Hao. The money was also used secretly to build local self-defense forces that would protect the congregations from the turmoil before the coming millenium (as well as from the French). Most important, tax money was used to claim and put into production abandoned land, which was then sold or rented cheaply to believers. The income from such sales and rentals, in turn, supported the supravillage organization. As congregation funds helped to finance agricultural improvements, peasants who belonged to a Hoa Hao congregation became increasingly free from their former total dependence on landlords. Dependence on landlords was further weakened by the establishment of stock-farm cooperatives that provided another source of draft animals.[62] By these means, the leadership acquired great power almost overnight. Fearful of the fanaticism—ritual murders were not unknown—and the mutual support of congregation members, landlords began to loosen their control over tenants and permitted them to enter the rice market on their own. They finally contented themselves with merely collecting rents, but little or no rents were actually paid as the peasants began to give their rice to the congregations—in effect daring the landlords to object. Alarmed by the threat of their power, the landlords soon

60. Author's research.
61. The exact rate of taxation has not yet been determined. The variation between areas and the general inflation of that period make accurate information difficult to obtain or assess.
62. Author's research.

sought to slow it by "finding faith" and joining congregations. By World War II, however, neither the landlords nor the French were able to slow Hoa Hao forces, which were powerful enough to prevent village authorities from harassing adherents or acting on behalf of large landlords.[63]

Soon the security teams emerged from underground. Effectively controlled by the Hoa Hao committees, they began to protect harvests and property; thus, the Hoa Hao displaced French courts as adjudicators of contested land. The security teams also defended against piracy: as the self-defense movement developed into actual armed units, the more adventurous military leaders (such as the legendary Ba Cut) raised a fortune for their religion (and themselves) by charging rich landlords and merchants huge sums to track down and destroy pirates and bandits. Throughout An Giang province, for example, there are still memories of the days when pirate heads were hung on stakes around villages to serve notice that the Hoa Hao armed forces were in the area and protecting their own.

It is noteworthy that the money was available among the peasants to finance a major organization. The peasants willingly paid heavy local "taxes" in a situation where they were able to place long-run faith in the credibility and viability of the movement and its leaders and to anticipate a return on their investment via insurance, protection, and welfare benefits.

As the movement increased in numbers, frequent conversions among the French-controlled provincial troops nullified or hindered the ability of the French to move against the Hoa Hao. Their several attempts to detain or deport So, for example, were unsuccessful. They were equally helpless to prevent the Hoa Hao from restoring and using as resistance centers the pagodas destroyed by the French in the nineteenth century.[64] The Japanese and So, on the other hand, exploited each other to mutual benefit. Desperate to obtain for their war effort as much rice as possible from Cochinchina, the Japanese willingly permitted So to travel the western region as long as he calmed the anxieties of the peasants and urged

63. Author's research; see also Dabézies, "Forces politiques au Viet Nam," pp. 138–139.
64. Savani, *Notes,* pp. 14–15.

them to continue rice production. (The Japanese, of course, were by no means entirely hostile to non-Communist, anti-French movements.)

As So's fame spread he began to attract urban activists searching for a movement. After the Communists destroyed the urban Trotskyite movement in 1945–1946, many Trotskyites sought to work with the Hoa Hao.[65] In 1945, So had standardized rules for local Hoa Hao communities. Now, due perhaps to Trotskyite influence, he undertook the formation of a political party. Disturbed by the fanaticism of his followers, So argued that "to lead a crowd by religion is to lead it by fanaticism, while [to lead] it by politics is to appeal to reason."[66] The platform of Dan Xa Dang, or Social Democratic Party, advocated socialism, large, commonly owned farms for those who wanted them, and a rejection of inequality. But So did not change his stance toward Marxism:

Because the Dan Xa Dang does not exceed the limit of national liberation and social reform, it does not reject any class within society, nor does it leave to any single class the right to exceed certain limits. It is against injustice and for the development of revolution in the country.[67]

The formation of the party finally convinced the Communists that So had to be eliminated. Shortly after the party's formation, he was assassinated by the Communist leadership of Cochinchina.

As a precaution to ensure against his return to life, So's body was hacked into three pieces, and each portion was buried in a separate grave. Still uncertain, and still apparently imbued with the local fear of spirit vengeance, the Communists later dug up the pieces to make sure that So was, indeed, dead.[68]

COMMUNISTS

Party Development

While some members of the Vietnamese elite converted to Catholicism and others allied themselves with the Cao Dai, still others turned to foreign countries for political ideas and training.

---

65. Author's research. Also Savani, *Notes,* pp. 11, 26.
66. Ibid., p. 24.
67. Ibid., appendix, p. 3.   68. Ibid., p. 29.

The victory of the Japanese fleet over Russia in 1905 stimulated a lasting interest in Japan as the first Asian power to best a Western country militarily; this interest was enhanced by Japan's modernization, as well as by its giving asylum to Prince Cuong De, a member of the royal family who preferred exile to French domination.[69] Eventually this led to such Japan-oriented political parties as the Dai Viet. A similar interest in Sun Yat Sen and the Chinese revolution led to the Vietnam Nam Quoc Dan Dang (VNQDD), a party modeled on—and sometimes guided and trained by—the Chinese Kuomintang (KMT). Members of all of these foreign-inspired parties manifested a high degree of personal heroism and bravery. Yet, although the Communists at times had fewer members and less elite support than did the other parties, they were, in the end, the only ones able to mobilize the peasantry. By examining the success of the Communists, we can see clearly, by contrast, the weaknesses and flaws of the losers—parties such as the Dai Viet and the VNQDD, which were able to field armies and capture elite sentiment, but were never able to move beyond that to village control and peasant mobilization.

Marxist ideology first entered Vietnam early in the twentieth century via Chinese translations. It was not well received, nor even understood. Confucian activists found social class a puzzling concept and questioned the ranking of persons by economic criteria.[70] The early appeal of communism, in fact, had little to do with Marxism—few of Marx's works were translated into Vietnamese or used among Party members. Attracted first and foremost by the prestige of the Russian Revolution, Vietnamese intellectuals were also responsive to the Communist concern with imperialism and to the writings of Lenin, in which they found a powerful tool for political organization and for overcoming fragmentation.[71]

69. For the early interest in Japan, see David Marr, *Vietnamese Anti-Colonialism 1885–1925.*

70. Woodside, *Community and Revolution,* p. 55.

71. This account is not intended as a comprehensive history of the Communist Party in Vietnam, and I have concentrated on those details most central to the Party's ultimate victory. For fuller accounts, on which this summary has relied heavily, see Huyny Kim Khanh, "Vietnamese Communism: The Pre-Power Phase (1925–1945)"; William Duiker, *The Rise of Nationalism in Vietnam 1900–1941,* and "The Revolutionary Youth League: Cradle of Communism in Vietnam," pp. 475–499, and "The Red Soviets," pp. 186–198, and "Building the United Front:

Ho Chi Minh, attracted to the Communists by their interest in colonialism and by Lenin's successes, was a founding member of the French Communist Party. Returning to Asia, he formed a Revolutionary Youth League (1925–1929) from several hundred young Vietnamese, most of whom were either members of preexisting, anticolonial organizations like the Tam Tam Xa (Heart to Heart Association) and the Tan Viet (Revolutionary Party) or lycée students expelled for anti-French activities. Ho, both personally and through his writings, was able to convince many members of these parties that Leninist theory was an advance over their own thinking about power and revolution. He was able to offer members of the Revolutionary Youth League training in political and military methods at various Communist or KMT academies in China.[72] From the Revolutionary Youth League emerged various Communist associations and, in 1929–1930, a Communist Party linked to the Communist International.

Soon after the Party was formed, the majority of its members were betrayed to the French and imprisoned or killed for their part in depression-era demonstrations, tax protests, and abortive uprisings.[73] At this same period the VNQDD also suffered decimation after its abortive attempt at a military uprising among native militia. The remnants of the latter party fled to China and remained a shadowy group until 1945; the Communists, however, were able to replenish their ranks. Many students, and some workers, returned from France committed to communism. Additionally, a few hundred Vietnamese were recruited in Vietnam and trained at the Toilers of the East University in Moscow. In 1936, when a Popular Front government came to power in France, it legalized limited Communist activity in Vietnam, and the Party again grew to a few thousand members. In 1939, the collapse of the Popular Front led to another French crackdown, and the majority of the open, avowed

---

The Rise of Communism in Vietnam, 1925–1954,'' pp. 3–26, and "The Comintern and Vietnamese Communism.'' Additional information on World War II comes from John T. McAlister, *Vietnam: The Origins of Revolution,* and King Chen, *Vietnam and China 1938–1954.* Unless expressly cited, all information on the policies followed in urban and rural areas is from personal research.

72. Khanh, "Vietnamese Communism" pp. 90, 112.

73. For the sake of brevity, as many dates and name changes as possible are here omitted.

Communist Party members were arrested. Then, in 1940, Vietnamese militia units, about to be sent to Cambodia from Cochinchina to repulse a Thai invasion, allied with local Communists and rallied rural support. The French quelled the uprising, and then decimated the Party in rural Cochinchina.[74] The Communist Party that organized the Viet Minh front and gained ascendancy from 1945 on was, therefore, the third rising of communism in Vietnam.

Thousands of Vietnamese joined the Communist Party before 1941, and most of them had their determination reinforced by French prisons. But whatever the intensity of their determination and their previous efforts, there is no reason to believe that they would have so dominated Vietnamese politics after 1945 had the Japanese not occupied Indochina, and had the Communists not fundamentally changed their approach after 1940. This analysis strongly supports Woodside's contention that without the emergence of a "second" Ho Chi Minh after 1940, there would have been no Communist revolution in Vietnam—that Communist success ultimately depended on Ho's changing from a "cosmopolitan ideologue" emphasizing global imperialism, class struggle, and the proletariat to a "back-woods insurrectionist" who dropped earlier views about culture and religion as nothing but tools with which people were oppressed.[75]

When Ho Chi Minh returned to Vietnam in 1941 after roaming Asia for years as a Comintern delegate, the preoccupation of the Soviet Union with the war in Europe gave him a freer hand to develop a local Communist strategy than at any previous time. The weaknesses that were the result of rigid Comintern directives and that had kept the Communists in a precarious position could now be overcome, and Ho, drawing on his Leninist training and Comintern experience, could reorient his strategy to local conditions.

The Viet Nam Doc Lap Dong Minh Hoi (Alliance for Vietnamese Independence), or Viet Minh Front, was formed by the Communists in 1941 at a low point for Vietnamese communism. The Party had rebuilt after the disaster of 1930–1931, only to have

74. Khanh, "Vietnamese Communism," pp. 308, 327–329; Duiker, *The Rise of Nationalism*, pp. 267–268.

75. Woodside, *Community and Revolution*, p. 220.

its urban branches destroyed throughout most of the country in 1940. All that remained was the skeleton of an underground party throughout the three regions of Vietnam, scattered cells in provincial capitals and industrial areas, and a small organization among tribal groups in the mountainous highlands between Vietnam and China.[76] Japan's defeat was foreseen, and the Front was oriented to the postwar period and to the rising tide of Vietnamese nationalism. It reflected a willingness on the part of the Party to work more seriously than in the past with intellectuals and the middle class and to develop a mechanism for the more effective utilization and mobilization of "reformist" possibilities among the peasantry.

From the very first days of the Revolutionary Youth League there had been distrust of intellectuals. Although intellectuals had been among the first to sacrifice themselves, they had nevertheless been viewed as "opportunists" and their grievances against the French either downplayed or ignored. Similarly, because the emphasis on workers had been paramount, there had been uneasiness after championing or allying with bourgeois groups.[77] The grievances of the middle class had been ignored, culture and religion had been seen as "weapons to keep the Vietnamese stupid,"[78] and nationalism had been seen as "archaic."[79]

As a result of these attitudes, the Trotskyites had been able to defeat the Communists in the electoral competitions for colonial council in Cochinchina and municipal council in Saigon. Most of the Trotskyite inner circle had learned their Marxism in France and were comfortable with urban electoral competition. Emphasizing the grievances of much of the Vietnamese electorate against the wealthy and privileged few, and unburdened with any need to make obeisance to parties in France or Russia, the Trotskyites were able to develop a large membership (over three thousand) in Cochinchina. Some French-educated Cochinchinese Communists allied themselves with the Trotskyites, but the national leadership and the Comintern, uncomfortable with the bourgeoisie, opposed to

76. Khanh, "Vietnamese Communism," pp. 349–356.
77. Ibid., pp. 88–89.
78. Woodside, *Community and Revolution,* p. 169.
79. Duiker, "Red Soviets," p. 196.

nationalism, and hostile to Trotskyites tried to stop such alliances and programs.[80]

Now at its lowest point, the Party decided to emphasize national liberation and to temporarily deemphasize class struggle. The move toward nationalism, coming at a time when decimation among the Trotskyites was even greater than their own, enabled the Communists, earlier than other major parties, to tap the large and growing national awareness among young intellectuals and the middle class that was stimulated by the wartime environment. Once-hostile writers, often uninterested in communism or class struggle, were more than willing to propagandize for national liberation and allied themselves with the Communists, who were then the only party interested in mobilization. Soon Viet Minh propaganda, drawing on Vietnamese legends and nationalist feelings, spread throughout the country, fanning an awakened nationalism.

Under the regnant Japanese, the French administered the country until 1945. But throughout the period of occupation, the Japanese constantly encouraged anti-French and non-Communist groups, such as Hoa Hao and the Cao Dai, and parties friendly to Japan such as the Dai Viet. The French responded by doubling the number of Vietnamese in high-level administrative positions and by beginning a number of programs for mobilizing the student population before the Japanese could sway them. While the Dai Viet and VNQDD members in the administration drifted toward positions in the capitals of Hue, Saigon, and Hanoi—and especially toward the positions that were high paying and prestigious—the more disciplined Communists directed their members and friends toward many positions in the provincial capitals, especially those directly concerned with mobilizing youth. Leadership of the enormously popular youth and sport program that the French developed throughout Cochinchina (the first legal youth program of any import) was dominated by Communists and their sympathizers. This program and its paramilitary successor under the Japanese were directed by three men, all of whom were either Communists or strong

80. Duiker, *The Rise of Nationalism,* pp. 238–258; Woodside, *Community and Revolution,* p. 170; Khanh, "Vietnamese Communism," pp. 230–308.

sympathizers from the beginning, and all of whom served in Ho Chi Minh's government after 1946.[81]

By 1943, Viet Minh propaganda was spreading throughout the country, Communists and Communist sympathizers were being placed in strategic locations throughout the administration, and servicemen's groups were being organized in many regiments.[82]

One area where the Communists had survived suppression was among the mountain minorities of Tonkin. The Communist Party was the only party with a comprehensive view of the Vietnamese nation and an awareness of the strategic importance of the non-Vietnamese mountain minorities. From 1932 on, there had been constant Communist activity in some of the mountain regions along the border between Tonkin and China. This area, and the support of the mountain tribes, were factors in Viet Minh success that cannot be stressed enough. While the other parties concentrated on the urban Vietnamese elite and rarely bothered with workers or peasants, the Communists were developing a large following in tribal areas, which were virtually inaccessible to the French and Japanese, but which were also right on the edge of the Tonkin delta.[83] Thus, while the VNQDD was amassing an army in China, while the Trotskyites were rebuilding in Saigon, and while the Dai Viet was arguing about the future in urban coffeehouses, the Viet Minh was developing a small army and an extensive network of bases and trails in north and central Vietnam. Indeed, when the Viet Minh entered Hanoi in 1945, non-Vietnamese troops were a substantial element of the small Viet Minh army, and Chu Van Tan, one of the key Communist military leaders, was himself a Tho-Ti who led the first guerrilla band in the mountain base area.

The mountain base so near to the Tonkin delta grew in importance as the Japanese occupation continued. As large tracts of land were forcibly diverted from rice production to jute, and as large quantities of peanuts and rice were commandeered for the war effort, famine entered Tonkin. As early as 1943, with American

81. White, "Revolution and Its Adherents," p. 27.

82. Woodside, *Community and Revolution,* p. 227.

83. McAlister, *Origins of Revolution,* chaps. 10 and 12, and "Mountain Minorities and the Viet Minh: A Key to the Indochina War," pp. 771–844.

planes bombing the rail lines to Saigon and preventing the shipment of food, there was starvation in the north. By 1944, there was mass starvation that finally took between five hundred thousand and two million lives in Tonkin. The Communists were the only political group willing or able to aid the Tonkinese peasantry, and they used the famine to build organizations in villages of Tonkin. With a few weapons, often with nothing but spears or an occasional grenade, Communists organized bands of desperate peasants to attack the Japanese granaries. Among the political parties, only the Viet Minh responded to the famine, and the distribution of Japanese rice among the participants in the raids was a powerful incentive for peasants to gather to the Viet Minh banner. Therefore, prior to March 1945—when the Japanese disarmed the French and proceeded to develop a Vietnamese government—the Viet Minh was already developing contacts through youth groups in Cochinchina and organizing peasant bands to gather food for survival in the north.

When the Japanese disarmed the French and organized a Vietnamese government, the Viet Minh stayed in the shadows, distributing its propaganda and waiting for disillusionment to follow the initial native euphoria. As they had expected, the Japanese gave only limited powers to their Vietnamese cabinet, and the Dai Viet, despite the offers of help from friendly Japanese officers, had no idea of how to take advantage of the sudden surge of passion sweeping the country. Dai Viet leaders were so unsure of what to do that they approached the Imperial Viceroy in Hanoi to ask for advice and support. After hearing the Dai Viet leaders, the disillusioned Viceroy fled Hanoi to join the Viet Minh in the mountains.[84]

In the aftermath of the Japanese coup, educated Vietnamese—particularly the young—recognized that France was not likely to be able to reassert its prewar dominion and that independence, or at least a completely new arrangement with the French, was certain. Many wanted only to help their country, to work for freedom and independence. Others wanted to secure their personal future, who-

84. Chen, *Vietnam and China*, p. 109.

ever emerged as victor. At the same time, all the parties were quietly searching out reliable new members to fill their ranks (membership in all parties swelled after the defeat of France; the increase was clearly related to heightened expectations of victory over a debilitated France). Indoctrinating new members among the enthusiastic, but as yet uncommitted, majority was slow work for all parties. But the Communists were able to outpace their rivals by brilliantly using those national salvation organizations that formed part of the Viet Minh front as half-way houses to coopt thousands of people unable or unwilling to sort out the ideological differences among parties. Eager to help their country and/or themselves, doctors, poets, soldiers, and bureaucrats attended the meetings of their respective national salvation associations to discuss what their members could do to create a new Vietnam and what role their professions should play in an independent society.

While the other elite groups floundered and slowly became disillusioned with the Japanese, the Viet Minh continued its attacks on granaries, began to woo Vietnamese militia units from the French services, and accelerated its propaganda effort with ever more strident and passionate demands for freedom and independence without the restrictions and restraints imposed by the Japanese. By July 1945, the Viet Minh presence was "ubiquitous": its flags were everywhere; Viet Minh songs were sung in schools and in the streets; and the Association of Vietnamese Students was leaning toward the Viet Minh.[85]

Then in late summer, after the Japanese surrender to the Allies, the Viet Minh, with a Communist Party now "swollen" to nearly five thousand, emerged from the backlands and mountains to mount the August Revolution. Over a period of weeks, they disarmed the Japanese, took over government buildings in regional and provincial capitals, and proclaimed a broad-based government of all Vietnamese. Soon thereafter, Vietnam was occupied by the Allies—the Chinese occupying the northern half of the country, the British the southern half. The next year was the most difficult of all for the Communists. In the north they confronted Chinese-supported

85. Khanh, "Vietnamese Communism," p. 423.

groups like the VNQDD as well as rampaging troops of Chinese war-lords.[86] In the south they soon confronted the French, returned to power by the occupying British, who helped them drive the Communists from Saigon.

But in the south, in the center, and in the north, the Communists—through the Viet Minh—were able to develop sufficient rural support to gain control of large areas of the countryside and to hold those areas against all other forces, Vietnamese or French, through a long war of resistance. The August Revolution was the beginning, not the end, of peasant mobilization. Thus, during the Japanese interlude and after the August Revolution, while Dai Viet and VNQDD members worried about personal power, cabinet seats, and portfolios in a joint government of all parties, the Communists developed meaningful and exciting activities for those eager to secure the future. This allowed them slowly to recruit the best of the elite for their government and party and to make an alliance with those who, although unwilling to become Communists, *were* willing to work with them at a different level of activism and commitment.

These fronts were crucial, not only because they coopted persons from other parties, but also because many of these people were willing to leave the cities and join the Viet Minh in the countryside when the postwar Chinese occupation of the north and the truce with the French came to an end. These allies helped to build the army and administration that were essential for the mobilization of the villages following the August Revolution. By devoting attention

86. The VNQDD arrived back in Vietnam with the KMT army and tried to mobilize a following. Although they were able to build a party, their inexperience and incompetence prevented them from attracting an elite via intermediate organizations. With no plans for the future, they were unable to give patriotic but apolitical members of the elite a conviction that alliance with the VNQDD would be efficacious. The Communists even managed to hinder their party-building at times by setting up dummy parties with coopted ex-members to draw people away. (Chen, *Vietnam and China*, p. 124.) Despite their friendly feelings for their (Vietnamese) ideological brothers, the KMT forces found themselves working most closely with the Viet Minh (and therefore with the Communists), who were best able to meet the demands of the occupying forces—both the "legal" demands for food and support and the *sub rosa* demands for gold and opium. Indeed, the Viet Minh ended by purchasing substantial numbers of weapons from KMT troops with opium they obtained in the highlands and donations they collected in Hanoi. (McAlister, *Origins of Revolution*, pp. 228, 246–255.)

to nationalism, culture, and the middle class, the Communists attracted an elite, its "revolutionary friends," whose energies could be channeled into mass organization.

The Viet Minh mobilization is a clear case of the importance of contributions, some of which were not stimulated by any expectation of future selective payoff. It emphasizes how important internalized feelings of duty or ethic can be. It also indicates how important it can be for an organization to manipulate information to convince persons that their contributions can be efficacious—as a way of increasing the level of contributions and as a way of diverting the contributions from other competing claims on the volunteered resources. That is, some persons felt the right and necessary thing was to contribute, others were convinced of this by the Communists, and many of each group were convinced by the Communists that their contributions would do the most good if channeled through the Viet Minh.

Village Mobilization: Annam

With the exception of a few key ports and other strategic points along the coast, the greater part of central Vietnam was never reoccupied by the French after World War II. Thus, even though opponents of the Communists could no longer rely on French support, the Party, through the Viet Minh, still did not achieve firm control of village administration until after 1950. Seizing power, in other words, was but the beginning of the process of gaining control of the villages and of actually bringing about redistribution in the countryside. Seizing power in the provincial and district capitals, for example, did not produce a lasting surge of volunteers among the peasantry. After the August Revolution, as the major Communist theoretician Truong Chinh noted, there were still many areas where even the young "consider the sabotage of roads, the building of earthen barricades, helping the army, as they did forced labor under the imperialist regime."[87] The problem of building support and overcoming free riders was as central to Viet Minh strategy as it was to Cao Dai, Hoa Hao, and Catholics: "How many able people still consider that the resistance war is the affair of the gov-

87. Truong Chinh, *The Resistance Will Win,* p. 206.

ernment and the army, and maintain the indifferent stand of 'doing nothing while your neighbor's house goes up in flames'?''[88]

During World War II, both the VNQDD and the Dai Viet were able to build contact nets of party members in Annam, nets that included the major provincial and district capitals, as well as scattered members in many villages. At the time of the August Revolution, they undoubtedly had as many weapons and more party members in the areas studied than did the Communists. Following the revolution, however, the Viet Minh quickly surpassed opposition membership with the support of province- and district-level front organizations. Whereas the Dai Viet and VNQDD limited their appeals to educated members of the elite—particularly administrators and officers of the militia—the Viet Minh targeted other groups in the population. Although they too sought to win members of the elite, they also made concentrated efforts to attract enlisted men and noncommissioned officers, locally powerful guilds like the weavers and fishermen, and machinists and skilled workers at scattered railroad yards and industrial sites. Of particular strategic importance for the Viet Minh's campaign to mobilize the peasantry was their success with the technical cadre who built and maintained the sea walls, bridges, dams, and irrigation works on which many villages depended for survival. The opposition attracted members from the militia, but the Viet Minh was particularly successful with the soldiers who returned to Vietnam following the defeat of France.

Although the Viet Minh had furtively propagandized villages throughout World War II, and although they quickly surpassed their opposition in membership following the August Revolution, they were not sufficiently integrated into the provinces at the time of the takeover to be able to place their own people in every village administration. Nor did they have sufficient power then to ensure that the existing village leadership would carry out their orders. As an intermediate step, therefore, they formed intervillage administrations, combining all the villages within a local market area into a larger "supervillage." Through these intervillage Viet Minh administrative committees, the Communists gradually developed the general support and organizational strength with which they were later

88. Ibid., p. 207.

able to take control of the individual villages and break the control of the notables. As the Communist Party was slowly and carefully built up, more and more redistributive policies and structural changes were introduced in the villages. But the policies that were first implemented were chosen to be—and were—so popular that little external power was needed to carry them out.

Immediately after the takeover, all schoolteachers and educated youth were "drafted" to begin literacy campaigns throughout the countryside. In some cases, villagers were not even allowed to enter the marketplace until they had learned the new words for the day. This was an important policy identifying the Viet Minh with progress and a generalized "antifeudalism," and it was overwhelmingly popular. Both teachers and peasants remember the literacy program for its contrast with the opposition of the previous mandarin bureaucracy and village administrations, which had so often— despite the Confucian respect for literacy—tried to stop the spread of education for the masses as threats to their own power. It is not clear how many older peasants actually learned to read, but many young persons did, and there is no doubt that teachers developed strong attachments to a regime that encouraged them. The Viet Minh collected large "donations" from the well-to-do (protection money, in the eyes of the rich) and used some of this money to support the teachers, which meant that for the first time the poor in many villages were able to afford education.

Immediate changes were made in the communal land system— changes that in the past had been resisted by the notables. Wives of men absent from the village were for the first time given a share of land. Before, when the men away from the village had been only poor laborers, their wives' demands had been scorned; now the absentees were often armed and members of the Viet Minh. Furthermore, all communal land that formerly had been diverted to private use by notables was returned to the village. The bidding system for the communal lands that were auctioned off for village expense money was then completely reformed. Only small parcels were auctioned, and payments for the parcels were made after the harvest rather than at the time of auction. This broke the back of the system whereby only the rich had benefited from the auction; it also

added to the money realized from the lands for the village treasury.[89] Thus, both the poor and the villages gained at the expense of
the rich. Even more revolutionary (and somewhat controversial)
was the policy of giving everyone who had lived in a village more
than five years the right to a portion of the communal land. For the
first time, therefore, there was no large, disenfranchised population
of outsiders who had fewer actual rights than established villagers
and who could be exploited by others.[90]

At the same time that the bidding system was changed to increase the benefits for the poorer peasants, an even more drastic,
and more popular, change was made in most of the villages studied:
The customary ladder of rank and seniority by which communal
lands were distributed was replaced. First, equalization committees
carefully reorganized the parcels to make them as equal in value as
possible (which, of course, coopted a few villagers and heads of
family into close working relationships with the intervillage committees). Then, random lotteries were instituted for the distribution
of the communal land. Instead of a regressive system in which the
rich picked first, in most villages a new system was introduced in
which everyone had an equal chance for every parcel.

This new lottery system, after an initial period of confusion and
tension, gained widespread support for the clear increase in equity
and benefits for so many villagers. In addition, it wrested a major
source of power from the village notables without exposing the Viet
Minh committees to charges of power grabbing.

Some villagers and administrators fled the area when the Viet
Minh took over. These "traitors"—corrupt administrators and village officials who had manipulated the French system for personal
gain—left behind them both land and animals, which were promptly
appropriated by the intervillage committees. Unlike the communal
lands, however, these were distributed by a committee selected at
the intervillage level and stocked with Communists and "progressive" elements. These resources became a source of patronage by
which a small and loyal following in the villages could be built. As

89. See Chapter 4, pp. 150–52.
90. It is not unreasonable to assume that there might have been serious resistance to this enfranchisement. It is hoped that further research will supply details.

a village base in each area began to develop through the favors and patronage of the intervillage committee, the standing notables were replaced by notables elected in open meetings by all villagers. Repeatedly, the Communist candidates overwhelmingly defeated their opposition, which lacked the sophistication to arrange agendas, stack meetings, or prepare slates.[91]

As soon as the Viet Minh gained administrative power within the villages, they instituted a change even more radical and more popular than their changes in the communal land system. The odious system of body and land taxes was replaced with a single, progressive income tax based on total family productivity and providing a standard exemption for every adult and child.[92] This meant that never again would tax demands squeeze anyone below subsistence. Ultimately, it also meant that when the pressures of war were most severe, the Viet Minh could extract more taxes from the villages than the French had ever done—and without reducing anyone to starvation. By judicious selections to the village committees in charge of assessments, the Communists were able to increase their control of the villages dramatically. The program itself won wide popular support, and serving on the assessment committee enhanced the prestige and following of its members.

Soon after the August Revolution, all debts for which the interest on the original loan exceeded 200 percent were declared paid in full by the Viet Minh. In reality, the debts were canceled because the creditors—often outside landlords who had built landed fortunes by manipulating taxes and assessments—fled. The Viet Minh also made serious attempts to impose maximum allowable interest rates, but the attempts were as unsuccessful as others had been in the past.

91. There was wide support for a lottery system to replace the ranking system for distributing communal lands, but every other issue involving the communal lands ended in either stalemate or unresolved conflict. There were attempts in some villages to turn all lands into communal lands, and this met with opposition from all classes (but not from all persons in each class). There were attempts to limit the distribution of communal lands to only the poor and landless. These also met with widespread opposition and conflict, as did the attempts to convert the communal land into private lands for the laborers, landless, and families of Communists and soldiers.

92. Supposedly, this change was instituted effectively in 1945, but the data suggest that it took several years before the administrative capacity and credibility to make the change actually existed.

An intermediate result was obtained, however, when village officials ceased to permit evictions before the harvest—that is, they no longer permitted a man to be deprived of the fruits of his labor. The Viet Minh-controlled administration was also unwilling to evict persons for small debts. These safeguards, combined with the progressive tax system and individual deductions, reduced the need for the high-interest, seasonal loans that had so often devastated the poor.

The results of a campaign to limit all rents to 25 percent of the crop are more ambiguous, and it is not clear how frequently the Viet Minh were able to control the transfers between tenant and landlord. In some villages, the Viet Minh actually collected the rent and paid the landlords in an attempt to prevent side payments, but in at least some such cases landlords were still able to demand under-the-table payments. What finally did have a clear effect was the increasing Viet Minh tax as the demands of war increased. In many villages, landlords found it to their advantage to sell most of their lands to tenants or poor relatives to avoid the increasingly confiscatory taxes for the upper-income brackets. This brought about something of a de facto land-to-the-tiller program even before the Communists actually organized any campaign against large landowners.

The Viet Minh also subsidized such village-level improvements as increasing the water storage and irrigation facilities. Many of the poorest smallholders could not afford either time or money to dig or improve water ponds on their property. Village neighborhoods often lacked a sufficient number of ponds to store water for later release into the fields because no one in the neighborhood had time, money, or leadership skills. Now the Viet Minh, with a village administration committed to long-run maximization of production (rather than to personal, short-run material aggrandizement), helped to finance and coordinate extensive additions to waterworks in poor neighborhoods; in many cases they even subsidized improvements on small parcels of land held by the poor. The long-run increases in productivity, to say nothing of the support such policies generated, more than repaid the small expenditures of the Viet Minh.

As a result of these changes, and in spite of the many problems, production is reported to have actually increased in many villages after liberation—clear testimony to the ability of the Viet Minh leadership to foster peasant faith in village-level action, to reshape economic incentives, and to increase the supply of collective goods.[93] Improving village resources, implementing a progressive tax system, and equalizing the distribution of communal lands are all classic methods for increasing productivity and ensuring security for the poorest peasants, but they could have been effected only by a leadership that had achieved considerable credibility and power prior to instituting such changes.

The Viet Minh, then, faced the same problems of rural organization as did the other movements discussed, for winning enormous popularity as the group responsible for declaring a free and independent Vietnam did not immediately or easily translate into the rural support necessary for the long and arduous resistance that was to ensue. That support was gained by slowly restructuring village government to increase productivity and taxes and to create a positive system of exchanges between village leaders and peasants that could be tapped for the resources and manpower necessary to build an army. As this was developing, the Communist Party itself was slowly growing in numbers and placing its members in key military and administrative positions. As Communist control increased, there was some movement toward much more radical policies of land reform. These policies, however, were not introduced into most of central Vietnam until late in the resistance war, and they were in a state of flux at the time of the French ceasefire in 1954. The Communist/Viet Minh success, therefore, was due more to the stripping of power from the notables and to progressive taxation than to any land redistribution, as narrowly conceived. Yet by the end of this period in Annam, there was a popular saying that "To marry a very poor man is like heaven; to marry a landowner is as bad as the fate of a cow."

Cochinchina

The Communists were more active in the rural areas of Cochinchina than they had ever been in the rural areas of Annam and Tonkin (except, perhaps, for Nghe An and Ha Tinh). At the time of

93. Our research, however, indicates that production dropped after 1950 as war demands and French embargoes increased in intensity.

liberation, furthermore, the peasants of Cochinchina were by far the most militant. Yet neither in terms of party membership nor village control were the Communists able to duplicate their successes of the other regions. Whereas in Annam and Tonkin they could capture villages and then remake them, in Cochinchina they had faced a far more complicated task of actually creating villages. Such a task was hampered by many factors that did not prevail in the other regions. In 1945, for example, their central organization was in almost complete disarray. Moreover, they had to contend with both a stronger French presence and the powerful forces of the Hoa Hao and Cao Dai. Given the strength of the opposition, the fact that the Communists achieved even limited success in Cochinchina is noteworthy.

The Communists were very active in the peasant movements and tax protests of 1930–1931. Throughout Cochinchina, these demonstrations led to violence against landlords and village offices and to the burning of tax rolls and land records. Six of these protests even led to the creation of nascent "soviets." Although not a single one of these demonstrations was as explosive or as long-lived as the Nghe An-Ha Tinh uprisings of northern Annam, they nevertheless covered the majority of the provinces of Cochinchina and involved tens of thousands of peasants. The movements were destroyed by the French, and most members of the Communist organization in the countryside were imprisoned. They were released in 1936 by the Popular Front government in France.

From 1936 to 1939, the Communists, building on old contacts, used the new, more liberal Popular Front standards of political activity to again develop extensive rural ties. When a call was raised in Saigon for an Indochina Congress to discuss the future of the colony, the Communists used the planned Congress—which never occurred—to reestablish rural networks. In 600 of the 1,300 villages of Cochinchina, Committees of Association were formed with the ostensible purpose of discussing grievances to be brought before the Congress. In fact, the Communists were forming small self-help fraternal organizations, one-fourth of whose members had been political prisoners. These organizations were built around friendship associations, groups to build straw huts, associations to celebrate the cult of the genii, and insurance systems. So quickly did these groups develop, and so popular were they in the countryside, that the official press was soon referring to them as the "new soviets" and saw in them a portent of future uprisings.[94] After the collapse of the Popular Front, these associations were smashed and many of their members arrested. Still more Communist organizations were smashed and more peasants arrested following the abortive 1940 uprising at the start of World War II, but the prisoners from that period were freed in 1945.

Yet another source of Communist supporters were the youth movements. During World War II the key leaders of the French youth and sports movement were either Communist or pro-Viet Minh, and many chapters of the village youth associations were organized by underground Communists or their supporters.[95]

Cochinchina was the area with the most antilandlord hostility and the most widespread demands for "land to the tiller." In much of the region, in fact, the August Revolution of 1945 was a widespread agrarian revolt during which land seizures were common.[96] By then many of the large estate owners had lost control of their tenants. In areas where there were small holders and local landlords, as well as large estates, a credit and marketing infrastructure independent of the large landlords had developed. This gave peasants access to alternate sources of credit, as well as to rice markets, which meant that any forced dependence on the large landlords was harder to maintain, particularly in the aftermath of the Japanese coup, when administrative breakdowns made it harder for big landlords to rely on village officials to police their tenants. Throughout Cochinchina, there was widespread retaliation against landlords, their clients, their agents, and the village officials with whom they had connived.

Lands were also seized by peasants who had been deprived of

94. Daniel Hemery, *Revolutionnaires vietnamiens et pouvoir colonial en Indochine: Communistes, trotskyistes, nationalistes à Saigon de 1932 à 1937*, pp. 318, 287, 327. Seventy percent of the committees were in villages around Saigon, Cholon, Hoc Mon, and Thudaumot; in Gia Dinh from Saigon to Hoc Mon nearly all villages had committees. This suggests the need for further study of the links between these committees and the earlier Nguyen An Ninh Association. On committees, see also Khanh, *Vietnamese Communism*, pp. 263–266.

95. Jayne Werner, *The Cao Dai*, p. 255; Khanh, *Vietnamese Communism*, pp. 345–346.

96. Donald Lancaster, *The Emancipation of French Indochina*, p. 421.

what they felt was their legitimate right to ownership of land. During the settling of Cochinchina, large portions of land had been subject to ownership disputes that arose from manipulations of French title processes. This was repeated during the depression of 1930–1931, and bureaucrats in the administrative centers profited from their fixed salaries to buy up land from smallholders who could not meet their tax payments (often because of manipulations by these same bureaucrats). Many of these smallholders now moved to reclaim their lands.

But in spite of widespread agrarian hostility to the landlords and bureaucrats, and in spite of the Communists' past political efforts and their many rural contacts, Cochinchina proved to be the weakest of the three areas of Vietnam for them, and they ended up controlling and organizing only about one-third of the population. If the Communists had done as well in Cochinchina as they had in Annam and Tonkin, there would have been no second Indochina war, for there would have been no conceivable base for a non-Communist government.[97]

One obstacle to their success in Cochinchina was the situation following the abortive uprising of 1940, which left the regional committee in disarray and without control of the provincial and local party apparatus it required to proceed effectively during the August Revolution. The distance of Cochinchina from the Party's mountain base in northern Tonkin, moreover, posed severe problems of communication and coordination.[98]

Another obstacle was French power in the south, restored almost immediately after World War II. Whereas the Chiang Kai-shek troops who occupied the northern half of the country were visibly anti-French, the British who reoccupied Saigon immediately released French officers and administrators from prison and helped them reestablish an administrative presence in Saigon and the provinces. This drove the Communists out of the cities and into remote areas before they could either ally themselves with (and dominate) or eliminate all their competition. Many of the Trotskyite leaders

97. Werner, *Cao Dai,* pp. 353, 339–344.
98. Truong Chinh, *The August Revolution,* pp. 35–36, in Truong Chinh, *Primer for Revolt.*

who were released from prison in 1945 (or who had managed to avoid imprisonment in 1939) were assassinated; many, however, escaped to plague the Communists. As Truong Chinh reviewed the August Revolution in the south, "because of the extremely intricate situation . . . it was not possible to carry out a systematic elimination of the counter-revolutionary elements on Jacobean or Bolshevik lines. . . . For a new-born revolutionary power to be lenient with counter-revolutionaires is tantamount to committing suicide."[99]

Although the Trotskyites had no mass base of their own after 1939, they added to the troubles the Communists had with the Hoa Hao and Cao Dai. Because they sought to hold together all three regions of the country, and because they wanted to be *the* political party to deal with France over the future of Vietnam, the Communists were restrained in their attitudes toward future relations between Vietnam and France. Lacking these prospects, the independent Trotskyites were bound by no such constraints. The moderate behavior of the Communists cost them little in the north, where the pro-Chinese VNQDD and the pro-Japanese Dai Viets were too incompetent at rural mobilization or alliance formation to pose a threat to the Viet Minh; nor did the behavior of either the Japanese or Chinese troops add to the power or prestige of the respective parties. In the south, however, where the competition was keener, Communist moderation was costly, and only one faction of the Cao Dai was willing to align itself with the Viet Minh.[100] With their rabid anti-French stance, the Trotskyites persuaded the remaining Cao Dai and the Hoa Hao sects to form their own front with them.[101]

Furthermore, while the Communists were having trouble establishing an effective alliance with the Hoa Hao and Cao Dai, many areas of Communist strength and many past and former Communists and militants were joining the competition. In the

99. Ibid., pp. 40–41.
100. Werner, *Cao Dai,* p. 256.
101. Hue-Tam Ho Tai, "The Evolution of Vietnamese Millenarianism," p. 230. The Trotskyites also had developed extensive personal contacts with the rural elite during their electoral campaigns for seats on the colonial council. (See Hemery, *Revolutionnaires vietnamiens,* pp. 248–275).

province-by-province history of the August Revolution compiled in Hanoi, a persistent Communist comment on the south was that participants in the 1930 and 1940 uprisings were being lost to the sects and that, for example, Hoa Hao propaganda was attracting ''a number of our comrades, whose consciousness was inadequate.''[102] When they formulated their plans for seizure and consolidation of rural power, the Communists emphasized the districts with the strongest tradition of protest and revolution. When the moment came, however, the areas where protest had been most extensive and rabid in 1930—the areas where soviets had actually been formed—were solidly Hoa Hao.[103]

There were many other groups in the region, all armed with weapons obtained from the Japanese. Besides the Hoa Hao, Cao Dai, Catholics, and Communists, there were many local sections of the youth movement that the Communists, despite their top-level infiltration of the youth movement, had not been able to control. Some of these groups were controlled by landlords and village officials who had placed their retainers in them to receive military training; others were little more than freelance extortion and protection groups who terrorized all sides equally. There were also sections of the Heaven and Earth Society that had never joined the Cao Dai; some VNQDD, Dai Viet, and Tan Dai Viet; the White Lotus Society; Trotskyites; groups of Chinese (who were Communist, but not yet allied with the Vietnamese Communist Party); the French-Vietnamese Colonel Jean LeRoy, who organized a Catholic militia and controlled (and sometimes terrorized) large parts of the Tan An-Ben Tre area; a brotherhood of railroad workers; gangs of rubber plantation workers; and even armed Boy Scouts.

An important part of Communist strategy was to bring as many of these groups as possible into the Viet Minh, but here too they faced competition. For awhile, the anti-Communist Nguyen Hoa Hiep was able to organize a division in the area near Saigon by attracting many of these small groups to his side.[104] In Bien Hoa province, for example, the railroad workers had for years main-

102. Ibid., pp. 221–222, 184, 170, 205.
103. Ibid., pp. 167–168, 225–226.
104. Werner, *Cao Dai,* pp. 277–278: Hue-Tam Ho Tai, ''The Evolution of Vietnamese Millenarianism,'' pp. 236–237.

tained a secret brotherhood associated with the Vietnamese branch of the Heaven and Earth Society. During the war, they raided several French armories and developed a small military force with which they attacked recalcitrant colonial administrators. After 1945, the workers were attracted to the Resistance; hostile at first to the Communists, they allied themselves loosely with a division formed by Nguyen Hoa Hiep from groups similar to their own. Hiep, however, was unable to maneuver politically and create a large and powerful military force. Nor was he able to use his military forces to take control of villages and develop new adminstrations. Disillusioned, the railroad workers—and the relatives and neighbors they had recruited—allowed themselves to be integrated into a Communist-controlled force. With their background of industrial discipline and organization, and with their secret society experience, three of the men from the railroad workers brotherhood —which never numbered more than a hundred men—soon rose to command their own Viet Minh military units.[105]

In addition to the areas controlled by the Hoa Hao and Cao Dai (both of whom eventually made peace with the French in return for control of their own territory), as well as the Catholics, the Communists faced opposition from landowners, many of whom actively collaborated with the French to protect their lands. Thus, French outposts and hostile landlords kept the Communists off balance in many areas where the peasantry was sympathetic to the Viet Minh. In an effort to gain effective control of such areas, they sought to reduce the strength of the opposition by appeasing the landlords. In short, they reversed their usual tactics and declared that anyone who seized private property would be severely punished. But the declaration went unheeded.[106] With no effective regional organization to control their own supporters, much less the many competing groups, the Communists were unable to stem the cries for agrarian reform and redress of grievances. "Land to the tiller" was the most potent political slogan in the countryside, and some local Communist groups began to redistribute land, cattle, and tools im-

---

105. Author's research. By 1970, at least three of these men had reached the level of regimental commander or provincial Party secretary.
106. Ellen Hammer, *The Struggle for Indochina 1940–1955*, p. 108.

mediately following the August Revolution.[107] Even the Catholic Colonel LeRoy instituted land reforms in the areas he controlled.[108] The Communist tactic of moderation in order to mitigate the strength of the opposition failed: it was unacceptable to a militant peasantry that found ready support from so many other political/ religious groups.

In Annam and Tonkin the challenge to the Communists was to restructure villages. In Cochinchina the challenge was to create villages. In the corporate areas of Annam and Tonkin villages controlled large amounts of water and land, as well as dikes, seawalls, irrigation or drainage canals. Political control of a neighborhood, of a few notables, or of lineages generally led either to the splitting of the village or to the support of the whole village. In the open villages of Cochinchina, however, where the public sector was small and the mode of production required little or no widespread cooperation, all the contending groups—Hoa Hao, Cao Dai, Catholics, Communists—had to create their villages, household by household, in order to control areas.

Given the obstacles, the Communists succeeded to an impressive extent.

As many large landlords began to side with the French, the Viet Minh village committees, reversing their former policy, ratified and defended (as well as extended) the distribution of property seized from collaborators. They also supervised the collection of rents by patriotic landlords in order to enforce rent ceilings. Although few large, urban-based landlords or landowning bureaucrats supported the Viet Minh, a considerable number of village-based landlords with 20 to 100 hectares did. Hating the large landlords and the French for pushing them around, many preferred a future of reduced landholdings under the Viet Minh to the colonial situation. Clearly, some of these landlords were protecting themselves against a Communist future. (Many of them, however, never tried to reclaim their lands after 1954, and many of their sons chose to become Viet Minh cadres rather than landowners under the French.)

107. Hue-Tam Ho Tai, "The Evolution of Vietnamese Millenarianism," pp. 230, 329, fn. 27.
108. Bernard Fall, "The Political Development of Vietnam: V-J Day to the Geneva Ceasefire," pp. 444–447.

These economic benefits resulted in numerous small-scale, voluntary actions on behalf of the Viet Minh. As long as the Viet Minh kept landlords, their clients, and their agents out of power, the peasants benefited economically. It was, therefore, important to the peasants that Viet Minh cadres not be captured. Indeed, the latter traveled almost everywhere in their villages unarmed, confident that someone would make the effort to alert them if the French entered the area. By contrast, village officials siding with the French could operate in most villages only when accompanied by several armed guards.[109]

But far more than either land reform or meeting subsistence requirements was required to develop a power base for the Viet Minh. The decline of the export trade meant that many villages had substantial surplus land. With land uncultivated—over 35 percent of the land in Cochinchina went out of production in 1946[110]—hunger and land shortages were not important short-run problems for most peasants. What attracted many unorganized peasants to the Viet Minh and gave the Party its initial entry into many areas were cotton cloth and cotton seeds for planting. Although there was enough to eat in all of Cochinchina during the period of instability that followed World War II, Japanese requisitions of fiber and disruption of international trade had produced a shortage of cloth. It was so complete that large amounts of rice could not be transported because there were no sacks to hold the rice. As will be noted in the following quotation, the cloth shortage even limited the time that peasants could spend outside their houses. Just as the Viet Minh distributed sweet potato and manioc seeds to peasants in Tonkin to help them back onto their feet after the floods, so the Viet Minh in Cochinchina signaled their concern for the peasantry with cotton seeds and attacks on stores of textiles. As one peasant recalled his first contact with the Viet Minh,

[During the war] we had money but there were no clothes available to buy anywhere. We had one pair of pajamas. . . . When my wife went to the market I would stay in the house and then when she came back I would

109. Jeffrey Race, *War Comes to Long An,* p. 3.
110. Davy Henderson McCall, "The Effects of Independence on the Economy of Viet Nam," p. 125.

wear the pajamas to the field. . . . The pajamas wore out and all we had
was a single rice sack. . . . When she wore the sack to market I stayed
home. . . . Then I wore the sack to the fields. The only time we could go
to the fields together was at night when no one could see us . . . we were
so ashamed. . . . Then the Viet Minh came to our village. . . . They had
some cloth and a few sacks and they brought some cotton seeds and taught
us how to plant them.[111]

Another popular action was the local court the Viet Minh established in each village to arbitrate disputes. Localizing and "Viet-
namizing" the courts gave the thousands of peasants engaged in
land disputes with large landowners an opportunity for local hearings in a language they spoke and without intimidation of witnesses. The comparative advantage of well-connected and powerful landowners declined, and there were countless reversals of
earlier decisions of village councils or French courts. Reversals occurred even in intrafamily disputes:

When Ba Qui's father died he left him six hectares of ricefield, but Mr. Ca
Dau, a relative of his, seized the land and made it his own. . . . When the
Viet Minh arose, Ba Qui sued Ca Dau. The Viet Minh invited all the
[prestigious men] in the village to a meeting, and they testified that the land
belonged to Ba Qui's father and that Ca Dau had seized the land and enjoyed the yield of the land for many years. Then the Viet Minh authorities
ordered Ca Dau to return the land to Ba Qui. This was done and Ba Qui
didn't demand any compensation payments. So the case was settled very
nicely. While Ca Dau had the land and enjoyed the yield of the six hectares
of ricefield, he used part of the income to worship Ba Qui's parents, and
this is why the authorities sympathized with him and didn't punish him.[112]

In the villages the Viet Minh organized peasants' and women's
associations. To pump life into them and to give villagers an incentive to join and to deal with the leaders of these associations, they
were given an important voice in all village decisions about land,
taxes, and marriage disputes. The peasants' association, for example, had a voice in arbitrating tax disputes and in assessing labor
drafts. The women's association was assigned a role in marital disputes; it also gave land and support to households headed by
women. The activities of the new local courts also served to in-

111. Author's research.
112. Rand Corporation Interviews with the NLF, interview DT-49, p. 2.

crease the prominence of the associations. Because their leaders represented the defendants in all court cases, the villagers had still another reason to remain on friendly terms with the leaders, building up obligations by attending meetings, contributing labor to group projects, and so on.

As in Annam, educational opportunities were greatly expanded. The literacy classes were enormously attractive and demonstrated to many the Viet Minh's break with the "feudal" past. One program was called "Six Months in Two Years": providing basic literacy adapted to the rhythms of rice agriculture, it spaced the six months of teaching over the slack portions of two years. Further, both to make the classes more attractive and to develop exchange relations with the Viet Minh that would continue after the end of classes, the classes were organized as vehicles of collective action and insurance for the students:

> We put them into groups of 20 or 30 people. Besides teaching them to read and write, we also helped them with their family or economic problems. For instance, if the house of a student has burned down, then the whole class and the whole unit will devote its effort to helping that particular student. Therefore the students are responsive to the class; they are eager to attend the class because the class is not only where the people learn, but also the place where we discuss other problems of collective interest.[113]

The literacy and self-help programs became an important recruiting ground for lower level officials and Party members. A major source of personnel for higher branches of the Viet Minh were the two large high schools (Thai Van Lung and Nguyen Van To) they established. Like the village classes, these schools were quite popular.

Additionally, a people's culture and art movement was founded. It recruited heavily from among the wandering troupes that performed traditional Sino-Vietnamese shows at village festivals, from vagabond musicians, and from village guitar teachers. Much like the bands at Tammany Hall election rallies, these groups helped attract large crowds for Viet Minh village rallies. With their tradi-

113. Simulmatics Corporation, "Studies of the Chieu Hoi Program," interview CH-5, 1966. This person was one of the organizers of the education and literacy programs during the Resistance and later became a member of a provincial Party committee.

tional arts and their newly developed skits and songs, they glorified the Resistance and ridiculed the basket carriers (the flatterers and clients of the rich) and Francophile Vietnamese.

These programs demonstrated the concern of the Viet Minh for the peasantry and were essential to the development of their armed forces. They led many young people to see a bright future with the Viet Minh, and the local cadres helped release youth for full-time participation in the struggle by taking care of their families. As one man who had spent his youth living as a buffalo boy in the home of a landlord recalled,

The Viet Minh came through on their promises. They actually took the land from the landlords and distributed it among their followers. Their propaganda struck a responsive chord in me because I hated the French . . . who were in league with the landlords that had oppressed and beaten me. . . . I thought in following them that I would have a brighter future . . . that I would get land to till, and my family could break out of its poverty. . . . [Before joining] I thought about my grandmother. I worried that she would live in misery if I went off and joined the army because no one would be left to look after her. I brought these apprehensions up with the cadres and they said that they were certain that the village authorities would take care of my grandmother. After I left my grandmother was given 0.6 hectare of ricefield.[114]

Despite their eventual success in many villages, the national Communist leaders, nearly all of whom came from Annam or Tonkin, found problems in Cochinchina that they did not encounter elsewhere. Ho Chi Minh's 1949 complaint about the failure to eradicate individualism in Cochinchina is indicative of the hold of "individualism" and a market orientation among the peasantry.[115] In some areas, the Viet Minh tried to manage all confiscated lands as communal land, allocated by the village Viet Minh committee. This was a decidedly unpopular measure among the peasantry—who demonstrated a marked preference for private property—and the Viet Minh quickly reverted to a policy of allotting confiscated lands to their supporters without placing any time limits on the allocation. The Viet Minh definitely preferred communal land as a prelude to collective agriculture, but as the head of Viet Minh economic and

114. Rand Corporation interview DT-101, p. 4.
115. Lancaster, *Emancipation of French Indochina,* p. 420.

financial services for Cochinchina stated, "the system [private property] is far from perfect. . . . It leads to over-fragmentation of property and to a very definite decrease in output. However, we have been obliged to stick to it because our entire political action among the peasants is based upon the right of each to individual property. We would have risked losing their support had we stopped breaking up landholdings."[116]

Furthermore, there was serious tension in some areas between the Viet Minh leadership and the peasantry over increased consumption. With a surplus of rice, many peasants in liberated areas resumed trade with the French-occupied cities for kerosene, cloth, fish sauce, and bean curd. Other peasants began to raise pigs and ducks for urban markets. The Viet Minh, who wanted to isolate the cities and starve them out, while keeping the liberated areas autonomous, went so far as to kill ducklings and piglets in order to curtail trade. These measures only aroused strong resentment and evasion. Eventually they had no choice but to allow the trade and relied instead on taxing it—tacitly ignoring the circulation of French piastres alongside their own Ho Chi Minh currency in liberated areas.[117] Paradoxically, this tension between peasant "bourgeois" economics and national liberation efforts was vastly ameliorated by French action. Concerned that the international rice trade was providing an important source of taxes for the Viet Minh, the French instituted an economic blockade of most of Cochinchina and severely cut rice exports.[118] Because there was less money, and therefore less interest in market goods among the peasantry, it was easy for the Viet Minh to manage (and isolate) the subsistence economy that ensued from the French action.

Given its competition, the disarray of the Communist Party in 1945, and the distance from the liberated areas of Tonkin, the success of the Viet Minh in developing liberated government in the south can be considered an achievement. To be sure, the peasants

116. Nguyen Than Vinh, quoted in Hammer, *The Struggle for Indochina*, p. 340.
117. Author's research. See also Rand Corporation interviews DT-148, DT-145.
118. Lancaster, *Emancipation of French Indochina*, p. 415. The blockade also caused nearly one million peasants to leave Viet Minh areas for Saigon or areas controlled by the sects.

of Cochinchina were less attracted by the ascetic discipline required of dedicated Communists, and party membership lagged in the region to such an extent that at one point of 180,000 members in the country, only 23,000 were in Cochinchina.[119] Moreover, there were differences of interest between market-oriented peasants and liberation-oriented Communists and an inability to make effective alliances with most of the Cao Dai and Hoa Hao. Nevertheless, the rural institutions that the Communists developed helped create villages in the liberated area, as well as remarkable support among non-Communist peasants and cadres. As Joseph Alsop wrote in 1954 when he visited a Viet Minh liberated area in Cochinchina,

The thing that impressed me most, in fact, was not the Communists' extraordinary feat of organizing, maintaining and expanding an independent state in southern Indochina without exterior support and in the teeth of French power. What impressed me most, alas, was the moral fervor they had inspired among non-Communist Viet Minh cadres and the stout support they had obtained from the peasantry.[120]

119. Document 1 of the appendices to "Working Paper on the North Vietnamese Role in the War in South Vietnam," Department of State, May 1968, is a report prepared by the Central Executive Committee of the Indochinese Communist Party in 1948 and details the "narrowness of development" of the Party in Cochinchina. See also Document 21, same series. (At the time of the Geneva Conference, this had risen to about 30,000, but this was still proportionately less than the other regions, even when only nonsect areas are considered.)

120. Joseph Alsop, *New York Herald Tribune,* December 31, 1954.

6

Peasant Movements and Collective Action

WHETHER RELIGIOUS or political, movements that change the basis of peasant society generate conflict and violence. As they develop, these movements fundamentally alter authority relations. These alterations spawn new conceptions of identity and self-worth.

In the case of Vietnamese Catholics, the profound impact of adopting the religion was compared to acquiring a new "occupation."[1] Similarly, after the Communists had been in control of Annam for several years, the paternalistic and hierarchical terms of address between common peasants and village leaders changed; village officials and peasants began to address each other in fraternal terms, "younger brother" to "older brother." Contrasting the new and the old, a peasant described village relations before liberation:

---

1. Virginia Thompson, *French Indochina*, p. 274.

If the village chief wore one type of clothes, then the villagers would refrain from wearing the same type. For example, if he wore wooden shoes to a ceremony or meeting, then the villagers would make a point to come to the same ceremony or meeting barefoot. . . . If he sat in the middle of a long bench, the villagers would never dare to sit down but would crowd in the rear and behind the bench. . . . The simple people were even afraid of walking at the same level with the village chief, and if they passed him they had to bow to him. . . . If he needed help repairing his house or clearing his garden, he would call on the villagers to come in and help him without ever being paid. The villagers would address him as *sir* while referring to themselves as *your humble servant*.[2]

From "your humble servant" to "younger brother" is indicative of the magnitude of the change brought about by these movements. These changes were ultimately massive, yet peasants did not start out conscious of the fact that they were about to accomplish massive works. Great works need not require great leaps by impassioned or outraged peasants.[3] The four movements studied here were built upon countless small steps that, added up, had an enormous cumulative impact on society and that generated passion and outrage. Rage was expressed and passions unleashed as new contexts decreased the risks of expressing age-old angers and/or as new options led to a reevaluation of old procedures as onerous, humiliating, and illegitimate.

I have argued that peasant investment logic includes both gambles and insurance, long-run investments and short-run investments. Further, I have argued that peasant investment logic applies to villages and patrons, as well as to markets. That is, instead of an investment logic for markets, on the one hand, and a normative logic for villages and patron-client relations, on the other, there is a similar investment logic for both situations. I now argue that these same principles apply to political and religious transformations of society: there is a unifying investment logic that can be applied to markets, villages, relations with agrarian elites, *and collective action* —whether the collective action is to build villages or to re-

---

2. Author's research.
3. This, however, is not to deny the importance of such "moments of madness" as the August Revolution. See Aristide Zolberg, "Moments of Madness," pp. 32–56.

build them as part of a new society. Whereas moral economy views of peasant protest and rebellion emphasize defensive reactions against threats to subsistence guarantees, loss of legitimacy for traditional elites, and moral outrage, I emphasize political entrepreneurs, incentive systems, free riders, and risk. The contrast is between moral propulsion and political competence.

MORAL ECONOMY AND REVOLUTION

To moral economists, peasant protests and movements are "defensive reactions" against massive threats to their traditional institutions.[4] In this view, capitalism turns labor, land, and wealth into market commodities, which (as noted in Chapter 1) is seen as but "a shorthand formula for the liquidation of encumbering social and cultural institutions."[5] As elite paternalism and "feudal" norms erode, peasant institutions and norms of reciprocity are stretched to the breaking point by the demands of capitalism and colonialism. As James Scott has argued, "Commercial agriculture and the growth of the state . . . was to steadily reduce the reliability of subsistence guarantees to the point where peasants had hardly any alternative but resistance."[6] Peasant protests are seen as restorative in nature: they seek to reinstate the traditional institutions and procedures menaced by capitalism; they are desperate responses to the threat to subsistence; they represent a collective response in the collective interest of the peasantry.

But the facts of peasant movements in Vietnam challenge this interpretation in three ways. First, the movements are antifeudal, not restorative. They seek not to restore traditional practices and institutions, but to *remake* them; they seek not to destroy the market economy, but to *tame* capitalism. Second, there is no clear relationship between subsistence threat (or decline) and collective response. Third, the issue is not the extent of threat to a class, but the risk to

4. Eric Wolf, *Peasant Wars of the Twentieth Century,* p. 282.
5. Ibid., p. 280.
6. James C. Scott, *The Moral Economy of the Peasant,* p. 40.

individual participants—and there is a clear distinction between individual and group (or class) rationality.

If peasant protests were defensive reactions to threats posed to "feudal" precapitalist institutions, there would be no widespread peasant movement in areas where traditional agrarian relations and/or traditional village forms survive intact. In Cochinchina, peasant protests would be a response to a change from "feudal" landlord-tenant relations—sharecropping, with shared risk, protective value, and a subsistence guarantee—to a "more straightforward and more painful cash-nexus contract with little or no social insurance for the weaker party."[7] In the denser eastern half of Cochinchina, there was just such a change from sharecropping to fixed-rent contracts, with the greater risk and uncertainty absorbed by the tenants. However, the Hoa Hao developed in the newer, less densely populated, western areas of Cochinchina, where the older, "feudal-type" sharecropping relations remained in effect. The Hoa Hao, that is, attracted its following in an area where supposedly legitimate, traditional practices still prevailed.

In southern Annam, traditional village forms and traditional "feudal-type" landlord-tenant relations also prevailed. Yet there the Communists succeeded not only in taking over nearly all the villages, but in wresting power from the traditional village elites by instituting important transformations in precolonial village procedures. These facts further support the argument that traditional village institutions and agrarian relations did not provide security and welfare (to say nothing of dignity) nearly so well as some observers have assumed. More equitable, just, and efficient procedures than were generally found in precolonial traditional institutions were possible and could win peasant support, as the precapitalist success of the Catholics demonstrated. Thus, the evidence suggests that a decay of old arrangements is not necessary to interest peasants in new and better procedures.

Traditional arrangements can be improved on and landlords outbid by persons willing to provide the same services at lower cost (and higher dignity). The growth of law and order and of centrally directed public works also means that less risk is assumed by land-

7. Ibid., p. 67.

lords and that their services are less crucial to peasants. Additionally, the acquisition of new skills by peasants and the expansion of communications networks make it possible for small fragmented movements to be linked into wider, more effective organizations. In 1916, a few years before the Cao Dai began to consolidate numerous small local sects into a regionwide movement, the director of the Sûreté Générale described the changes taking place in sects and secret societies. Whereas in the past their activities had been localized, "the new conditions of modern life, the multiplication of means of communications, have favored the development of broader groups. Better-organized or better-led associations tend to aggregate and absorb the sporadic societies which exist over the whole country."[8]

What constitutes a subsistence crisis changes as organizations expand, communications improve, and new skills are developed. Some events provoked collective action in Cochinchina but not elsewhere in Vietnam. In Cochinchina there was widespread protest activity in 1913 and 1916 against corvée labor which came during harvests and against the draft of men to fight in World War I.[9] In Cochinchina during the Depression, there were widespread protests when tax payments forced many smallholders to lose title to their land. In Tonkin, on the other hand, a great number of persons lost their land, many even had to flee their villages, and there were no subsistence crisis uprisings.[10]

In short, all four of the movements that serve as illustrations in Chapter 5 address themselves to peasant security and welfare, but they are counterevidence to the argument that peasant uprisings focus on restoring old rules of elite behavior. New conditions, new options, new skills and opportunities can create situations in which long-standing practices come to be viewed as arbitrary, capricious, or intolerable.

There is no direct relation between short-term subsistence crises and collective action. In examining conditions in the same region at different points in time, the evidence does not suggest that the

8. Hue-Tam Ho Tai, "The Evolution of Vietnamese Millenarianism," p. 109.
9. Ibid., pp. 116, 120.
10. Vu Quoc Thuc, "L'Economie communaliste," pp. 201–202.

greatest political activity will occur at the time of greatest subsistence threat. The peasant protests of 1930–1931, in the northern Annam provinces of Nghe An and Ha Tinh, are the most frequently cited examples of massive protest against subsistence threats or economic crisis. Famine conditions resulting from severe drought precipitated widespread protest against French taxes. Ultimately, the protests became a conflagration that led to the formation of peasant "soviets" and to complete loss of French control over a wide area for more than a year.[11] Here, indeed, is a subsistence crisis leading to protest in which hungry peasants forcibly confiscated food supplies from villagers with food reserves. In this same area, however, there had been an even worse famine at the turn of the century. At that time, thirty thousand persons died; yet there was no widespread protest.[12] The difference between the two reactions was not level of misery: it was organization, particularly communication and coordination. By 1930, there were more than three hundred Communists (including cadres trained in Thailand, China, and Russia) actively working among the industrial workers in the area, and urban labor organization was already making an impact. Osborne could therefore conclude, "In terms of the organization necessary to arrange protest marches and even, on one occasion, a carefully coordinated attack on a French post making use of infantry tactics of fire and movement, the concept of a jacquerie is not appropriate."[13]

Nor is there a direct relation between extent of subsistence threat and political activity when two regions are compared at the same point in time. Although Annam and Tonkin (aside from Nghe An and Ha Tinh) were generally peaceful during the Depression period, there was widespread protest throughout Cochinchina, just as there

11. Scott, *Moral Economy,* pp. 127–150. See also Milton Osborne, "Continuity and Motivation in the Vietnamese Revolution: New Light from the 1930s," pp. 37–55; Tran Huy Lieu, *Les Soviets du Nghe-Tinh;* William Duiker, "The Red Soviets of Nghe-Tinh: An Early Communist Rebellion in Vietnam," pp. 186–198.

12. Henri de Monpezat, *Deux Années de délégation au Conseil Superieur des Colonies: Annam, Tonkin,* pp. 81–82, cited in Nguyen Van Phong, *La Société vietnamienne de 1882 à 1902,* p. 330.

13. [Sic]. Osborne, "Continuity and Motivation," p. 43. There was also a "Brave Death Squad," which risked death to obtain boats to ferry protest marchers across a river. (Khanh, "Vietnamese Communism," p. 158.)

was far more tumult there during the entire colonial era.[14] But threat to subsistence cannot account for the difference in levels of tumult between the areas. The average income levels for every class were higher in Cochinchina than in Tonkin. If there were a direct relation between subsistence threat and rebellion, there would have to be much more variance to income in Cochinchina than in Tonkin, else peasants in Cochinchina would not drop to the danger line more often than the peasants in Tonkin. Scott, for example, infers that there was much more variance in Cochinchina because it lacked corporate villages; therefore, Cochinchinese peasants hit the danger line more often than peasants elsewhere. This assumes that the corporate villages of Tonkin and Annam had such wide-ranging patterns of reciprocity and distribution that it was possible for them to "redistribute pain" and absorb shocks, that although the Tonkin average income may have been close to the line the village could hold everyone above danger. Thus, the relatively well-off Cochinchinese, lacking corporate villages, are assumed to have hit the danger line more often than the poor but corporate peasants of Tonkin.[15] But the analysis of taxes and land in Chapter 4 suggests that Scott's view of the ability of the corporate village to withstand subsistence threats is too optimistic.[16] Although there is no direct evidence on variance in incomes from either region, there is considerable *indirect* evidence to suggest that the Tonkinese peasants were far more affected by subsistence crises than were the peasants of Cochinchina, that Tonkinese touched the danger level far more often than Cochinchinese. The rate of infant mortality was higher in Tonkin, and the average family size was smaller; caloric intake was lower (*despite the colder climate*); the incidence of tuberculosis, hookworm, and trachoma were far greater.[17] In short, the data

14. See, for example, Ralph Smith, "The Development of Opposition to French Rule in Southern Vietnam, 1880–1940," pp. 94–129.

15. Scott, *Moral Economy,* pp. 82, 202–203.

16. To quote Vo Nguyen Giap and Truong Chinh, "There are many people, especially foreigners, who are very enthusiastic about the communal land system. They think that communal land partially guarantees the livelihood of the peasants. . . . Communal land is distributed unfairly or monopolized and usurped by village notables" [*The Peasant Question (1937–1938),* p. 83, see also pp. 78–84].

17. For basic sources on demographic data, see "French Indochina: Demographic Imbalance and Colonial Policy," Population Index, 11 (1945), no author, and A. Terry Rambo, "A Comparison of Peasant Social Systems of Northern and South-

strongly argue that more peasants, in spite of their corporate villages, touched the danger level in Tonkin than in Cochinchina, with its open villages. Thus, subsistence, danger-level crises cannot account for greater political activity in Cochinchina.[18]

The class most threatened by subsistence crises (both short and long run) are the landless agricultural laborers. Were there a direct relation between crisis and activity, this class would be the most active politically. But the class most threatened need not be the first to act, even when it is the most "politically conscious" group. Giap and Truong Chinh found that the landless peasant laborers of Vietnam were, in fact, the class most enthusiastic for change.[19] Yet the Vietnamese experience confirms the almost universal finding that agricultural laborers are harder to organize or less likely to protest than are tenants, and that tenants, in turn, are often far less active than are landowning middle peasants.[20] As with threat, polit-

ern Vietnam: A Study of Ecological Adaptation, Social Succession and Cultural Evolution," pp. 169–217. Rambo has collected extensive data on the differences in standards between Tonkin and Cochinchina. In colder Tonkin, average caloric intake was 1,800; in Cochinchina, 2,100 (p. 100). The incidence rate for trachoma was 70 percent in Tonkin, 30 percent in Cochinchina. The presence of liver flukes was "very high" in Tonkin, "not present" in Cochinchina. Hookworm incidence was 50 to 55 percent in Tonkin, 15 to 25 percent in Cochinchina; tuberculosis was "common" in Tonkin, "less common" in Cochinchina (p. 101). (Dr. John S. Marr of the New York City Bureau of Preventable Diseases has kindly identified for author which diseases of the many listed by Rambo are meaningful indices of living standards—as opposed to diseases that are a function of ecological zones.) In addition, agricultural laborers in Tonkin received about one-fourth the pay of agricultural laborers in Cochinchina (p. 101). Woodside notes, furthermore, that it was only after 1931 that peasants in Cochinchina began to grow sweet potatoes on any scale to supplement rice, whereas sweet potatoes and manioc had been a staple in Tonkin since the nineteenth century (Woodside, *Community and Revolution*, p. 123). Finally, it was cheaper for the giant rubber plantations on the malarial fringes of Cochinchina to dragoon men from Tonkin through labor recruiters than to hire labor at market prices in Cochinchina itself.

18. In Burma as well, the greater political activity of commercialized areas cannot be accounted for by short-term subsistence crises (that is, starvation). Although there were widespread protests in the commercial areas during the Depression, Michael Adas has noted that few, if any, starved "even when the slump was at its worst in the early 1930s. A tenant's or laborer's family might have less rice to consume and little money to spend on *pwes* or other amusements, but normally food and shelter could be found" *(The Burma Delta,* p. 203). In contrast, during an earlier crisis in the Burmese agricultural subsistence area, a government report noted that "they died in the fields gnawing the bark of trees; they died on the highways while wandering in search of food; they died in their homes" (ibid., p. 45).

19. Giap and Truong Chinh, *Peasant Question,* p. 17.

20. Hamza Alavi, "Peasants and Revolution," pp. 241–277. However, migrant laborers, because they work away from home, are able to be more militant in their

ical consciousness is not directly translatable into political competence.[21]

Thus, whether we compare the same region at two points in time, different regions at the same time, or different classes, the facts of Vietnam do not confirm a direct relation between subsistence threat (or crisis) and political activity.[22]

Shifting the premise from threat to risk leads to a shift in focus from group rationality to individual rationality. The tendency of moral economists to equate the two implies that individual and group (or class) interests will be identical. The evidence, however, supports the contrary assumption. As William Hinton has observed, peasant society exhibits

an all-prevading individualism engendered by the endless, personal struggle to acquire a little land to beat out the other fellow in the market place. Peasants individually driven to bankruptcy viewed economic disaster not as a social but as a personal matter, to be solved in isolation by whatever means came to hand. This essentially divisive and selfish approach made cooperation between peasants on any level other than the family extremely difficult, greatly increased the leverage of the gentry's divide-and-rule tactics. . . .[23]

Whether a self-interested peasant will or will not contribute to a collective action depends on individual—not group—benefits. If there are individual calculations, then the fact that a group or class is in an improving or declining economic situation is not sufficient to explain the presence or absence of political protest. One must also know whether or not the individual member of the group or class expects *individual* participation in collective action to be of

---

home village than are agricultural laborers who live and work in the same village, and they are often more militant in their home village than where they work. (This was the pattern in Crystal City, Texas, and it was also the pattern in Vietnam.)

21. Jeffrey Paige, *Agrarian Revolution: Social Movements and Export Agriculture in the Underdeveloped World,* p. 41.

22. Furthermore, the French presence was stronger in Cochinchina than in either Annam or Tonkin; it was also stronger in Nghe An and Ha Tinh in 1930 than circa 1900. Therefore, the "level of repression" was higher in the more active time period and region. If agricultural laborers were more repressed than other classes, the "repression" came neither from the French nor from large landowners, but from within "the peasantry"—from the tenants and middle peasants who employed them. Note, in contrast, that Scott sees as the main deterrent to revolt the (collective) risks of rebellion, which are "largely proportional to the coercive power of the state" (*Moral Economy,* p. 195).

23. William Hinton, *Fanshen,* p. 55.

ultimate *individual* benefit. Class benefits from action do not necessarily mean that there are individual reasons to participate: the resources for collective action will be applied only when free-rider problems are overcome.

THE POLITICAL ECONOMY OF REVOLUTION

The basic question for successful organization is how, and under what conditions, can the resources for a collective project be gathered together and applied? Although the four case studies illustrate a variety of responses to the challenge, all clearly indicate that any attempt to organize for group action must recognize the distinction between individual and group and must provide effective leadership, as well as sufficient incentives, to overcome individual resistance to collective action.

When a direct link is made between individual morality and the morality of a class, the implicit assumption is that peasants are easily motivated to uphold norms and support one another by individual action; they are assumed to be willing to devote time and resources to common efforts for the good of their class.[24] In direct contrast to this assumption, Giap and Truong Chinh found peasants acutely aware of the trade-offs involved when allocating resources to further either individual or common interests:

Peasants also have the mentality of private ownership. . . . They are suspicious of talk of collective work. Most of them do not like the idea of contributing money for common goals. Traditional peasant organizations . . . are all characterized by individual profit for each member of the group. None have a social nature, *i.e.*, a common advantage for the entire group or for society. . . . We have yet to see peasants spontaneously organize societies which have a common usefulness.[25]

This means that peasants do not necessarily act to further their group or common interests, that they often opt for individual interests over common interests, and that there is a free-rider problem. Thus, there is a marked proclivity for individual-level adaptations

24. Scott, *Moral Economy*, p. 160, for example, generalizes from individual morality to class morality.
25. Giap and Truong Chinh, *Peasant Question*, p. 21.

to common problems whenever the only result of group action is "common advantage for the entire group or for society." As long as the only results of contributing to the common goals are common advantages, the peasant may leave the contributions to others and expend his scarce resources in other ways. Collective action requires more than consensus or even intensity of need. It requires conditions under which peasants will find it in their individual interests to allocate resources to their common interests—and not be free riders.

Under what conditions can resources for collective endeavor be aggregated? Mancur Olson has stated the argument in its classic form: " . . . unless there is coercion or some other special device to make individuals act in their common interest, rational, self-interested individuals will not act to achieve their common or group interest."[26]

This formulates the collective-action problem in its most elegant and straightforward fashion. If an individual assumes that his contribution to a collective good has no perceptible impact on the contributions of others, and if the collective good is so expensive that an individual's contribution will have no perceptible impact on the level of the collective good supplied, then special incentives are needed to produce any action toward group goals (the *by-product theory* of collective goods.)[27]

As framed by Olson, the by-product theory implies that efforts to organize for action can succeed only when the leadership provides selective incentives from whose proceeds the collective goods are financed. However, even for nonexcludable goods, this formulation

---

26. Mancur Olson, *The Logic of Collective Action*, p. 2.

27. The by-product theory is best illustrated by the (simplified) example of the American Medical Association. The Association produces major collective goods, particularly political power, for the medical profession. Since the results of the AMA's influence on tax and health legislation, for example, are available to all doctors, membership in the Association is not required to receive its collective benefits. But a doctor receives *selective, noncollective* benefits from his membership that justify payment of dues. If the AMA can provide members with valuable information about new medicines or tax loopholes, or if it can monopolize the services of malpractice specialists, then it is in the individual doctor's interest to join the organization. Thus, no one pays anything for collective goods: they are provided by the organization as a by-product of the sale of memberships for individual benefits. (See Olson, *Logic of Collective Action*, pp. 137–141.)

is too restrictive. Contributions can occur (1) because persons contribute for reasons of ethic, conscience, or altruism; (2) because it pays to contribute on a pure cost-benefit basis; (3) because of selective incentives (excludable benefits), which can be either positive or negative; or (4) because it pays to contribute, given that the contributions of others are contingent on one's own contribution.[28]

When persons have decided to contribute on the grounds of ethics, altruism, or conscience, a would-be leader need offer no selective incentives. Instead, what must be offered persons searching for the best way to expend their contributions is efficacy. That is, a leader must be able to convince persons that making the contribution through a particular organization or a particular form of participation is the most beneficial. During the August Revolution, there were many persons in Hanoi and Saigon who felt it their duty to fight for national salvation. Among these persons, the Viet Minh substantially outrecruited other organizations because it was able to convince them that their contributions would do the most good if channeled through the Viet Minh. (As my analysis has indicated, however, situations in which contributions are widespread are infrequent in peasant society.)

Selective incentives to induce participation also are not needed whenever it pays to contribute on a straight cost-benefit calculation. Olson deals with the pure case of collective goods that benefit all equally and from whose benefits no one can be excluded. Thus, while implicit in Olson's analysis, excludability is separate from the pure problem of collective goods. There are also many collective projects where some benefits can be restricted to participants. In this case, no special selective incentives beyond those tied to the collective project are needed to induce participation. One can contrast an insurance scheme, a planting or harvesting cooperative, or a blood bank—all of which have collective goods aspects *and* whose benefits can be restricted to members—to an expedition to kill a marauding tiger, a plot to kill a landlord, or construction of a dike—the benefits from which accrue to participants and nonpar-

28. Norman Frohlich and Joe Oppenheimer, *Modern Political Economy,* chap. 3; Norman Frohlich et al., "Individual Contributions to Collective Goods: Alternative Models," pp. 310–329.

ticipants alike. And, of course, the quintessential excludables often involve religion: religious organizations offer not only insurance programs, moral codes, and courts—all of which are initiated locally, have low start-up costs, and require only leadership—but also provide the important long-run, individual benefit of salvation for members. This was exactly the model that the Jesuits employed so effectively in the seventeenth century and into the twentieth century, and it is ultimately much like the model used by the Communists. *Ceteris paribus,* maintaining membership is easier if to be excluded from an organization is to lose valuable benefits.

Excludability is related to the problem of self-enforcement and to situations in which selective incentives, either positive or negative, are needed for leadership to overcome free-rider problems. A group is not self-enforcing when a member gains more benefits by dropping out than by voluntarily remaining in the group. If an immediate benefit can be derived from defection, an organization formed to pursue a goal can survive only if there is sufficient coercion available to the leadership to enforce discipline, or enough resources to make defection less valuable than remaining in the group. An insurance scheme, for example, is self-enforcing: when a member fails to pay or do his share, he loses his benefits. In direct contrast is the problem of organizing a work stoppage among laborers in order to raise their wages. If all the laborers in an area were to simultaneously withhold their labor from their fellow villagers who are tenants or smallholders, the laborers' share of the crop could be increased. But such coordinated action is not self-enforcing, for there is an incentive for any individual laborer to defect and offer his labor. He will reason that if everyone else withholds his labor, wages will inevitably rise; he will therefore receive the future benefits of the collective action as well as the wages he receives as a strike-breaker.

Where defection brings benefits, a second consideration is the ease with which defections can be monitored. It is easy to detect defectors during a labor boycott, and when resources are available the defectors can be dealt with. There are many times, however, when it is difficult to detect defections and to apply sanctions to maintain group solidarity. This applies to the problem of interest rates. Virtually every writer on peasant society refers to exorbitant, usurious interest rates. If all peasants could agree to borrow only at a given rate and at no higher rate, the interest rate would come down, and nonmarket methods would govern the allocation of credit. But no one in Vietnam, from the Catholics in the seventeenth century to the Viet Minh during the resistance, was able effectively to put a ceiling on interest rates, for defection (secretly paying the higher rates to get more credit at the expense of the group) was the strategy chosen by enough peasants to thwart boycotts.

Directly affecting the amount of resources needed to prevent defection is the extent to which opposing interests and resources can be mobilized against nascent organizations. Whereas an insurance scheme or a well-digging group are unlikely to generate immediate, local opposition, attempts to raise laborers' wages do have built-in opposition from all tenants and smallholders. Tenants and smallholders are financially able to hold out more easily than laborers, and they are in a better power position because they control more resources. Similarly, tenant movements to destroy or weaken landlords are likely to be more successful in areas where there is no class of permanent laborers for the landlords to use against the tenants. In the north and in the denser parts of Annam, where there was a permanent laboring class, there was always someone waiting for a tenant to make a wrong move, so that he could take his place. In such situations, tenant movements are very difficult to organize. In the less densely populated, newer parts of Cochinchina where there was no permanent laboring class, organizing tenants was easier, and collective efforts to constrain landlords were more successful. It was easier, moreover, for the Hoa Hao to bring about de facto rent reductions because of a labor scarcity in its area. There were no fights between laborers and tenants about whether to merely drive the big owners off the land and ratify the tenant's ownership, or to divide the land equally among tenants and laborers. All that was required to emasculate the large landowners was to intimidate their agents (clients), sometimes with considerable (and popular) violence. Indeed, the Hoa Hao recognized the virtues of a favorable man/land ratio and established "border patrols" to prevent peasants from moving into the area unless they were either members, or related to members, of the Hoa Hao.

People will also contribute whenever they believe their contribution will make a big enough difference. There are two main variants to consider: (1) a contribution which might influence other persons to contribute and which therefore has an important perceptible effect on the overall level of contributions, and (2) situations where every little bit is seen as a crucial step in a long process. After land was distributed and rents reduced in Cochinchina, peasants commonly went out of their way to warn Viet Minh cadres that French soldiers or agents were in the area; they did not risk free riding on warnings by waiting for someone else to notify the cadre. This illustrates a major point: if a large overall goal can be broken into many small independent pieces, all of which are necessary, the free-rider problem can be overcome, for if each person has a monopoly on a necessary factor for the final goal, all contributions are essential.

Effective leaders may provide only selective incentives; but by coordination of contributions, by manipulation of information, or by breaking up a large overall goal into numerous steps with critical thresholds, they may also elicit contributions not tied directly to selective incentives.[29] Olson's tidy formulation, therefore, can be expanded from a situation where collective goods are financed solely from funds raised by leaders through selective incentives to situations where collective goods are financed by convincing persons that their contributions will have a perceptible effect.

For pure incentive situations or for contributions justified on grounds of perceptible effects, participation (be it a purchase or a contribution) is a gamble. The value of a contribution to a peasant depends not just on the value of the collective good, but also on how likely it is that others will contribute. Yet other situations also often involve gambles. For example, with selective incentives

29. These two situations, of course, merge together as an organization becomes institutionalized. When there is long-run faith in an organization's survival, strict reciprocity and immediacy of connection between contribution and incentives will become relaxed as persons come to believe that contributions and selective returns will even out over time.

there are cases where peasants must estimate the probability of actually receiving the selective incentive. The potential consequences of failing to contribute to a potentially successful movement undoubtedly stimulated the purchase of Viet Minh "war bonds."

Risk is involved both in purchasing incentives and in contributions, but particularly when peasants are making a contribution they can be expected to evaluate their actions as they would evaluate lotteries. This means a more complex comparison of any action—to contribute or not to contribute. In both cases there is consideration of success or failure of the collective good being supplied with or without the individual's contribution.

This risk aspect of the decision to participate in the collective action can be contrasted with the loss-of-legitimacy, moral-propulsion aspects of the moral economy approach. Whereas the moral economy approach suggests that peasants compare what *is* with what *ought* to be, the political economy approach emphasizes that peasants weigh the risk of trading the status quo for a lottery between successful action and failure. Of course, *no contribution* is also a risky situation with lottery elements.

In all situations, then, collective action involves risk and uncertainty. It is logically incorrect to equate intensity of need with the likelihood of collective response without also considering the ability of individuals to gamble on an improvement in the status quo. A peasant with a small surplus can more readily afford to take risks than can a peasant truly against the margin: the peasants of Cochinchina were bigger risk-takers vis-à-vis politics and markets than were the "needier" peasants of Tonkin and Annam.

This also serves to reemphasize the importance of looking at both long-run and short-run dimensions of security and subsistence. Cochinchinese peasants who joined Hoa Hao congregations were making a short-run investment to improve their long-run security. By establishing local congregations and undermining the large landholders' total power, with the attendant long-run uncertainty that such total dependency implied, they were making more secure their long-term access to land. In this sense, the Hoa Hao was a preemptive movement against possible future crises. A differential propensity to make short-run investments or gambles for long-run benefits is reflected in the pattern, common to all four movements, for young people to be more eager to volunteer for activity than were older persons with family responsibilities.[30]

POLITICAL ENTREPRENEURS

When a peasant makes his personal cost-benefit calculations about the expected returns on his own inputs, he is making subjective estimates of the credibility and capability of the organizer, "the political entrepreneur,"[31] to deliver. The problem of the supply of collective goods and the choice among alternative patterns of supply make "mechanisms for coordination of expectations and the pooling of resources" a central issue.[32] Hence, the importance of the leader as a political entrepreneur—someone willing to invest his own time and resources to coordinate the inputs of others in order to produce collective action or collective goods—cannot be underestimated.

Whether the entrepreneur is directly exchanging immediate individual benefits for peasant inputs or trying to convince the peasant that his actions can have a perceptible and profitable impact on the collective good, he must be concerned with increasing the peasant's estimates of the efficacy of his contribution to secure the promised returns. This means that the peasant's subjective estimates of the would-be entrepreneur's capability and credibility will directly influence the entrepreneur's ability to organize peasants, and that, *ceteris paribus,* a situation with more credible organizers is likely to be a situation with more effective organizations.

A would-be leader must convince a peasant that he is not going to take his money and run, supplying neither the collective goods

30. Amending the moral economy assumptions to include the long-run and short-run views of security and subsistence produces another problem. If, that is, all persons are propelled to action by long-run, as well as short-run, subsistence crises, then laborers—who are usually unable to have as large a "complete family" (and thus ensure children for their old age) as do tenants and smallholders—should be the first to rise in protest.

31. Frohlich and Oppenheimer, *Modern Political Economy,* chap. 5. Also, Norman Frohlich, Joe Oppenheimer, and Oran Young, *Political Entrepreneurship and Collective Goods.*

32. Frohlich et al., *Political Entrepreneurship,* p. 25.

nor the promised incentives.[33] It was noted earlier that most peasant cooperation, organization, and insurance involved relatively immovable assets—that peasants seldom gave another peasant money to hold for the future because the peasant could always run away with the money or spend it on himself or his family. Clearly, overcoming this obstacle was for all four organizations a major feat, which could not have been accomplished without trustworthy political entrepreneurs. How does an organizer convince a peasant that his goals are credible, that not only can he and will he do what he promises with the peasant's contributions, but that if he does what he promises, the peasant's lot will be bettered?

A leader must, first of all, be able to use terms and symbols his targets understand. In contrast to the religious organizers, most of the early political organizers failed to communicate with the peasants they sought to enlist. Educated in Europe or in the French schools of Vietnam, these urbanites dealt with concepts and outlooks which no peasant could relate to his world. Significantly, the first successes of these organizers, whether Communist or Trotskyite, were among urban workers and the middle class, to whom their appeals were comprehensible. Although the rural challenge was substantial everywhere, the problems were especially severe in the villages of Tonkin and Annam. As Gourou noted, educated Vietnamese could not relate to the rhythms and styles of village politics in Tonkin. When an educated person is back in his native village,

The religious life of the commune no longer has any hold on him and the intrigues of its political life do not interest him. . . . The rationalist and materialist education which they have received does not allow them to preserve their faith in village genii; their knowledge of the outside world reveals to them the meanness of the political life of the village.[34]

Although the educated also encountered obstacles in Cochinchina, it is noteworthy that from 1920 on, successful Western-oriented organizers, such as Nguyen An Ninh and the Communists, were far more active there than in Tonkin. The greater flow of

33. Ibid., chap. 1.
34. Pierre Gourou, *Les Paysans du delta tonkinais: Etude de géographie humaine*, p. 220.

urban-rural communication, wider provision for education, and greater interest in new ideas throughout the countryside increased the possibilities for successful communication.

The great success of religious movements vis-à-vis the Communists before the latter began to utilize cultural themes underscores, even more than the failed appeals of Westernized organizers, the cultural bases of competence and credibility estimates made by the peasants. So long as the Communists argued only in terms of material incentives and neglected to add an ethnic, Vietnamese content to their discussions of the future, they were unable to present a credible vision of that future to the peasants; hence, their early failures at organization. The religious movements, on the other hand, brought visions of the future consonant with peasant beliefs, and peasants were able to relate these visions to their contemporary actions.[35]

The religious movements, furthermore, had moral codes and sanctions that were critical, not only for binding groups of peasants together, but also for increasing each peasant's estimate that contributions would go for the purposes claimed. It can be argued that a major factor in the credibility of both the Communist and religious movements over the century, in contrast to the failed bourgeois organizations, was the self-abnegation of the leadership. The self-denial of Communist organizers, the celibacy of missionary priests, the scorn of conspicuous consumption by Hoa Hao organizers, were striking demonstrations to peasants that these men were less interested in self-aggrandizement than were the visibly less self-denying organizers from other groups. Thus, another way to raise the peasant's subjective estimate of the credibility and capability of an entrepreneur is to increase the probability that he is actually going to use the resources for common rather than selfish purposes.

Another way of encouraging credibility is to use leaders already well known to the target group. As Christine White has noted, the Communists eventually were able to use members of urban, leftist organizations in their native villages and therefore to move from

35. Alexander Woodside, *Community and Revolution*, p. 188. The methods peasants use to assess competence and credibility are not unique to them. American voters use similar cues, or information shortcuts, when faced with assessing the competence and credibility of presidential candidates.

urban success to rural entrée.[36] Whereas the Western-educated urbanites often lost the ability to communicate with peasants, they could reach them through urban workers—who could still communicate with the other peasants, particularly because the majority of the urban work force maintained families in the villages and was therefore still tied to local politics and rituals. Similarly, all three religions utilized preexisting religious organizations to make contact with persons able to relay their message and vouch for them with other villagers.

Credibility, moral codes, and visions of the future, then, all affect a peasant's estimate that his investment will either contribute directly to a collective goal or will bring an acceptable return of individual benefits.

Examination of the examples of successful organization indicates that one consideration in particular may have been crucial for effective mobilization of the peasantry: in all four cases, the initial organization of peasants focused on local goals and goods with immediate payoffs. This suggests that an important way to increase the peasants' estimate of success and, therefore, the probability of contribution is to decrease the scope of the project for which he is being recruited—and thus shorten the interval before benefits are received. The profits derived from local organizing can then be directed by the leadership to larger, more national goals and projects, which take longer to pay off. Peasants in the late 1960s still laughed about the early attempts by young Trotskyites and Communists to organize them for a national revolution, for industrialization, or even for a world revolution! Only later, when peasants (and workers) were organized around smaller and more immediate goals, were larger organizational attempts successful. This was the strategy used by the Catholics in the seventeenth century, and it proved the most effective strategy again in the twentieth century.

When an entrepreneur, intent on organizing around concrete local issues, approaches a group of peasants, what features of possible issues are crucial? And how does the "organizability" of an issue vary from region to region? Examining relevant properties of

---

' 36. Christine White, "Revolution and Its Adherents: The Development of the Revolutionary Movement in Vietnam," p. 66.

different local issues (local collective goods, in Olson's terms) helps to clarify why affluent peasants can be initially more militant than poorer peasants, and why the hardest groups to organize initially can be in the long run the most radical, dedicated, and committed.

For example, the start-up costs of a project and whether peasants are required to pay before or after collective ends are achieved (that is, whether or not there is outside financing) may determine the potential value of a local issue to organizers. Poor peasants might find their individual benefits from an undertaking very high and might be willing to pay enormous amounts to achieve the benefits, but only if they are able to pay after the fact ("on time") out of the profits. When the Communists seized control of village government in much of Annam and Tonkin, many projects that increased production and repaid themselves many times over were possible because the Communists then had resources to finance projects and did not require the beneficiaries to pay in advance. They provided the leadership for "poor neighborhoods" to dig additional water ponds and drainage ditches and used previously collected taxes in the village treasury for the extra food needed to fuel the workers. The funds were easily repaid from increased production. Much of the strongest and deepest support for the Communists came ultimately from areas (and classes) where there had been little or no pre-1945 political activity, where people were roused politically only after the Communists were in power and able to give them benefits that they were then willing to pay for and fight to keep.

Even when an organization produces divisible goods for individual consumption, there are collective-goods aspects to the organization itself. Systems of incentives or mechanisms for sharing costs are collective goods which leadership can supply to the benefit of the leader and peasantry. When improved leadership makes possible the incentive systems or cost-sharing mechanisms for self-help projects such as insurance programs and livestock cooperatives, it is possible to produce benefits for the peasants as well as a "revolutionary surplus" which can then be used to support a supravillage organization and applied to broader organizational objectives. All the successful groups, religious and political, developed large-scale, national movements from local organizations that produced a "revolutionary surplus" used for expanding the overall organization. As Woodside describes this pattern, the Communists, who were eventually to become far more successful than the other groups, perceived

the rather simple sociological truth that a large movement could derive cohesion and even dynamism from multitudes of small-group attachments which fell short, in practice, of attachments to the movement's most complex central ideologies and philosophical doctrines—provided that these small group attachments were associated with concrete local issues.[37]

This approach leads to an enlargement of Olson's central formulation. Discussions of collective goods usually address the problem of whether a particular good will or will not be provided to a group. In practice, many collective goods can be provided in many different ways. Improving the quality of available leadership, for example, can change the way the good is provided, increase benefits for all participants, and supply large amounts of "profit" for the organizers—profit which the leaders may use to further additional national goals of their own.

Many of the collective goals within peasant society can be achieved, furthermore, within groups of widely varying sizes and structures. Thus, insurance and agricultural efforts can be organized so as to supply benefits with or without exclusion, either inside or outside of a market mechanism. With little savings and money, with a lack of trained leadership, and with costly and unreliable mechanisms for enforcing contracts, it is not surprising to find insurance and agricultural cooperatives supplied on a quasi-collective basis rather than on a market basis. Large groups are workable, given problems of excludability and defection, only when there is skilled leadership or enforceable contracts. Almost all the small, insurance-type organizations discussed in Chapter 3 can be organized by very small groups of peasants. But the security and viability of the insurance could be improved immeasurably if a larger group were involved. A large insurance company, that is, is more

37. Woodside, *Community and Revolution,* p. 179. See also Olson, *Logic of Collective Action,* pp. 62–63.

likely in the long run to provide the promised benefits than is a small company with few members. Although they may be erratic and offer low-quality insurance compared to villagewide or even intervillage associations, the small group arrangements have the virtue of requiring less capable leadership and are often the only organization possible. As Olson has noted, small groups need few if any special incentives or leadership because there is such a notable effect of each member's contribution on the overall output of the group.[38] In a small mutual aid group, if one member gains a free ride, the loss of his contribution will be perceptible to all and the group will dissolve.

Without skilled leadership or enforceable contracts, exclusion is only possible in small groups. In an eight-man planting cooperative, if a peasant drops out of the group after the other seven have spent the day helping him plant his crops, he will be blackballed from all similar groups as unreliable. So, while small groups may be far less rewarding over a number of years than larger groups, they are viable when there is little or no trusted leadership because there are minimal problems of coordination and incentives.

If a skilled leader can convince peasants to join a larger mutual aid group, there is a potentially substantial profit both for the peasants and the leader. The Hoa Hao and the Communists both established villagewide labor pools into which everyone was required to contribute a few days of labor. This labor was used for emergency purposes to supplement the small labor groups in special situations such as a small local flood or a rampaging water buffalo. Furthermore, all four organizations established supravillage exchange programs whereby resources were transferred to villages in different areas as the need arose, giving local villages or congregations access to insurance systems in case of natural disaster or war-related damage in their immediate area. But before such systems could be established, the organizations had to overcome the peasants' ambivalence about strong local leadership. All the extended schemes that helped the peasants were also potential sources for abuse of power by unscrupulous entrepreneurs. The closer to the margin and

38. Olson, *Logic of Collective Action*, pp. 22–35, especially pp. 33–34.

the more cautious the peasants, the longer it took to establish the credibility required to build broad-based projects. It took the Communists five years to accomplish in Annam what the Hoa Hao achieved in far less time in a more affluent area.

There are, however, occasions when collective action can occur without leadership or organization. When there are few internal conflicts of interest, when the job requires some particular skill or the area is isolated so that strikebreaking is difficult, when persons live together in one community so that they can communicate easily and decide on "the last straw" and defections can be monitored easily, when work can be put off without destroying the product so that crucial wages will not be lost, there can be collective action such as slowdowns, wildcat strikes, or protest marches with little or no formal leadership to supply incentives or even to provide information.[39] The demands expressed by such collective action, however, will be limited to highly visible, universal demands and thus are likely to reflect the lowest common denominator of a group, not the full range of interests of its members or even the most important preferences of the members. Thus, when a group engages in collective action and protest, one should not infer from such demonstrations of collective ability and common interest that the group will be able to function as a moral economy in the more mundane areas of village life. As a colonial newspaper noted in 1896,

A whole village comes to an admirable understanding in order to pillage a convoy of Chinese junks or to plunder the house of a rich neighbor. Discretion will be well guarded even in the case of success. . . . But ask this same village to group together to store their rice in one central warehouse and assure themselves of quick and certain benefits. Disorder and bickering will quickly break out in the midst of the group. In a week they will be calling each other thieves.[40]

39. These conditions are most obviously met among rubber plantation workers where protests often are similar to the moral economy model. Paige, *Agrarian Revolution*, pp. 50–58; Chandra Jayawardena, "Ideology and Conflict in Lower Class Communities," pp. 418–423. Note also that Cesar Chavez started with vineyard workers in California.

40. *Le Courier de Saigon,* quoted in Guy Gran, "Vietnam and the Capitalist Route," p. 523.

CONCLUSION

Why do good fences make good neighbors? One answer is that building a good fence requires collective effort, and sharing the effort with neighbors helps to develop workable patterns of interaction which lead to sustained interaction and collective benefits. Good fences also make good neighbors because they establish precise boundaries, and thus ease the difficulties of accounting between peasants and help settle the conflicts which need to be resolved for cooperative patterns to develop between peasant households. The subsistence crises faced by peasants can lead to a common outlook, but the dangers and risks which all peasants face also generate an awareness of possibilities for harm inherent in relations beyond the household, be they market, village, or patron-client exchanges. Aversion to risk, conflicts, and distrust among peasants mean that a common moral outlook need not lead to a moral economy.

In developing my approach, I have modified two views of peasant society. A free-market economics approach, even when amended to take account of peasant aversion to risk, cannot explain the patterns of stratification and production in the precolonial, colonial, and revolutionary eras in Vietnam without considering collective goods and leadership, political coalitions that shape markets, and the infrastructure of the economic system, including taxes, courts, land titles, law and order, and insurance. The moral economy approach, while fully cognizant of the risks and dangers of markets and the importance of villages and patron-client relations for peasant survival, requires modification as well to take account of the ways in which aversion to risk, conflicts between public and private forms of investment, and conflicts among the peasantry limit the quality and extent of insurance and welfare embedded in peasant institutions.

By stressing the common investment logic of intravillage, patron-client, and market relations, I have attempted to show that given the actual performance levels of patrons and villages, neither decline nor decay of peasant institutions is necessary for peasants to enter markets. Further, peasant support for revolutions and protests may represent political competence, not decline and decay.

Bibliography

ABBREVIATIONS

HRAF - Human Relations Area File
RIJE - Revue Indochinoise Juridique et Economique (Hanoi)
BSEI - Bulletin de la Société des Etudes Indochinoises
BEFEO - Bulletin de l'Ecole Française d'Extrême Orient

Abelson, Robert P. "Social Psychology's Rational Man," in G. W. Mortimore and S. I. Benn, eds., *The Concept of Rationality in the Social Sciences*. London: Routledge, Kegan and Paul, 1976.

Acheson, James M. "Limited Good or Limited Goods: Response to Opportunity in a Tarascan Pueblo," *American Anthropoligist* 74 (1972):1152–1169.

Adas, Michael. *The Burma Delta: Economic Development and Social Change on an Asian Rice Frontier, 1852–1941*. Madison: University of Wisconsin Press, 1974.

Alavi, Hamza. "Peasants and Revolution," in Jonathan Saville and Ralph Miliband, eds., *The Socialist Register*. London: Merlin Press, 1965.

Alsop, Joseph. *New York Herald Tribune*. December 31, 1954.

Appleby, Andrew B., "Agrarian Capitalism or Seigneurial Reaction? The Northwest of England, 1500–1700," *American Historical Review* 80 (June 1975):574–594.

Arrow, Kenneth. *Social Choice and Individual Values*. New Haven: Yale University Press, 1963.

Ault, W. O. "By-Laws of Gleaning and the Problems of Harvest," *Economic History Review* 14, 2nd ser. (1961–1962).

————. *Open-Field Farming in Medieval England*. London: George Allen and Unwin, 1972.

Bailey, F. G. "Decisions by Consensus in Councils and Committees with Special Reference to Village and Local Government in India," Association of Social Anthropologists of the Commonwealth, monograph #2: *Political Systems and the Distribution of Power*. London: Tavistock Publications, 1965.

————. *Gifts and Poison*. Bristol: Basil Blackwell, 1971.

Banfield, Edward C. *The Moral Basis of a Backward Society*. New York: Free Press, 1968.

Barry, Brian. *Sociologists, Economists and Democracy*. London: Macmillan, 1970.

Barth, Frederick. "Segmentary Opposition and the Theory of Games: A Study of Pathan Organizations," *Journal of the Royal Anthropological Institute of Great Britain and Ireland* 89 (1959):5–21.

Bates, Robert H. "The Issue Basis of Rural Politics in Africa," *Social Science Working Paper No. 102*. California Institute of Technology. Pasadena, California, October 1974.

————. "Political Science and Anthropology: The Study of Rural Politics in the Developing Areas," *Social Science Working Paper No. 112*. California Institute of Technology. Pasadena, California, February 1976.

————. *Rural Responses to Industrialization: A Study of Village Zambia*. New Haven: Yale University Press, 1976.

Beals, Alan. "Interplay among Factors of Change in a Mysore Village," in McKim Marriott, ed., *Village India*. Chicago: University of Chicago Press, 1955.

Bell, Clive, and Pinhas Zusman. "A Bargaining Theoretic Approach to Cropsharing Contracts," *American Economics Review* 66 (September 1976), pp. 578–587.

Bell, Sir Hesketh. *Foreign Colonial Administration in the Far East*. London: Edward Arnold, 1928.

Blau, Peter. *Exchange and Power in Social Life*. New York: Wiley, 1964.

Blok, Anton. *The Mafia of a Sicilian Village 1860–1960: A Study of Violent Peasant Entrepreneurs*. New York: Harper and Row, 1975.

Blum, Jerome. "The European Village as Community: Origins and Functions," *Agricultural History* 45 (1971):157–178.

————. "The Internal Structure and Polity of the European Village Community from the Fifteenth to the Nineteenth Century," *Journal of Modern History* 43 (December 1971):541–576.

———. *Lord and Peasant in Russia: From the Ninth to the Nineteenth Century*. Princeton, New Jersey: Princeton University Press, 1961.

———. "The Rise of Serfdom in Eastern Europe," *American Historical Review* 42 (July 1957):807–836.

———. et al. *The Emergence of the European World*. 2nd ed. Boston: Little, Brown, 1970.

Bodard, Lucien. *The Quicksand War*. Boston: Little Brown, 1967.

Boserup, Ester. *The Conditions of Agricultural Growth: The Economics of Agrarian Change under Population Pressure*. Chicago: Aldine, 1965.

Breman, Jan. *Patronage and Exploitation*. Berkeley and Los Angeles: University of California Press, 1974.

Brenner, Robert. "Agrarian Class Structure and Economic Development in Pre-Industrial Europe," *Past and Present*, 70 (1976):29–75.

Brocheux, Pierre. "Grands Propriétaires et fermiers dans l'ouest de le Cochinchine pendant la période coloniale," *Revue Historique* 499 (July–September 1971):59–77.

Buchanan, James M., and Gordon Tullock. *The Calculus of Consent*. Ann Arbor: University of Michigan Press, 1962.

Buttinger, Joseph. *The Smaller Dragon: A Political History of Vietnam*. New York: Praeger, 1958.

———. *Vietnam: A Dragon Embattled*. New York: Praeger, 1967.

Buu Duong. "The Confucian Tradition in the History of Vietnamese Education," Ph.D. dissertation, Harvard University, May 1958.

Cadiere, Leopold, *Croyances et pratiques religieuses des vietnamiens*. Vol. 1. Saigon: Imprimerie Nouvelle d'Extreme-Orient, 1958.

Campbell, J. K. *Honour, Family and Patronage*. New York: Oxford University Press, 1974.

Cancian, Frank. *Economics and Prestige in a Maya Community*. Stanford, California: Stanford University Press, 1971.

Carrasco, Pedro. "The Civil-Religious Hierarchy in Meso-American Communities: Pre-Spanish Background and Colonial Development," *American Anthropologist* 43 (June 1961):483–497.

Chambers, J. D. "Enclosure and Labour Supply in the Industrial Revolution," *Economic History Review*, 2nd ser., 5 (1952–1953):318–343.

———. and G. E. Mingay. *The Agricultural Revolution 1750–1880*. London: B. T. Batsford, 1970.

Chappoulie, Henri. *Rome et les missions d'Indochine au XVII siècle*. Paris: Bloud et Gay, 1943.

Chen, King. *Vietnam and China 1938–1954*. Princeton: Princeton University Press, 1969.

Chesneaux, Jean, "The Historical Background of Vietnamese Communism," *Government and Opposition* 4 (winter 1969):119–135.

————. *The Vietnamese Nation: Contribution to a History.* Trans. Malcolm Salmon. Sydney: Current Book Distributors, 1966.

Chirot, Daniel. *Social Change in a Peripheral Society.* New York: Academic Press, 1976.

Clark, Colin, and Margaret Haswell. *The Economics of Subsistence Agriculture.* New York: St. Martin's Press, 1967.

Cobb, R. C. *The Police and the People: French Popular Protest, 1789– 1820.* Oxford: Clarendon Press, 1970.

Collier, William A., et al. "Choice of Technique in Rice Milling on Java—A Comment," *Bulletin of Indonesian Economic Studies* 10 (March 1974):106–120.

————. et al., "Agricultural Technology and Institutional Change in Java," Staff Paper 75–1, Agricultural Development Council, New York, New York, pp. 169–194.

————. et al., "Recent Changes in Rice Harvesting Methods: Some Serious Implications," *Bulletin of Indonesian Economic Studies* 9 (July 1973):36–45.

Collins, E. J. T. "Labour Supply and Demand in European Agriculture, 1800–1880," in E. L. Jones and S. L. Woolf, eds., *Agrarian Change and Economic Development.* London: Methuen, 1969.

Colson, Elizabeth. *Tradition and Contract.* Chicago: Aldine, 1974.

Cotter, M. G. "Toward a Social History of the Vietnamese Southward Movement," *Journal of Southeast Asian History* 9 (March 1968):12–24.

Coulton, G. G. *The Medieval Village.* Cambridge: At the University Press, 1926.

Dabézies, Pierre. "Forces politiques au Viet Nam," thèse de droit, Université de Bordeaux, 1955.

Dalton, George. *Economic Anthropology and Development.* New York: Basic Books, 1971.

Dgo Duy Anh, *Vietnan Van-hoa su cuong.* Saigon: Khai Tri, 1951.

Davis, Lance E., and Douglas C. North, with the assistance of Calla Smorodin. *Institutional Change and American Economic Growth.* Cambridge: At the University Press, 1971.

Day, Clive. *The Dutch in Java.* New York: Oxford University Press, 1966.

De Gruilly, Paul. *Le Droit du glanage.* Paris: V. Giard et E. Briere, 1912.

De Roover, Raymond. "The Concept of the Just Price: Theory and Economic Policy," *Journal of Economic History* 18 (1958):418–434.

Deutsch, Karl W. *Nationalism and Social Communication.* Published jointly by Cambridge: MIT Press and New York: John Wiley, 1953.

De Vries, Jan. "Peasant Demand Patterns and Economic Development: Friesland, 1550–1750," in Eric L. Janes and William Parker, eds., *European Peasants and Their Markets.* Princeton: Princeton University Press, 1975.

———. *The Economy of Europe in an Age of Crisis, 1600–1750*. Cambridge: Cambridge University Press, 1976.

Do Thanh, "Cai luong huong chinh," *Nam Phong* (Hanoi), September 1925:219–220.

Dore, R. P. *Land Reform in Japan*. London: Oxford University Press, 1959.

Duiker, William J. "Building the United Front: The Rise of Communism in Vietnam: 1925–1954," in Joseph Zasloff and McAlister Brown, eds., *Communism in Indochina*. Lexington, Massachusetts: D. C. Heath, 1975.

———. *The Comintern and Vietnamese Communism*. Southeast Asia Program, Monograph #37. Athens, Ohio: Ohio University Center for International Studies, 1975.

———. "The Red Soviets of Nghe-Tinh: An Early Communist Rebellion in Vietnam," *Journal of Southeast Asian Studies* 4 (September 1973):185–198.

———. "The Revolutionary Youth League: Cradle of Communism in Vietnam," *China Quarterly* 13 (July–September 1972):475–499.

———. *The Rise of Nationalism in Vietnam 1900–1941*. Ithaca: Cornell University Press, 1975.

Dumont, René. *La Culture du riz dans le delta du Tonkin*. Paris: Société d'Editions Geographiques, Maritimes, et Coloniales, 1935.

———. *Types of Rural Economy: Studies in World Agriculture*. London: Methuen, 1957.

Duncanson, Dennis. *Government and Revolution in Vietnam*. New York: Oxford University Press, 1968.

Elvin, Mark. *The Pattern of the Chinese Past*. Stanford: Stanford University Press, 1973.

Fainstein, Norman I. and Susan S. *Urban Political Movements*. Englewood Cliffs, New Jersey: Prentice-Hall, 1974.

Fall, Bernard. "The Political Development of Vietnam: V-J Day to the Geneva Ceasefire," Ph.D. dissertation, Department of Political Science, Syracuse University, 1954.

Fenoaltea, Stefano. "Fenoaltea on Open Fields: A Reply," *Explorations in Economic History* 14 (1977):405–410.

Fitzgerald, Frances. *Fire in the Lake: The Vietnamese and the Americans in Vietnam*. Boston: Atlantic-Little, Brown, 1972.

Foster, George. "Interpersonal Relations in Peasant Society," *Human Organization* 19 (winter 1960–1961):174–180.

———. "Peasant Society and the Image of Limited Good," *American Anthropologist* 67 (April 1965):293–315.

Fournier-Wailly, C. "Les Institutions traditionelles et la justice indigene en Annam et au Tonkin," HRAF #119. *Bulletin du Comité de l'Asie Française* 9 (1909):328–339.

Franklin, S. H. *The European Peasantry: The Final Phase*. London: Methuen, 1969.

Friedman, Edward. *Backward toward Revolution: The Chinese Revolutionary Party*. Berkeley and Los Angeles: University of California Press, 1974.

Friedman, Milton, and Savage, L. G. "The Utility Analysis of Choices Involving Risk," *Journal of Political Economy* 56 (1948):279–304.

Frohlich, Norman. "Self-Interest or Altruism, What Difference?" *Journal of Conflict Resolution* 18 (March 1974):55–73.

———— and Joe A. Oppenheimer. "Entrepreneurial Politics and Foreign Policy," *World Politics* 24 (October 1971):151–178.

————. "I Get By with a Little Help from My Friends," *World Politics* 23 (October 1970):104–120.

————. "The Carrot and the Stick: Optimal Program Mixes for Entrepreneurial Political Leaders," *Public Choice* 19 (fall 1974):43–61.

————. *Modern Political Economy*. Englewood Cliffs, New Jersey: Prentice-Hall, 1978.

————, and Oran Young. *Political Entrepreneurship and Collective Goods*. Princeton: Princeton University Press, 1971.

———— et al. "Individual Contributions to Collective Goods: Alternative Models," *Journal of Conflict Resolution* 19 (June 1975):310–329.

Fukutake, Tadashi. *Asian Rural Society*. Seattle: University of Washington Press, 1967.

Galjart, Benno. *Itaguai: Old Habits and New Practices in a Brazilian Land Settlement*. Wageningen: Centre for Agricultural Publishing and Documentation, 1968.

Geertz, Clifford. *Agricultural Involution: The Process of Ecological Change in Indonesia*. Berkeley and Los Angeles: University of California Press, 1966.

————."Comments on Benjamin White's 'Demand for Labor and Population Growth in Colonial Java,'" *Human Ecology* 1 (1973):237–239.

————."Ideology as a Cultural System," in David E. Apter, ed., *Ideology and Discontent*. New York: Free Press, 1964.

————."Religion as a Cultural System," in Michael Banton, ed., *Anthropological Approaches to the Study of Religion*, London: Tavistock Publications, 1966.

————."The Wet and the Dry: Traditional Irrigation in Bali and Morocco," *Human Ecology* 1 (1972):23–39.

Gheddo, Piero. *The Cross and the Bo-Tree: Catholics and Buddhists in Vietnam*. Trans. Charles Quinn. New York: Sheed and Ward, 1970.

Gitlitz, John S. "Hacienda, Comunidad, and Peasant Protest in Northern Peru," Ph.D. dissertation, Political Science Department, University of North Carolina, Chapel Hill, 1975.

Goody, Jack. "Restricted Literacy in Northern Ghana," in Jack Goody, *Literacy in Traditional Societies*. Cambridge: At the University Press, 1968.

Gotsch, Carl H. "Technical Change and the Distribution of Income in Rural Areas," *American Journal of Agricultural Economics* 54 (May 1972):326–341.

Gourou, Pierre. *Land Utilization in French Indochina*. HRAF #2. Washington: Institute of Pacific Relations, 1945.

———. *Les Paysans du delta tonkinois: Etude de geographie humaine*. HRAF #1. Paris: Editions d'Art et d'Histoire, 1936.

Gran, Guy. "Vietnam and the Capitalist Route to Modernity: Village Cochinchina 1880–1940," Ph.D. dissertation, Department of History, University of Wisconsin, 1973.

Graziano, Luigi. *A Conceptual Framework for the Study of Clientelism*. Western Societies Program Occasional Paper no. 2. Ithaca, New York: Cornell University Press, 1975.

Gusfield, Joseph R. "Tradition and Modernity: Misplaced Polarities in the Study of Social Change," *American Journal of Sociology* 72 (January 1967):351–362.

Hammer, Ellen. *The Struggle for Indochina*. Stanford: Stanford University Press, 1955.

Hanks, Lucien. *Rice and Man: Agricultural Ecology in Southeast Asia*. Chicago: Aldine Press, 1972.

Harsanyi, John C. "Rational-Choice Models of Political Behavior vs. Functionalist and Conformist Theories," *World Politics* 21 (July 1969):513–538.

Hemery, Daniel. *Revolutionnaires vietnamiens et pouvoir colonial en Indochine: Communistes, trotskyistes, nationalistes à Saigon de 1932 à 1937*. Paris: François Maspero, 1975.

Henry, Yves. *Economie agricole de l'Indochine*. Hanoi: Governement General de l'Indochine, 1932.

H. G. "L'Evolution des institutions communales au Tonkin," RIJE 18 (1942):246–256.

Hickey, Gerald C. "Social Systems of Northern Vietnam: A Study of Systems in Contact," Ph.D. dissertation, Department of Anthropology, University of Chicago, 1958.

———. *Village in Vietnam*. New Haven: Yale University Press, 1964.

Hill, Christopher. *The World Turned Upside Down*. New York: Viking Press, 1972.

Hill, Frances. "Millenarian Machines in South Vietnam" *Comparative Studies in Society and History* 13 (July 1971):325–350.

———. "Nationalist Millenarians and Millenarian Nationalists: Conflict or Cooperation in the New Jerusalem?" *American Behavioral Scientist*

#16 (November–December 1972):269–288.

Hilton, Rodney, *Bond Men Made Free: Medieval Peasant Movements and the English Rising of 1381.* London: Temple Smith, 1973.

————. "Medieval Peasants—Any Lessons?" *Journal of Peasant Studies* 1 (January 1974):207–219.

————. "Peasant Society, Peasant Movements and Feudalism in Medieval Europe," in Henry Landsberger, *Rural Protest: Peasant Movements and Social Change.* New York: Barnes and Noble, 1973.

Himes, Norman. *Medical History of Contraception.* Baltimore: Williams and Wilkins, 1936.

Hinderink, Jan, and Mübeccel B. Kiray. *Social Stratification as an Obstacle to Development.* New York: Praeger, 1970.

Hinton, William. *Fanshen.* New York: Random House Vintage Books, 1968.

Hirschman, Albert O. *Exit, Voice and Loyalty.* Cambridge, Massachusetts: Harvard University Press, 1970.

Hobsbawm, E. J. *Primitive Rebels.* New York: W. W. Norton, 1965.

Hok-Lam Chan. "Chinese Refugees in Annam and Champa at the End of the Sung Dynasty," *Journal of Southeast Asian History* 7 (September 1966):1–10.

Homans, George C. *English Villagers of the Thirteenth Century.* New York: W. W. Norton, 1975.

Hue-Tam Ho Tai. "The Evolution of Vietnamese Millenarianism," Ph.D. dissertation, Department of History, Harvard University, 1977.

Hunter, Guy. *Modernizing Peasant Societies: A Comparative Study in Asia and Africa.* New York: Oxford University Press, 1969.

Huynh Kim Khanh. "Vietnamese Communism: The Pre-Power Phase 1925–1945" Ph.D. dissertation, Department of Political Science, University of California at Berkeley, 1972.

Huynh Phu So. *Sam Giang cua Duc Huynh Giao Chu.* Compiled by Hoa Hao faithful. Saigon, 1962.

————. *Suu Tap Thi Van Giao Ly cua Duc Huynh Giao Chu.* Compiled by Hoa Hao faithful. Saigon, 1962.

Isoart, Paul. *Le Phénomène national vietnamien: De l'Independance unitaire à l'independance fractionée.* Paris: Librarie Générale de Droit et de Jurisprudence, 1961.

Jay, Robert. "Local Government in Rural Central Java," *Far Eastern Quarterly* 15 (February 1956):216–228.

Jayawardena, Chandra. "Ideology and Conflict in Lower Class Communities," *Comparative Studies in Society and History* 10 (1967–1968):413–446.

Johl, S. S. "Gains of the Green Revolution: How They Have Been Shared," *Journal of Development Studies* 11 (July 1975):178–189.

Jumper, Roy, and Nguyen thi Hue. *Notes on the Political and Administra-*

tive History of Vietnam, 1802–1962. East Lansing, Michigan: Michigan State University Vietnam Advisory Group, 1962.

Kartodirdjo, Sartono. *Protest Movements in Rural Java: A Study of Agrarian Unrest in the Nineteenth and Early Twentieth Centuries.* Singapore: Oxford University Press, 1973.

Kaufman, Howard K. *Bangkhuad: A Community Study in Thailand.* Locust Valley, New York: J. J. Augustin, 1960.

Kessinger, Tom. *Vilyatpur 1848–1968.* Berkeley and Los Angeles: University of California Press, 1974.

Kherian, Gregoire. "Les Méfaits de la surpopulation delataique," RIJE #7 (Hanoi), 1938:476–505.

Kikuchi, Masao, Luisa Maligalig-Bambo, and Yujiro Hayami. "Evolution of Land Tenure System in a Laguna Village," paper no. 77–11, Agricultural Economic Department, International Rice Research Institute, July 1977.

Kresser, Paul. *La Commune annamite en Cochinchine.* HRAF #56. Paris: F. Loviton, 1935.

Laidler, Harry W. *Boycotts and the Labor Struggle.* New York: John Lane, 1913.

Lam Le Trinh. "Village Councils—Yesterday and Today," *Viet-My* #3, September 1958.

Lancaster, Donald. *The Emancipation of French Indochina.* London: Oxford University Press, 1961.

Lande, Carl. "Networks and Groups in Southeast Asia: Some Observations on the Group Theory of Politics," *American Political Science Review* 67 (March 1973):103–127.

Langlois, Walter. *Andre Malraux: The Indochina Adventure.* New York: Praeger, 1966.

Le Roy Ladurie, Emmanuel. *Montaillou, Village occitan de 1294 à 1324.* Paris: Editions Gallimard, 1975.

———. *The Peasants of Languedoc.* Urbana: University of Illinois Press, 1974.

Le Thanh Khoi. *Le Vietnam: Histoire et civilisation.* Paris: Les Editions de Minuit, 1955.

Letwin, William. "The Contradictions of Serfdom," *Times Literary Supplement* (March 25, 1977):373.

Lewis, Henry T. *Ilocano Rice Farmers.* Honolulu: University of Hawaii Press, 1971.

Lewis, Oscar. *Life in a Mexican Village, Tepotzlan Restudied.* Urbana: University of Illinois Press, 1951.

———. *Pedro Martinez: A Mexican Peasant and His Family.* New York: Random House, 1964.

———. *Tepotzlan: Village in Mexico.* New York: Henry Holt and Co., 1960.

Lipton, Michael. "The Theory of the Optimizing Peasant," *Journal of Development Studies* 4 (April 1968):327–351.

Long, Millard. "Credit for Small Farmers: Indonesia, Malaysia, Thailand," unpublished paper.

Lopez, Robert. *The Commercial Revolution of the Middle Ages 950–1350.* Englewood Cliffs, New Jersey: Prentice-Hall, 1971.

McAlister, John T., Jr. "Mountain Minorities and the Viet Minh: A Key to the Indochina War," in Peter Kunstadter, ed., *Southeast Asian Tribes, Minorities and Nations.* Vol. 2. Princeton: Princeton University Press, 1967.

———. Vietnam: *The Origins of Revolution.* New York: Alfred A. Knopf, 1969.

———. and Paul Mus. *The Vietnamese and Their Revolution.* New York: Harper and Row, 1970.

McCall, Davy Henderson. "The Effects of Independence on the Economy of Viet Nam," Ph.D. dissertation, Department of Economics, Harvard University, 1961.

McCloskey, Donald N. "The Economics of Enclosure: A Market Analysis," in William N. Parker and Eric L. Jones, eds., *European Peasants and Their Markets.* Princeton: Princeton University Press, 1975.

———. "English Open Fields as Behavior toward Risk," in Paul Uselding, ed., *Research in Economic History,* vol. 1. Greenwich: JAI Press, 1976.

———. "Fenoaltea on Open Fields: A Comment," *Explorations in Economic History* 14 (1977):124–170.

———. "The Persistence of English Common Fields," in William N. Parker and Eric L. Jones, eds., *European Peasants and Their Markets.* Princeton: Princeton University Press, 1975.

Maddison, Angus. *Class Structure and Economic Growth: India and Pakistan since the Moghuls.* New York: W. W. Norton, 1971.

Mamdani, Mahmood. *The Myth of Population Control: Family, Caste and Class in an Indian Village.* New York: Monthly Review Press, 1972.

Marr, David. *Vietnamese Anti-Colonialism 1885–1925.* Berkeley and Los Angeles: University of California Press, 1971.

Marshal, Carter. "Health, Nutrition and Roots of World Population Growth," *International Journal of Health Services* 4 (1974):677–690.

Melin, Pierre. *L'endettement agraire et la liquidation des dettes agricoles en Cochinchine.* HRAF #121. Paris: Libraire Sociale et Economique, 1939.

Migdal, Joel S. *Peasants, Politics and Revolution.* Princeton: Princeton University Press, 1974.

———. "Why Change? Toward a New Theory of Change among Individuals in the Process of Modernization," *World Politics* 26 (January 1974):189–206.

Moerman, Michael. *Agricultural Change and Peasant Choice in a Thai Village.* Berkeley and Los Angeles: University of California Press, 1968.

———. "A Thai Village Headman as a Synaptic Leader," *Journal of Asian Studies* 28, no. 3 (1969):535–549.

Monet, Paul. *Français et annamites entre deux feux.* Paris: Editions Rieder, 1928.

Moore, Barrington, Jr. *Social Origins of Dictatorship and Democracy.* Boston: Beacon Press, 1967.

Moore, M. P. "Co-Operative Labour in Peasant Agriculture," *Journal of Peasant Studies* 2 (April 1975):270–291.

Mortimer, Rex. "Strategies of Rural Development in Indonesia: Peasant Mobilization Versus Technological Stimulation," prepared for seminar on "Peasant Organization in Southeast Asia," sponsored by Rural Development Panel of the Southeast Asia Development Advisory Group of the Asia Society, New York, September 25–27, 1975.

Mus, Paul. "The Role of the Village in Vietnamese Affairs" *Pacific Affairs* 12 (September 1949):265–272.

———. "Vietnam: A Nation Off Balance," *Yale Review* 41 (summer 1952):524–538.

Newby, Howard. "The Deferential Dialectic," *Comparative Studies in Society and History* 17 (1975):139–164.

Nghiem Dang. *Vietnam: Politics and Public Administration.* Honolulu: East-West Center Press, 1966.

Ngo Vinh Long. *Before the Revolution: The Vietnamese Peasants under the French.* Cambridge: MIT Press, 1973.

Nguyen Huu Khang. *La Commune annamite: Etude historique, juridique, et économique.* Paris: Tepac, 1946.

Nguyen Khac Vien. *A Century of National Struggles.* Vietnamese Studies no. 24. Hanoi: Xunhasaba, 1970.

———. *Experiences vietnamiennes.* Paris: Editions Sociales, 1970.

———. *Tradition and Revolution in Vietnam.* Berkeley, California: Indochina Resource Center, May 1975.

———, ed. *Traditional Viet-Nam: Some Historical Studies.* Vietnamese Studies no. 21. Hanoi: Xunhasaba, 1969.

Nguyen The Anh. "Quelques Aspects économiques et sociaux du problème du riz au Vietnam dans la première moitié du XIXe siècle," BSEI (1967):5–22.

Nguyen van Khoan. "Essai sur le dinh et le culte du genie tutelaire des villages du Tonkin," HRAF #133. BEFEO 30 (1950):107–139.

Nguyen van Phong. *La Société vietnamienne de 1882 à 1902.* Paris: Presses Universitaires de France, 1971.

Nguyen van Vinh. *Les Réformes agraires au Vietnam.* Brussels: Librairies Universitaires Urstpruyst, 1961.

Niehoff, Arthur H., and J. Charnel Anderson. "Peasant Fatalism and Socio-Economic Innovation," *Human Organization* 25 (winter 1966):273–282.

North, Douglas C. "Institutional Change and Economic Growth," *Journal of Economic History* 31 (March 1971):118–126.

——— and Robert P. Thomas. "The Rise and Fall of the Manorial System: A Theoretical Model," *Journal of Economic History* 31 (December 1971):777–803.

Oliver, Victor L. *Cao Dai Spiritism: A Study of Religion in Vietnamese Society*. Leiden: E. J. Brill, 1976.

Olson, Mancur. *The Logic of Collective Action*. Cambridge, Massachusetts: Harvard University Press, 1965.

Ortiz, Sutti R. *Uncertainties in Peasant Farming: A Colombian Case*. New York: Humanities Press, 1973.

Ory, Paul. *La Commune annamite au Tonkin*. HRAF #130. Paris: Augustin Challamel, 1894.

Osborne, Milton. "The Vietnamese Perception of the Identity of the State: Absolute Ideals and the Necessity to Compromise." *Australian Outlook* 23 (April 1969):7–17.

———. "Continuity and Motivation in the Vietnamese Revolution: New Light from the 1930s," *Pacific Affairs*, n.d., pp. 37–55.

———. *The French Presence in Cochinchina and Cambodia: Rule and Response (1859–1905)*. Ithaca: Cornell University Press, 1969.

———. "Truong Vinh Ky and Phan Thanh Gian: The Problem of a Nationalist Interpretation of Nineteenth-Century Vietnamese History," *Journal of Asian Studies* 30 (November 1970):81–93.

Overmeyer, Daniel L. *Folk-Buddhist Religion: Dissenting Sects in Late Traditional China*. Cambridge, Massachusetts: Harvard University Press, 1976.

Paige, Jeffrey. *Agrarian Revolution: Social Movements and Export Agriculture in the Underdeveloped World*. New York: Free Press, 1975.

Pasquier, Pierre. *L'Annam d'autrefois*. HRAF #48. Paris: Augustin Challamel, 1907.

Perkins, John. "The Adoption of Quoc Ngu Romanization in Vietnam: 1860–1925," senior thesis, Department of History, University of Michigan, 1972.

Pham Cao Duong. *Thuc trang cua gioi nong dan Viet-Nam duoi thoi Phap thuoc*. Saigon: Khai-Tri, 1965.

Phan Thi Dac. *Situation de la personne au Vietnam*. Paris: Centre National de la Recherche Scientifique, 1966.

Pitt-Rivers, Julian. *The People of the Sierra*, 2nd ed. Chicago: University of Chicago Press, 1971.

Polanyi, Karl. *The Great Transformation*. New York: Rineholt, 1957.

Popkin, Samuel. "Corporatism and Colonialism: Political Economy of Rural Change in Vietnam," *Comparative Politics* 8 (April 1976):431–464.

Postan, M. M. *The Medieval Economy and Society*. London: Weidenfeld and Nicolson, 1972.

Potter, Jack. *Capitalism and the Chinese Peasant: Social and Economic Change in a Hong Kong Village*. Berkeley and Los Angeles: University of California Press, 1968.

———. *Thai Peasant Social Structure*. Chicago: University of Chicago Press, 1976.

Powell, Sumner Chilton. *Puritan Village: The Formation of a New England Town*. Garden City, New York: Doubleday, 1965.

Rabidhadana, Akin. *The Organization of Thai Society in the Early Bangkok Period, 1782–1873*. Southeast Asia Data Paper #74. Ithaca: Cornell University Press, 1969.

Rabushka, Alvin, and Kenneth A. Shepsle. *Politics in Plural Societies: A Theory of Democratic Instability*. Columbus, Ohio: Charles E. Merrill, 1972.

Race, Jeffrey. *War Comes to Long An*. Berkeley and Los Angeles: University of California Press, 1972.

Rambo, A. Terry. "A Comparison of Peasant Social Systems of Northern and Southern Vietnam: A Study of Ecological Adaptation, Social Succession and Cultural Evolution," Ph.D. dissertation, Department of Anthropology, University of Hawaii, 1972.

Rhodes, Alexandre de. *Rhodes of Vietnam. The Travels and Missions of Father Alexandre de Rhodes in China and Other Kingdoms of the Orient*. Trans. Hertz Solange. Westminster, Maryland: Newman Press, 1966.

Robequain, Charles. *The Economic Development of French Indochina*. London: Oxford University Press, 1941.

Rockwell, Joan. "The Danish Peasant Village," *Journal of Peasant Studies* 1 (July 1974):409–461.

Rogowski, Ronald. "Culturalist and Deprivationist Theories of Revolution: A Rationalist Critique and Alternative." Prepared for delivery at the 1975 Annual Meeting of the American Political Science Association, San Francisco, California, September 1975.

———. "Rationalist Theories of Politics: A Midterm Report," *World Politics* 30 (January 1978):296–323.

Roseberry, William. "Rent, Differentiation, and the Development of Capitalism among Peasants," *American Anthropologist* 78 (March 1976):45–58.

Rosen, George. *Peasant Society in a Changing Economy*. Urbana: University of Illinois Press, 1975.

Rouilly, Marcel. *La Commune annamite*. HRAF # 60. Paris: Les Presses Modernes, 1929.

Roumasset, James. "Risk and Uncertainty in Agricultural Development," Agricultural Development Council Seminar Report #15, October 1977.

Sabean, David. "The Communal Basis of Pre-1800 Peasant Uprisings in Western Europe," *Comparative Politics* 8 (April 1976):355–365.

————. "Family and Land Tenure: A Case Study of Conflict in the German Peasants' War (1525)," *Peasant Studies Newsletter* 3 (January 1974):1–20.

————. "German Agrarian Institutions at the Beginning of the Sixteenth Century: Upper Swabia as an Example," *Journal of Peasant Studies* 3 (October 1975):76–88.

Sacks, I. Milton. "Communism and Nationalism in Viet Nam: 1918–1946," Ph.D. dissertation, Department of Political Science, Yale University, 1960.

Sansom, Robert. *The Economics of Insurgency in the Mekong Delta of Vietnam*. Cambridge, Massachusetts: MIT Press, 1970.

Sarkisyanz, E. *Buddhist Backgrounds of the Burmese Revolution*. The Hague: Martinus Nijhoff, 1965.

Savani, A. M. *Notes sur le Phat Giao Hoa Hao*. Unpublished ms., 1951.

Schelling, Thomas C. "Choosing the Right Analogy: Factory, Prison or Battlefield," in Douglas E. Knight, Huntington W. Curtis, and Lawrence J. Fogel, eds., *Cybernetics, Simulation and Conflict Resolution*. New York: Spartan Books, 1971.

————. "Hockey Helmets, Concealed Weapons, and Daylight Saving: A Study of Binary Choice with Externalities," *Journal of Conflict Resolution* 17 (September 1973):381–428.

————. *Strategy of Conflict*. New York: Oxford University Press, 1963.

Schmidt, Steffen W. et al., eds., *Friends, Followers and Factions: A Reader in Political Clientelism*. Berkeley and Los Angeles: University of California Press, 1977.

Schram, Stuart R. "Mao Tse-tung and Secret Societies," *China Quarterly* 27 (July–September 1966):1–13.

Schreiner, Alfred. *Les Institutions annamites en Basse Cochinchine avant la conquête française*. 3 vols. Saigon: Claude et Cie, 1901.

Schultz, Theodore, W. *Transforming Traditional Agriculture*. New Haven: Yale University Press, 1964.

Scott, James C. "The Erosion of Patron-Client Bonds and Social Change in Rural Southeast Asia," *Journal of Asian Studies* 33 (November 1972):5–37.

————. "Exploitation in Rural Class Relations: A Victim's Perspective," *Comparative Politics* 7 (July 1975):489–532.

————. *The Moral Economy of the Peasant*. New Haven: Yale University Press, 1976.

———. "Patron-Client Politics and Political Change in Southeast Asia," *American Political Science Review* 66 (March 1972):91–113.

———. "Peasant Revolution: A Dismal Science," *Comparative Politics* 9 (January 1977):232–248.

———. "Protest and Profanation: Agrarian Revolt and the Little Tradition, Part I," *Theory and Society* 4 (spring 1977):1–38, and "Protest and Profanation: Agrarian Revolt and the Little Tradition, Part II," 4 (summer 1977):211–246.

——— and Benedict J. Kerkvliet. "How Traditional Patrons Lose Legitimacy: A Theory with Special Reference to S. E. Asia," *Cultures et Developpement* 5 (1973).

———. "The Politics of Survival: Peasant Response to 'Progress' in Southeast Asia," *Journal of Southeast Asian Studies* 4 (September 1973):241–268.

Shelton, Walter J. *English Hunger and Industrial Disorders.* London: Macmillan, 1973.

Shubik, Martin. *Strategy and Market Structure.* New York: Wiley, 1959.

Silverman, Sydel F. "Agricultural Organization, Social Structure, and Values in Italy: Amoral Familism Reconsidered," *American Anthropologist* 70 (February 1968).

———. "Exploitation in Rural Central Italy: Structure and Ideology in Stratification Study," *Comparative Studies in Society and History* 12 (July 1970):327–339.

Smith, Donald Eugene. *Religion and Political Development.* Boston: Little, Brown, 1970.

———, ed. Religion, *Politics and Social Change in the Third World.* New York: Free Press, 1971.

Smith, Ralph B. "An Introduction to Caodaism, Part I: Origins and Early History, Part II. Beliefs and Organizations," *Bulletin,* School of Oriental and African Studies, University of London, vol. 33, pp. 335–349 and 573–589, respectively.

———. "The Development of Opposition to French Rule in Southern Vietnam 1880–1940," *Past and Present* 54 (December 1972):94–129.

———. *Viet Nam and the West.* Ithaca: Cornell University Press, 1971.

Solomon, Richard H. *Mao's Revolution and the Chinese Political Culture.* Berkeley and Los Angeles: University of California Press, 1971.

Steinberg, David Joel, ed. *In Search of Southeast Asia: A Modern History.* New York: Praeger, 1971.

Stigler, George J. "A Theory of Oligopoly," *Journal of Political Economy* 72 (February 1964):44–59.

Stoler, Ann. "Class Structure and Female Autonomy in Rural Java," *Signs,* Special Issue: Women and National Development, 3 (autumn 1977):75–89.

Stone, Lawrence. "The Disenchantment of the World," *New York Review of Books,* December 2, 1971.

Sturtevant, David R. *Popular Uprising in the Philippines 1840–1940.* Ithaca: Cornell University Press, 1976.

Swartz, Marc J. "Bases for Political Compliance in Bena Villages," in Swartz et al., eds., *Political Anthropology.* Chicago: Aldine, 1966.

Taboulet, George. *La Geste française en Indochine.* Paris: Adrienne-Maissonneuve, 1955.

Takahashi Akira. *Land and Peasants in Central Luzon.* Tokyo: Institute of Developing Economies, 1969.

Tambiah, S. J. *Buddhism and the Spirit Cults in North-East Thailand.* Cambridge: At the University Press, 1970.

Tarrow, Sidney. *Peasant Communism in Southern Italy.* New Haven: Yale University Press, 1967.

Tawney, R. H. *The Agrarian Problem in the Sixteenth Century.* Burt Franklin Research and Source Works Series #13. New York: Sentry Press, 1912.

Thaxton, Ralph. "The World Turned Downside Up," *Modern China* 3 (April 1977):185–228.

Thirsk, Joan. *English Peasant Farming.* London: Routledge and Kegan Paul, 1957.

Thompson, Kenneth. *Farm Fragmentation in Greece.* Monograph #5. Athens: Center of Economic Research, 1963.

Thompson, Virginia. *French Indochina.* New York: Macmillan, 1937.

Tilly, Charles. *The Formation of National States in Western Europe.* Princeton, New Jersey: Princeton University Press, 1975.

Timmer, C. Peter. "Choice of Technique in Rice Milling on Java," *Bulletin of Indonesian Economic Studies* 9 (July 1973):57–76.

———. "Choice of Technique in Rice Milling on Java: A Reply," *Bulletin of Indonesian Economic Studies* 9 (July 1973):121–126.

———. "The Turnip, the New Husbandry and the English Agricultural Revolution," *Quarterly Journal of Economics* 83 (August 1969):375–395.

Titow, J. Z. *English Rural Society 1200–1350.* London: George Allen and Unwin, 1969.

Toan Anh. *Nep cu lang xom Viet Nam.* Saigon: Khai-Tri, 1968.

———. *Tin Nguong Viet Nam.* Saigon: Khai-Tri, 1967.

Toquero, Zenaida, et al. "Estimating the Elasticities of Home Consumption and Marketable Surplus for a Subsistence Crop: Rice in the Philippines," *American Journal of Agricultural Economy* 57 (November 1975):705–709.

Tran Duy Nhat. "Ban ve huong chinh xu bac ky," *Nam Phong* (Hanoi), May 1922, p. 362.

Tran Huy Lieu. *Les Soviets du Nghe-Tinh de 1930–1931.* Hanoi: Editions en Langues Etrangères, 1960.

Truong Buu Lam. "Comments and Generalities on Sino-Vietnamese Relations," in Edgar Wickberg, ed., *Historical Interaction of China and Vietnam: Institutional and Cultural Themes*. Lawrence, Kansas: University of Kansas Center for East Asian Studies, 1969.

————. "Patterns of Vietnamese Response to Foreign Intervention: 1858–1900." Monograph #11, Southeast Asia Studies, Yale University Press, 1967.

————. "The Vietnamese Village in the Colonial Period." Unpublished paper.

Truong Chinh. "The August Revolution" and "The Resistance Will Win" in Truong Chinh, *Primer for Revolt*. New York: Praeger, 1963.

Tuma, Elias. *Twenty-Six Centuries of Agrarian Reform*. Berkeley and Los Angeles: University of California Press, 1965.

Utami, Widya, and John Ihalauw, "Some Consequences of Small Farm Size," *Bulletin of Indonesian Economic Studies* 9 (July 1973):46–56.

Van de Walle, Etienne. "Comments on Benjamin White's 'Demand for Labor and Population Growth in Colonial Java,'" *Human Ecology* 1 (1973):241–244.

Vella, Walter F., ed. *Aspects of Vietnamese History*. Asian Studies at Hawaii, no. 8. University of Hawaii: University Press of Hawaii, 1973.

Vo Nguyen Giap. *Unforgettable Days*. Hanoi: Foreign Languages Publishing House, 1975.

———— and Truong Chinh. "The Peasant Question (1937–1938)," Trans. Christine Peltzer White. Data Paper #94, Southeast Asia Program. Ithaca: Cornell University Press, 1974.

Vu Quoc Thuc. *L'Economie communaliste du Vietnam*. Hanoi: Press Universitaire du Vietnam, 1951.

Vu van Hien. *La Propriété communale au Tonkin: Contribution a l'étude historique, juridique et économique des cong-dien et cong-tho en pays d'Annam*. HRAF #117. Paris: Presses Modernes, 1939.

————. "Les Institutions annamites depuis l'arrivée des français: L'Impôt personnel et les corvées de 1862 à 1936," RIJE 13 (1940):84–107.

Wagley, Charles. "Economics of a Guatemalan Village," *Memoirs of the American Anthropological Association* 58 (1941):76.

Ward, Benjamin. "Majority Rule and Allocation," *Journal of Conflict Resolution* 4 (December 1961):379–389.

Waswo, Ann. *Japanese Landlords: The Decline of a Rural Elite*. Berkeley and Los Angeles: University of California Press, 1977.

Weisser, Michael. *Peasants of the Montes*. Chicago: University of Chicago Press, 1976.

Werner, Jayne S. "Cao Dai: The Politics of a Vietnamese Syncretic Religious Movement," Ph.D. dissertation, Department of Politics, Cornell University, 1976.

Wertheim, W. F., and The Siauw Giap, "Social Change in Java 1900–1930," *Pacific Affairs* 35 (fall 1962):223–247.

White, Benjamin. "Demand for Labor and Population Growth in Colonial Java," *Human Ecology* 1 (1973): 217–236.

———. "The Economic Importance of Children in a Javanese Village," in Moni Nag, ed., *Population and Social Organization*. The Hague, Paris: Mouton, 1975.

———. "Production and Reproduction in a Javanese Village," Ph.D. dissertation, Department of Anthropology, Columbia University, 1976.

White, Christine. "Revolution and Its Adherents: The Development of the Revolutionary Movement in Vietnam." Unpublished manuscript, 1973.

White, Louise G. "Rational Theories of Participation: An Exercise in Definitions," *Journal of Conflict Resolution* 20 (June 1976):255–279.

Whyte, William Foote. *Street Corner Society*. Chicago: University of Chicago Press, 1943.

Wickberg, Edgar. *Historical Interactions between Vietnam and China: Cultural and Institutional Patterns*. Lawrence, Kansas: University of Kansas Press, 1969.

Wolf, Eric. "Aspects of Group Relations in a Complex Society: Mexico," *American Anthropologist* 58 (December 1956):1065–1078.

———. "Close Corporate Communities in Meso-America and Java," *Southwestern Journal of Anthropology* 13 (spring 1957):1–18.

———. "Introduction," in Norman Miller and Roderick Aya, eds., *National Liberation: Revolution in the Third World*. New York: Free Press, 1971.

———. "Kinship, Friendship, and Patron-Client Relations in Complex Societies," in Michael Banton, ed., *The Social Anthropology of Complex Societies*. ASA Monographs. London: Tavistock Publications, 1966.

———. *Peasants*. Englewood Cliffs, New Jersey: Prentice-Hall, 1966.

———. "Peasant Rebellion and Revolution," in Norman Miller and Roderick Aya, eds., *National Liberation: Revolution in the Third World*. New York: Free Press, 1971.

———. *Peasant Wars of the Twentieth Century*. New York: Harper and Row, 1969.

———. "Review Essay: Why Cultivators Rebel," *American Journal of Sociology* 83 (November 1977):742–750.

———. "Types of Latin American Peasantry: A Preliminary Discussion," *American Anthropologist* 57 (June 1955):452–471.

Woodside, Alexander. *Community and Revolution in Modern Vietnam*. Boston: Houghton Mifflin, 1976.

———. "The Development of Social Organizations in Vietnamese Cities in the Late Colonial Period," *Pacific Affairs* 64 (spring 1971):39–63.

———. "Some Features of Vietnamese Bureaucracy under the Early Nguyen Dynasty," *Harvard University East Asia Papers on China* 19, December 1965.

———. *Vietnam and the Chinese Model: A Comparative Study of Vietnamese and Chinese Government in the First Half of the Nineteenth Century.* Cambridge, Massachusetts: Harvard University Press, 1971.

———. "Vietnamese Buddhism, the Vietnamese Court and China in the Early 1880s," in Edgar Wickberg, *Historical Interactions between Vietnam and China: Cultural and Institutional Patterns.* Lawrence, Kansas: University of Kansas Press, 1969.

Womack, John, Jr. *Zapata and the Mexican Revolution.* New York: Alfred A. Knopf, 1969.

Yang, C. K. *Religion in Chinese Society.* Berkeley and Los Angeles: University of California Press, 1967.

Zinsser, Hans. *Rats, Lice and History.* Boston: Little, Brown, 1967.

Zolberg, Aristedes. "Moments of Madness," in Ira Katznelson et al., eds., *The Politics and Society Reader.* New York: David McKay, 1974.

Index

Acheson, James M., 93n
Adas, Michael, 21n, 76n, 250n
Adjudication: by Cao Dai leaders, 201;
  by Catholic priests, 189, 192; by
  Communist courts, 238; by Hoa Hao
  security teams, 212; by missionaries,
  130; need for, 108; by village
  council, 36, 92
Administrative class, Confucian exam
  system for, 86–87
Administrative council, in colonial
  villages, 159–161
Age, 93; of village council members,
  110
Aged, insurance for, 47, 49, 56, 101
Agrarian elite, 2. *See also*
  Landlord-tenant relations
Agrarian relations: Cao Dai changes in,
  196–200; and stratification during
  colonial rule, 153–158
Agrarian revolt, 231

Agricultural: cooperatives, 264;
  institutions, 76–77; involution, 12
Agricultural production: in colonial
  period, 134, 135, 168–169, 170,
  171; on private land, 104–105
Agriculture: collective, 240; and
  distribution of resources, 56–58;
  harvesting and gleaning in medieval
  villages, 51–53; improved
  techniques for, 12, 29, 34, 68;
  innovations in, 66–67;
  intensification of, 12, 68, 169;
  open-field, 36; in precolonial
  Vietnamese villages, 90–91;
  scattered vs. consolidated plots,
  49–51, 105; subsistence vs.
  commercial, 171–172. *See also*
  Commercialization of agriculture;
  Communal land
Alavi, Hamza, xi, 73n, 78n, 250n
Alcohol taxes, 136

289

Designer: Al Burkhardt
Compositor: Typesetting Services of California
Printer: The Murray Printing Co.
Binder: The Murray Printing Co.
Text: VIP Times Roman
Display: VIP Ultra Bodoni